Using Drawings in Clinical Practice

Clinicians are always in need of enticing techniques to engage clients on a daily basis, especially those who are nonverbal or initially opposed to feedback. *Using Drawings in Clinical Practice* provides a rich variety of drawing directives to enhance the diagnostic process. In this highly illustrated text, clinicians will discover the tools they need to interact effectively with their clients. The book places special emphasis on intake interviewing and psychological testing, where the potential for uncovering hidden conflicts and therapeutic direction is especially poignant. Case studies provide a comprehensive overview of how to introduce simple drawings and gain remarkable insights. *Using Drawings in Clinical Practice* is a crucial guidebook for professionals who seek new ways to facilitate meaningful communication and interactions in their practice settings.

Gerald D. Oster, PhD, has worked in a variety of inpatient and outpatient settings for more than 35 years. He is currently providing therapy and assessment services in private practice; he also supervises graduate students in psychological testing. In the past, he held the titles of clinical associate professor of psychiatry and psychology internship director. He has co-authored numerous books and professional publications, including *Using Drawings in Assessment and Therapy: A Guide for Mental Health Professionals*.

Using Drawings in Clinical Practice
Enhancing Intake Interviews and Psychological Testing

Gerald D. Oster

NEW YORK AND LONDON

First published 2016
by Routledge
711 Third Avenue, New York, NY 10017

and by Routledge
2 Park Square, Milton Park, Abingdon, Oxon, OX14 4RN

Routledge is an imprint of the Taylor & Francis Group, an informa business

© 2016 Gerald D. Oster

The right of Gerald D. Oster to be identified as author of this work has been asserted by him in accordance with sections 77 and 78 of the Copyright, Designs and Patents Act 1988.

All rights reserved. No part of this book may be reprinted or reproduced or utilised in any form or by any electronic, mechanical, or other means, now known or hereafter invented, including photocopying and recording, or in any information storage or retrieval system, without permission in writing from the publishers.

Trademark notice: Product or corporate names may be trademarks or registered trademarks, and are used only for identification and explanation without intent to infringe.

Library of Congress Cataloging in Publication Data
Oster, Gerald D.
  Using drawings in clinical practice : enhancing intake interviews and psychological testing/Gerald D. Oster.—1 Edition.
  pages cm
  Includes bibliographical references and index.
  1. Projective techniques. 2. Drawing, Psychology of. 3. Mental illness—Diagnosis. 4. Art therapy. I. Title.
  RC473.P7O88 2016
  616.89'1656–dc23
  2015019625

ISBN: 978-1-138-78032-3 (hbk)
ISBN: 978-1-138-02406-9 (pbk)
ISBN: 978-1-315-77084-0 (ebk)

Typeset in Sabon
by Florence Production Ltd, Stoodleigh, Devon, UK

With the recent passing of our dog, Buster,
we are now left without pets in our home for the first time.
All of our animals provided us with much love and positive energy over the
years to help us overcome whatever crises or tears that arose.

I now want to dedicate this book in memory of their lasting companionship.

In memory of

REGGIE & BUSTER
Our beloved family dogs

and

SYBIL & HANNAH
Our beloved family cats

Contents

Foreword by Eliana Gil — xi
Preface — xiii
Acknowledgments — xix
About the Author — xxi

1 Drawings in Everyday Practice — 1

    Case Study—Sarah E. 2
    Using Drawings in Clinical Settings 3
    Why Use Drawings? 4
        Case Study—Cheyenne R. 5
    Drawings Can be Reassuring 7
        Case Study—Paul K. 7
        Case Study—Alice W. 9
    Strengthening Insight and Problem-solving 10
    Disclosing Temperament 11
        Case Study—Sam K. 12
    Identifying Goals and Motivation 14
    Talking Through Images 14
    Vital Points 15
    Expansion of Interpersonal Engagement 16
    Stimulating Inspiration 17
        Case Study—Marcia T. 18
    Concluding Remarks 20
    References 23

2 Foundations of Clinical Drawings — 25

    Historical Aspects of Clinical Drawing 25
    Images of Psychological Maturation 26
    Developmental Sequences 27
    Cognitive Maturation 32
        Case Study—Greg B. 33
    Emotional Indicators 34
        Case Study—James D. 35
    Symbols of Mental Illness 37
    Freud and Jung 37
    Creative Pursuits in Psychotherapy 38

Case Study—Elizabeth G. 38
Art Therapy as a Discipline 41
Interactions of Art Therapy and Psychology 42
    Case Study—Lakandra E. 43
    Case Study—Charlotte P. 45
Controversies in Drawing Interpretation 46
From Psychology to Art Therapy Assessments 47
  Silver Drawing Tests 48
  Diagnostic Drawing Series 48
  The Person Picking an Apple from a Tree 49
Enhancement to Assessment 50
Cautionary Tales 50
Concluding Comments 51
References 52

3   House–Tree–Person and Variations   56

Human Figures and Everyday Objects 56
House–Tree–Person 57
House Drawings 58
    Case Study—Kelli R. 58
    Case Study—Karl C. 61
The Tree 63
    Case Study—Sakura R. 64
    Case Study—Sierra A. 66
Human Figures 66
    Case Study—Joseph S. 68
    Case Study—Melissa B. 70
    Case Study—Monique W. 73
Kinetic–House–Tree–Person 74
    Case Study—Mandy S. 74
Draw-a-Person-in-the-Rain 75
    Case Study—Toni N. 77
Family Drawing Procedures 81
  Draw-a-Family 81
    Case Study—Marla B. 82
  Kinetic-Family-Drawing 83
    Case Study—Arlene G. 84
  Family-Centered-Circle-Drawing 86
    Case Study—Eddie C. 87
  Mother-and-Child 89
    Case Study—Alan W. 90
References 91

4   Alternative Drawing Directives   94

Broadening the Interpersonal Encounter 94
Timelines 95
    Case Study—Lauren F. 96
Genograms 97
    Case Study—Nosian H. 98

Family Shield 99
    Case Study—Albert J. 100
Draw Your World 101
    Case Study—Amku L. 101
Draw Yourself with Friends 103
Kinetic School Drawings 103
    Case Study—Kesandra B. 104
Draw Your "Ideal" Self 105
    Case Study—Carla S. 106
Draw Your (Current) Mood 106
    Case Study—Consuela L. 108
Defining and Resolving Problems 110
    Case Study—Alysha G. 110
Before, During, and After Crises 112
    Case Study—Loren Y. 112
Ending Remarks 113
References 114

5 Using Drawings During Clinical Interviews   115

Information Gathering 115
    Case Study—Jacob D. 117
Conducting an Initial Interview 119
    Case Study—Lori S. 119
Behavioral Observations 121
    Case Study—Eduardo L. 122
    Case Study—Randall M. 123
The Crux of the Interview 123
Types of Clinical Interviews 124
  Intake Interviews 124
    Case Study—Marilyn C. 126
  Mental Status Exam 126
    Case Study—Breanna P. 129
Trauma Interviews 130
Clinical Administration PTSD Scale 131
    Case Study—Kienna T. 132
Trauma Symptom Inventory 133
    Case Study—Nina F. 134
Trauma Symptom Checklist for Children 135
    Case Study—Leyana G. 136
Sexual Abuse Indicators in Drawings 137
    Case Study—Louis R. 138
Benefits and Limitations 139
    Case Study—Cheryl N. 140
Family Evaluations 142
Sharing of Conflicts 143
    Case Study—Jason A. 143
An Enhancement to Practitioners 145
References 146

6 Comprehensive Psychological Evaluations — 148

Case Study—Max T. 148
Case Study—Janette B. 148
Psychological Testing within the Assessment Process 149
Requests from Treating Professionals 150
  Case Study—Carlos B. 151
Responding to Referral Questions 151
  Case Study—Malcolm S. 153
Identifying Presenting Problems 153
The Role of Psychologists 154
  Case Study—Deborah M. 155
  Case Study—Charles L. 155
Puzzles that Need Solutions 156
Principles of Psychological Testing 157
Components of Psychological Evaluations 157
Selecting a Test Battery 158
  Intellectual Assessment 159
  Academic Achievement 159
  Neuropsychological Testing 160
  Personality Inventories 160
  Behavior Rating Scales 161
  Projective Techniques 161
Drawings in the Test Battery 162
  Case Study—Janice L. 163
  Case Study—John R. 165
The Psychological Report 167
Summaries of Psychological Evaluations 168
  Case Study—Marvin S. 168
  Case Study—Allison T. 172
Closing Words 175
References 175

Index — 177

Foreword

Eliana Gil, PhD, ATR, Gil Institute for Trauma Recovery and Education, LLC, Fairfax, VA

Dr. Oster and I share a deep appreciation of the potential benefits of utilizing art during assessment and treatment of children and adults. This book focuses on the assessment phase of treatment, that time when clinicians seek to gain an adequate understanding of the client seeking treatment in order to tailor a treatment plan. This is particularly challenging when clients are very young, hesitant to communicate verbally, or unwilling or unable to identify their thoughts and feelings through words.

Thus clinicians who work with children are well advised to grow a repertoire of nonverbal strategies that might invite and engage their young or ambivalent clients in the process of exposing themselves gradually and without reservation. The expressive arts (sometimes thought of as alternative therapies) have gained popularity due to their practicality and usefulness in real-life clinical settings. In fact, music, drama, dance, play, sand, and art therapies, to name a few, are successfully integrated into hospitals, residential centers and group homes, senior centers, and a variety of other programs serving those in need.

I am very fond of books that provide the content described in the title. Thus I was pleased and excited to find that Dr. Oster delivered on his stated promise: He gives us a comprehensive manual for using drawings in our clinical practices and enhancing intake interviews as well as psychological testing. I think this book will greatly increase clinical understanding of how encouraging and allowing creative and graphic expressions, and later demonstrating clinical curiosity, can greatly maximize clinical rapport and client comfort.

There is a solid historical backdrop that sets the context for the rationale or utilizing drawings in assessment and enlightening examples of how drawings have inherent benefits such as strengthening client insight and problem-solving, identifying motivation, making deeper emotional connections, and stimulating inspiration. This last factor, in particular, has always provided clients with an intangible, yet powerful feeling that moves them forward, stimulates them towards more introspection, and mobilizes energy for treatment. Indeed, drawing and painting and engaging in the expressive arts in general opens up additional avenues for accessing internal resources and externalizing images that then elicit reflection and possible action.

Dr. Oster documents some standard drawing assessment strategies and provides some interesting expanded ideas. For example, while he dedicates time to the House–Tree–Person assessment instrument, he also offers variations that are novel and hold great promise. All assessment techniques are presented through case presentations that enliven the material and provide the reader with a bird's eye view of how drawings are powerful aids in the assessment process.

Being a trainer and an advocate of utilizing arts in assessment and treatment, I know first-hand that clinicians approach the use of clinical art with trepidation. Sometimes clinicians view drawings as puzzles that cannot be easily solved. Paradoxically, most clinicians always have paper and art materials in their offices if they are working with children and teens but are often less likely to ask adults to draw. However, once clients cooperate and draw, most untrained clinicians don't know how to proceed. They often worry about either misinterpreting what they see, or become frustrated when children or youth don't want to say more about the drawings they've made. This book will help greatly in that regard as the ample case studies reflect how clinicians can use the drawings in their decision-making process during the assessment phase.

I have long been a fan of Dr. Oster's work. In fact, his earlier works peaked my interest in learning more. It was reading his books that led me to seek out additional, structured training in art therapy. I was fortunate to move to the DC area and was able to have lunch with Barry Cohen, himself a brilliant art therapist with an established interest in the treatment of trauma through art. I am eternally grateful to Barry for suggesting that I become a Registered Art Therapist, a process that cemented my respect and appreciation for the potential use of art in both assessment and treatment of individuals across the life span. Most of my actual experience has been with children, however, and I very much resonate with the tone and depth of this book, as well as Dr. Oster's assertions about drawings enhancing our understanding and connection to our clients, many of who cannot use words to signal their distress. This book is comprehensive, focused, creative, and enlightening. Thanks again to Dr. Oster for renewing my excitement for the use of art in clinical work!

Preface

Since the early 1980s, I have had the opportunity to collaborate with other behavioral health professionals regarding the clinical uses of drawings during interviews, assessments, and psychotherapy. Through writings and lectures, as well as utilizing graphic images in my practice for over 35 years, I have discovered that the act of constructing illustrations and talking through these images about problems, moods, and relationships has enlarged my framework enormously. And for my clients, these quick paper-and-pencil sketches have certainly made the sessions more enjoyable and meaningful, as they have strengthened the possibilities of enhancing emotional expression and communication.

Initially, these experiences were stimulated by art therapist Patricia Gould (now Patricia Crone), who co-wrote our original best-selling book *Using Drawings in Assessment and Therapy*, which is now in its second edition and we are beginning to work on a third. By presenting her evaluations within the state hospital where we both worked at the time, the staff and I gained an enormous appreciation for the striking and informative artwork of those vulnerable individuals who were attempting to express themselves more fully and channel their feelings in a more adaptive framework. I was fascinated by the unique pictures presented and wondered about the metaphorical meanings.

From this introduction to art evaluations and therapy, as well as subsequent readings and attending workshops on the topic, I began to introduce drawing directives during my beginning assessment and therapy sessions, especially when these sessions were met with initial resistance. I still remember and am equally amazed at the exceptional images presented and the subsequent discussions with the clients that ensued in addition to the insight gained! These brief nonverbal activities certainly opened a new avenue for me, and provided an alternative path toward the gathering of important historical information and generated many possible hypotheses about personality characteristics and emotional resources of the client in distress.

The present book, *Using Drawings in Clinical Practice*, is a culmination of these experiences and previous writings and lecturing on the topic. Besides my books with Patricia Gould Crone, I also had the opportunity to co-write a similar book with social worker Sarah Montgomery (*Clinical Uses of Drawings*) and have included aspects of using drawings in other books that I and my colleagues have written on child and adolescent testing and psychotherapy. I also continue to read and learn on a daily basis about exploring new ways to add drawings to the clinician's toolbox from other authors and practitioners. This life-long pursuit has kept me enthused about the topic and allows me to share new discoveries with colleagues and the psychology graduate students with whom I have the honor and pleasure to supervise.

As this new book emphasizes, the alternative nonverbal techniques (such as drawing directives) that have been created over the past century have re-energized the field of clinical interviewing, psychological testing, and psychotherapy. Clinicians who have actively integrated drawings within the evaluative process have valued the richness of responses and the engagement it has brought to the diagnostic and treatment planning encounter. By introducing a unique situation into the arena of evaluations, the resulting graphic products truly speak a different language, add flexibility to clinician–client interactions, and build cohesion and trust (which becomes a crucial factor for accurate understanding to occur). This novel approach offers an exciting pathway to producing tangible markers for remembering important events, revealing hidden conflicts, and establishing a wider scope for viewing problem solutions.

Drawings have certainly enriched my *Life as a Psychologist* (Oster, 2006). This key ancillary technique that I have used during assessment and therapy sessions has always enhanced conversations that have resulted in evocative and perceptive interactions. Nonverbal methods, such as constructing graphic images, have gained a solid foothold in behavioral health treatment and have increased enthusiasm among a wide range of practitioners who welcome the addition of unique clinical procedures during mental status exams, diagnostic screenings, intake interviews, and psychological testing. When these types of opening are utilized within these situations, they remain alluring in their ability to emphasize and portray hidden worries and conflicts, and in allowing a greater potential for the deeper understanding of the inner psyche. Many professional counselors, psychologists, social workers, expressive therapists, and other health and mental health caretakers believe that the added knowledge gained during the construction of drawings becomes salient to the clients' struggles and provides concrete symbols of emotions, self-esteem, and social competence.

Treating professionals always needs a more comprehensive clinical toolbox to engage clients, especially those who are resistant to sharing personal information. Sometimes words alone do not provide enough possibilities for effective communication to occur. By introducing drawings to the interview and assessment process as a way to broaden interpersonal interactions, a different strategy has been introduced that offers countless opportunities for expressing feelings and thoughts. This valuable mechanism is especially helpful for clients suffering from past abuse or neglect, or for families in current disarray.

In my everyday clinical practice and my supervisory sessions with psychology graduate students, I have found the use of drawings to be a fun, collaborative, and effective method to engage and enlighten those more difficult feelings, perceptions, and events that are otherwise too painful to speak out loud. By initiating drawing activities to the diagnostic and early treatment process, my students and I have truly discovered an exciting method to expediently bring difficult issues to the surface that would otherwise have been overlooked during standard interviews and evaluations or beginning therapy sessions. These revelations have accelerated our abilities to intervene and assist individuals to better understand their inner fears and gain possible resolutions to change.

As my students and I continue to be astonished by the impact of simple directives in assessment and therapy, we have discovered how easily a basic drawing can readily provide fruitful material on aspects of development and maturation, emotional and cognitive functioning, and expression of hidden trauma, as well as convey ambivalent or contradictory feelings and perceptions about a client's world. Whether it be standardized instructions to "Draw a House, Tree, or Person," which have dominated psychological research on the clinical uses of drawings, or more expanded directives, such as "Draw your: mood; a mother and child; or solutions to a problem," the utilization of visual images has found a substantive place for the sharing of personal secrets and experiences within the diagnostic and therapeutic process. While other nonverbal modalities (such as music, dance, and other art media) can certainly be used in channeling hidden thoughts, concerns, and conflicts, portraying one's inner images through pencil-and-paper constructions (or talking about them) are certainly one of the most economical and easily applied. And drawings actually do represent a different language in revealing psychological well-being and are certainly "worth a thousand words," as they enlarge the framework for interpersonal interactions, as well as supply metaphorical meanings to common experiences.

Using Drawings in Clinical Practice focuses on introducing drawing directives within the clinical interview and psychological assessment process and is intended to expand on previous books that met with much enthusiasm among behavioral health professionals for expanding alternative, nonverbal methods to engage and communicate more effectively with clients of all ages. These prior volumes produced renewed attention among practitioners and researchers for finding straightforward approaches that could highlight and elucidate significant emotional problems within diagnostic sessions, as well as document therapeutic treatment progress. Over these many years, I have had the opportunity to correspond with many clinicians about new drawing directives and outcomes, lead workshops on introducing drawings into the therapeutic realm, and expand the view of psychology graduate students who were initially skeptical of creative applications to enhance psychological testing.

This book will solidify these experiences and update the literature on drawings since the last edition (2004). It will mostly emphasize the beginning process of treatment (that is, assessment and clinical interviewing); for it becomes a time of formulating diagnoses and outlining avenues of treatment. It is during these initial sessions where I have discovered the exciting world of graphic constructions and the potential for uncovering hidden conflict and solidifying recommendations for interventions. And as I have also found through these experiences, clients do not have to artistically express themselves to convey hidden images, they can merely talk about them.

This practical guidebook to the utilization of drawings during the initial phase of information gathering is replete with numerous case studies and graphic images. It will provide a broad historical overview of a variety of drawing procedures that have been used during evaluations and interviewing and provide evidence to emphasize their advantages. This volume will cogently explain how simple drawing tasks that only take a few moments within a session can assist and enhance interviews and psychological testing of children, teenagers, and adults. It will also update both beginning and seasoned professionals' libraries with recent literatures and new solutions for overcoming client resistance. Richly illustrated within a "how-to" approach, these chapters will cover important aspects to introducing drawings during the initial segments of treatment and offer ways to facilitate meaningful communication of problematic thoughts and behaviors.

Drawing with pencil and paper makes it a direct and readily available technique for a myriad of practitioners, including psychologists, social workers, and professional counselors, in addition to expressive therapists. The sole use of pencil and paper makes it distinct from the art therapy professions who have a much more substantial background in the creative arts and use a myriad of material that is not usually comfortable to other behavioral health disciplines and is typically outside of their skill realm. All of these clinicians, though, have shown their hunger for knowledge and their eagerness to learn fresh techniques to engage the less verbal or resistant client who they must see on a daily basis in their respective practices. This book will hopefully be valued not only as a basic instructional guide to the varied uses of graphic images within the diagnostic process, but will also be viewed as an excellent educational manual to better understand the inner world of individuals beset by psychological conflicts. The intended audience of graduate students and behavioral health practitioners will undoubtedly be impacted by vivid case descriptions, enriched in their increased knowledge of interview and assessment guidelines and procedures, and delighted with a visual language that will make this text a highly stimulating and valuable resource.

This book will be divided into six chapters that cover the historical basis, research, and applications of the importance and value of introducing drawings into the clinical interview and diagnostic process. Chapter 1 begins with the presentation of a case study that provides a striking example of a young girl's depression and the depths of her inner pain. It shares with the reader her ability to demonstrate through her drawings that she clearly needed help in overcoming her negatively biased view of her interactions with peers and adults. Other stories follow that equally validate how effectively graphic images can underscore presenting problems and core issues that need to be discovered during initial interviewing and psychological testing. The pages within this book are filled with narratives that share how the introduction of drawings to this evaluative process allows for a secure stage to be developed that actively facilitates memories, thoughts, and feelings that may otherwise be too painful to address directly by standardized scales and questionnaires.

Also, the idea of "talking through images" will be introduced. At times, the introduction of drawings into the diagnostic or therapeutic arena will meet with strong resistance. When this roadblock occurs, examiners or interviewers can offer an alternative opportunity— that is, asking clients to verbally describe their inner images or representations of the various drawing directives that are being requested, as opposed to actually portraying their "problem" or "world" on paper. Many intriguing examples of these requests and responses will be provided. It is often a relief to the client (and perhaps the clinician) that talking about inner images can be similarly effective in providing a hidden landscape of distress.

The second chapter will introduce the reader to the historical sequence of the many uses of drawing activities and other nonverbal techniques within therapeutic questioning and assessment. It will describe how drawings were first used to assess normal development, how they became an essential part of clinical interviewing and psychological testing, and how they have been utilized through the years in a variety of therapeutic formats, especially during the beginning phases of treatment. Examples and case studies will be used to emphasize how the introduction of drawing methods can expand formal diagnostic interviews. A review of past literature and the names of standardized drawing directives will be introduced. Foundations of developmental theory, drawing interpretations within psychological assessment, clinical diagnoses and the revised edition of *Diagnostic and Statistical Manual of Mental Disorders* (DSM-5), and updated research will be offered. It will also detail how psychology and art therapy have been integrated over the years.

Chapter 3 will accentuate the historical progression of how the house, tree, and person were chosen as widely used figures in assessment and how their immense interpretive value came about in practice and research. These common objects of everyday life were the first drawings to be added to the psychological testing examination and have been the most comprehensively researched throughout the assessment literature. Thus, it requires a separate section and a more in-depth investigation. The addition of the modifications to the standard instruction, such as Draw-A-Person-In-The-Rain (D-A-P-R; in the rain), is a more recent and fascinating variation among this sequential focus of figure and object drawings, and has demonstrated its own unique benefits to interpretation during interviews and evaluations. Other alternative formats to accessing information have also been included. Popular methods, such as the "Kinetic H-T-P" to other directives, like "Mother and Child" drawings, have allowed for these minimally threatening methods to promote the sharing and the gathering of subjective experiences that might not have been revealed so readily during interview or assessment sessions. A simple request to draw can provide a maximally absorbing and unique introduction to an evaluative situation. For the clinician interpreting these drawings, or the clients who verbally share their own insights of the constructions, these images and interactions initiate an important process of communication that offers the opportunity to investigate the conflicts, worries, and anxieties that have resulted in these experiences occurring.

The next chapter (Chapter 4) offers ancillary directives that enlarge the scope of using drawings in gathering important information during the initial stages of evaluation and treatment. Through numerous examples and case studies, these pages will enrich and stimulate readers to creatively think about how they can utilize drawings and craft new directives into their own clinical practices. These pages will examine the standard drawing commands of common nonverbal techniques, such as timelines and genograms, as well as inspire more creative paths to gain supplemental information about client concerns and symptoms. The chapter will review basic instructions and expand possibilities in a very practical approach that will attract practitioners to drive beyond their typical way of approaching information gathering.

Chapter 5 will focus on different aspects of clinical interviewing and how to integrate drawings into the screening process. The clinical interview establishes an exchange between clients and behavioral health workers. In order to make this time effective, clinicians need to: a) make this human contact comfortable; b) establish rapport efficiently; c) build a working alliance; d) instill hope that problems being faced can be overcome; and e) provide clear goals and helpful interventions. Practitioners who find themselves in this position require numerous strategies to discover the background history, support system, presenting symptoms, and the resilience of the person sitting in front of them. To assist in this elaborate process, both structured and unstructured clinical interview formats have been constructed and are used to gain valuable information that determines treatment direction. This chapter covers various interview styles in gathering pertinent evidence and examines such techniques as the mental status exam, as well as trauma inventories and interview formats that allow distress individuals a framework to address disturbing thoughts and feelings. Family evaluations are also included to examine the past or current household dynamics that are contributing to the presenting symptoms. And, of course, drawings are introduced to facilitate this process.

The concluding chapter (Chapter 6) will concentrate on the referral needs for psychological testing and review the common tests that constitute a typical assessment battery. Once these referral questions have been clarified, interviews conducted, and diagnostic impressions considered, questions might still remain regarding the need for specific information and documentation that will determine a particular classroom accommodation, degree of deterioration in functioning, or the need for specialized residential, rehabilitative, or aftercare programs. Through self-report questionnaires, behavioral observations, and the administration of intellectual and neuropsychological tests, educational batteries, personality inventories, and projective techniques (like drawing directives), a comprehensive depiction of functioning based on normative data and the examiner's judgment and experience is created from client responses that can detail specific strengths and weaknesses and more accurately summarize and clarify diagnostic conjectures. This final section of the book will examine these issues and discuss the value of adding drawings to the psychological battery. Through the abundance of information gathered during this process, goals for therapy and other treatment interventions can then be accurately established.

Upon completing this book, clinicians will have obtained a broad overview of how to introduce a wide variety of nonverbal directives to expand communication during clinical interviewing and psychological testing. Gaining comfort in these drawing-based measures adds immensely to the process of information gathering. Even when talking through these images, clinicians will have discovered an alternative method for interacting with their distressed or traumatized clients and have the opportunity to become effective change agents. By its highly illustrated examples, this practitioner guidebook offers many possibilities for clinicians to integrate these creative methods into their own working style. And finally, by emphasizing the relational aspects of change that is so inherent to applying experiential methods to the evaluative and therapeutic arena, *Using Drawings in Clinical Practice* will highlight the obvious advantages of adding nonverbal activity to clinical interviews and psychological testing sessions.

REFERENCES

Oster, G. D. (2006). *Life as a psychologist: Career choices and insights*. Santa Barbara, CA: Praeger.

Oster, G. D., & Crone, P. (2004). *Using drawings in assessment and therapy* (2nd ed.). New York: Taylor & Francis.

Oster, G. D., & Gould, P. (1987). *Using drawings in assessment and therapy*. New York: Brunner/Mazel.

Oster, G. D., & Montgomery, S. S. (1996). *Clinical uses of drawings*. Northvale, NJ: Jason Aronson.

Acknowledgments

Over the many years in my professional life as a psychologist, I have interacted with wonderful people who have nurtured my curiosity and continue to play an important part in my growth. Many of these people I met during my undergraduate and graduate school years and still maintain contact with them on a regular basis through a Sunday morning blog. I have also had the fortune of communicating with work colleagues at various settings, including state and private hospitals, residential treatment and counseling centers, group practices, and in my own private setting. Some of these gifted individuals (including psychiatrist Stewart Gabel, psychologists Joan Offerle and Joshua Semiatin, and professional counselor Marcie Brooks) were kind enough to add encouraging words to promote this book. All have, and still, impact me to varying degrees in my learning, and I owe them much credit in my continuing work.

For the past nine years, I have also had the fortune of providing psychological assessment supervision to graduate students around the D.C. and Baltimore areas two mornings a week and this time has always been very special to me. They have always been receptive to new experiences, such as introducing drawings within their client sessions and have been amazed by the results. All of these individuals have been intelligent and enthusiastic in their willingness to learn new ways to expand their awareness surrounding the process of interviewing and assessment. Their motivation, humor, and high-level work ethic have always inspired me to continue in this pursuit. To them, I owe my continuing youth and resistance towards retirement.

There are, of course, specific people that I want to acknowledge who have influenced my path and interest in drawings. Foremost is art therapist Patricia Gould Crone who initially provided exposure to the power of visual images during the early 1980s, as she presented in clinical rounds at the state hospital where we both worked at the time. Coming from a traditional psychology program, this novel approach to expression certainly stimulated me to write about what I had experienced. With her assistance, we wrote our first edition of "Using Drawings in Assessment and Therapy" (1987) and through this work we were able to enhance many other professionals in pursuing and adding nonverbal expressions of thoughts and feelings to their clinical repertoire. One such individual, psychologist and art therapist, Eliana Gil, has certainly strengthened the field of creative pursuits in her own work, expanding the areas of play therapy and interventions for traumatized individuals. I especially want to thank her for taking the time to write such a supportive foreword to this volume. Other art therapists who I have connected with over the years, especially Cathy Malchiodi, Rawley Silver, Shirley Riley, and Diane Safran, have also contributed to my enthusiasm.

In writing this book, I also need to recognize many talented people at Routledge Mental Health/Taylor and Francis Group for their support, ideas, and timely editing. It was during my early discussions with editor Anna Moore (who originally requested a third edition of our "Using Drawings" book) that this separate volume was conceived. Another person I want to acknowledge who provided structure through this process is Zoey Peresman, editorial assistant, as she frequently asked my opinion throughout the entire course of publication. Other equally important individuals that assisted in finalizing the book included the production staff and copy editors in New York and London; that is, George Warburton, Quentin Scott, and Katherine Hemmings. To all of your excellent and professional work, I want to thank you for a job well done.

Finally, I need to acknowledge the continuing encouragement of my immediate family. We were all much younger in our life cycle when I began writing about drawings during the mid-1980s. In fact, my wife, Jo Warwick, who was a student in psychology at the time, has watched me "evolve" as a psychologist, writer, and flute player for over 30 years, and will be there observing me as we approach our retirement years. She has also provided me pleasure in watching her transition into a special education teacher and offers me many remarkable stories in her pursuit of thoughtful and meaningful interventions for her students. Our two children, who are now in their late 20s, were only infants during the 1980s. We have both watched in amazement as they have grown into interesting individuals of their own, though outside of our professional pursuits. Our son, Aaron Oster, who is now 29, has followed a career in sports media and now spends his time working in radio as producer and reporter for professional and college sports. He also writes columns in the Baltimore Sun and Rolling Stone on professional wrestling. Our daughter, Corriane (Corri) Oster, now 26, discovered her passion through musical theater and now works in development at a nonprofit theatre in Florida with weekends acting at Disney World. A very different life from our own, but we could not be more thrilled for them.

About the Author

After receiving his PhD in Psychology at Virginia Commonwealth University (1981), Dr. Oster worked in a variety of research settings, inpatient hospitals, and outpatient centers, including the University of Maryland at Baltimore Counseling Center and Medstar Montgomery Medical Center. During that time, he held the titles of Clinical Associate Professor at the University of Maryland Medical School, as well as Director of Psychology Internship Training at the Regional Institute for Children and Adolescents (RICA-Rockville). Upon "retiring" from the State of Maryland system after 20 years, he has maintained a full-time private practice with subcontracting arrangements providing psychological testing to a community hospital as well as a group practice. He also provides supervision to graduate students in psychology (20 hours/week externs) at a residential treatment center in Baltimore. During these times, he and his graduate students from local universities review referrals, gather background information, and select the various tests (including drawing directives) to include in psychological assessment batteries. Afterwards, they spend much time in test interpretation and report writing, as well as enjoying the process of gaining diverse insights from their own extensive experiences.

Besides his clinical work, Dr. Oster has written or co-authored 10 books including the last two as ebooks—*Unmasking Childhood Depression* and *From ABCs to IEPs*. Other than his focus on drawings (including one text with social worker Sarah Montgomery, LCSW-C), he has co-authored texts on psychological testing (*Understanding Psychological Testing in Children* and *Assessing Adolescents*), teenage depression (*Understanding and Treating Adolescent Depression and Their Families* and *Overcoming Teenage Depression*), child therapy (*Difficult Moments in Child Psychotherapy*), and psychology career options (*Life as a Psychologist*). In his earlier years, he also published numerous articles in peer-reviewed journals on such diverse topics as learned helplessness, cognitive distortions, textbook errors, and animal drinking behavior, and has taught both undergraduate and graduate courses in child and lifespan development.

The first edition of *Using Drawings in Assessment and Therapy* (with Patricia Gould Crone in 1987) was acclaimed as a pioneering text in combining both the psychological and art therapy literature. It was later provided status as a monthly selection in professional book clubs. Before the second edition was released in 2004, Dr. Oster was also able to publish a similar text in 1996 (*Clinical Uses of Drawings*) with Sarah Montgomery. Again, it was this emphasis on multidiscipline audiences that derived the most interest. Subsequently, he provided lectures and workshops on the various aspects of using drawings in assessment and therapy to social workers, professional counselors, psychologists, expressive therapists, and even to medical students.

Dr. Oster has been married for over 30 years and has two adult children. His wife is a middle school special education teacher and his children continue to grow through their respective entertainment careers in sports media and non-profit theatre. Dr. Oster also plays flute in a community band.

1 Drawings in Everyday Practice

1.1

CASE STUDY: Sarah E.

Sarah E. was an 8-year-old, third grade student referred for psychological testing by her parents to gain a clearer understanding of her intellectual, educational, and emotional strengths and vulnerabilities. Her parents wanted to clarify whether attention weakness, information processing deficits, or other learning or emotional problems might be hindering her potential. They described Sarah's mood as being generally anxious and sad, as well as irritable and defensive. They also noted that she lacked self-confidence, as she was easily frustrated and often quit activities before she had really expended much effort.

Although Sarah's parents seemed unsure about the severity of her problems, they noted that Sarah appeared to misperceive her situation very negatively in comparison to her peers. For instance, Sarah remarked that she was "the worst reader in class," and told her parents that her "report card would be terrible." In fact, she had always been on at least grade level. Sarah also misconstrued her surroundings and tended to over-generalize the situation in a pessimistic manner. Within this context, Sarah often stated that "everything is horrible," and that "I'm no good."

During the initial interview, the parents stated that they viewed Sarah as interpersonally popular due to her outward appearance of having many friends. By contrast, Sarah portrayed herself as not getting along with peers and as frequently being bullied. She also described herself as the only "unhappy" individual in her family (even with her parents present in the same room!). There seemed to be diametrically opposed beliefs between the parents' perceptions of Sarah's viewpoints and her own self-image. Because of Sarah's moodiness and their concerns about her, the parents had already scheduled an outpatient therapy appointment. They now wanted additional documented information derived from a psychological evaluation to provide the future therapist with a detailed comprehensive picture regarding Sarah's daily struggles, in addition to her affective and academic needs.

As part of the assessment process, Sarah was asked to construct a series of drawings that would characterize her self-view and her problems. Even before listening to all the requested drawing directives (which consisted of various pictures, such as: the House–Tree–Person; her family and friends; herself in school; and problems she may have experienced and how to resolve them), Sarah hastily constructed this exemplary image to portray herself and her mood (see Figure 1.1). This very expressive illustration of a "sad butterfly" truly represented her outward appearance, as well as her perceived negatively biased status (a cute and outgoing persona with a sad inner life). Sarah was quick to share the very gloomy and misleading perceptions of her world and attempted to offer many insights into her distress.

Sarah's unhappiness was very apparent in this graphic depiction. And her willingness to share her negative thoughts through her drawings (even with her parents when they were brought together to review the results) was both enlightening and heartbreaking. In fact, this creative channel of expressing her thoughts and feelings through pencil-and-paper drawings made the feedback to her parents more tangible and poignant! Sarah later constructed several more images during the evaluative session with multiple indicators of excessive misery, sensitivity, and lowered confidence that were consistent with several self-report questionnaires and other personality techniques that related to her sadness and fragile self-concept. On these latter inventories and measures, she depicted herself as overly "lonely" and unable to cope with even minor everyday stressors.

Elaborating on her worries and concerns after the drawings and other aspects of the psychological testing were completed, Sarah described herself as having variable mood dispositions. She indicated that her typical day was waking up "okay," then becoming increasingly sadder throughout school, and by the end of the day feeling the "need to cry." The introduction of drawing directives to the psychological battery, especially at the beginning of the interview and assessment session, allowed many alternative avenues for Sarah to share her excessive degree of emotional upset and made it easier for the parents to actually "see" her marked despair. It would appear that any future therapeutic interventions would not only focus on her negative thoughts and feelings (in addition to family education about the distortions in thinking that depression can produce), but also provide more effective adaptive skills to help Sarah reduce her everyday tension (such as principles of yoga and mindfulness).

USING DRAWINGS IN CLINICAL SETTINGS

Because psychologists, social workers, expressive therapists, professional counselors, and behavioral health workers of all persuasions work in a wide variety of settings with myriad populations, they continue to require multiple methods for enhancing communication and understanding the difficult stories that are being revealed to them from each and every client (Oster & Gould, 1987; Oster & Montgomery, 1996; Oster & Crone, 2004). These clinicians need to quickly and efficiently assess the individuals before them, identify their core issues and conflicts, and establish a trusting and authentic relationship that will allow a free flow of meaningful interactions. As part of initial intakes, diagnostic interviews, psychological evaluations, or beginning therapeutic interventions, it becomes crucial to have a rich and diverse "clinical toolbox" of nonthreatening techniques and methods that will augment the collaboration between a client in distress and a supportive individual who will direct the flow of information that is being gathered, both verbally and nonverbally (Brooke, 2004). The introduction of drawings into this elaborately structured "dance" is an important adjunct to the interview and assessment process and provides greater insight into the cumulative narrative that is taking place during an initial session and subsequent evaluation.

Over the past century, graphic images of people, places, objects, or symbols have provided a fertile ground for interpretation about recognizing meanings or metaphors of underlying struggles during clinical questioning and psychological testing (Hammer, 1997; Handler & Thomas, 2013). Drawings and the process of drawing have also provided clients in distress with an easier and less threatening way of discovering and communicating negative affect and disturbing thoughts during the early stages of treatment (Malchiodi, 2012). Creating, viewing, and discussing drawings during evaluative sessions permit a safer platform to facilitate memories that may otherwise be too painful to address directly.

The use of visual metaphors as adjuncts to the clinical interview and psychological assessment process expresses an inner world that would otherwise not be revealed and shared. Making time (usually only a few minutes) to introduce these nonverbal techniques allows for nonintrusive and effective methods to truly help clients who are anxious, sad, and worried to expand the scope of their thinking and increase their spontaneous feedback. By using drawings within sessions, clinicians have observed that every picture that is created is unique to that person and offers the individual a distinct shift in perspective (that is, a new "door of perception") that has the potential to change an internal dialogue to activate potential problem solutions. When this inner representation is transformed onto a piece of paper or merely verbalized (for instance, "tell me what drawing of your anger would look like"), numerous possibilities arise for added insight and new understandings with subsequent interpersonal adjustments through the assessment and therapeutic process. With this alternative format of providing drawing suggestions included in the gathering of new information about the individual during clinical interviewing and psychological testing, countless opportunities surface for added flexibility toward self-disclosure, freer communication, and keener insight.

Using drawings in assessment and beginning therapy sessions has always had the benefit of being less invasive for clients who have problems accessing certain emotions, especially painful ones they are trying to hide and protect. Their applications during interviews and evaluations were often seen as especially useful for those individuals who presented as nonverbal or confused (Rubin, 2001; Wadeson, 2010). And during the long history of clinical practice, the utilization of pictures has been particularly salient when utilized with specialized populations, such as: substance abusers, who may feel more defensive and inhibited in seeking change (Bivans, 2013), or for those individuals who have suffered medical traumas (Malchiodi, 2014). Much literature over the past century has also demonstrated that there are many people (from high-risk youngsters to the fragile elderly) who may find drawings an easier, safer, and distinctive way to explore painful issues and troubling recollections that have impacted their maturational growth or present functioning (Oster & Crone, 2004). By establishing a symbolic space within an intake or assessment interview or beginning therapy session to express internal anguish, graphic images have been found to offer limitless openings to uncover significant psychic blockages and to inspire clients to notice and begin practicing a wider range of possibilities toward positive change.

By requesting drawing directives within the clinical interview, psychological assessment, and diagnostic process, a heightened amplification is generated within the client's stories. These symbols that describe inner conflicts (or shared aspects of the client's world) can greatly assist all health and mental health workers who require an alternative way to overcome initial resistance they are facing, or who are attempting to offer a more in-depth understanding of the evolving narratives that are being offered to them. These nonverbal pictures offer clues to underlying turmoil, apprehensions, and secretive dialogues that are sometimes not so easily expressed by words alone and almost always enhance the interpersonal exchange. Through these visual reference points, clients in distress can begin to expand their descriptions of their thoughts, feelings, and perceptions rather than attempt to place only verbal labels on their inner life.

WHY USE DRAWINGS?

Clinicians continually need to reenergize themselves with new techniques for extending beginning interviews, observing various performances during psychological testing, and examining diagnostic questions. Additionally, clients require more pathways to express themselves during the evaluative and beginning treatment process than merely talking about their problems to promote awareness and growth. And behavioral health professionals must discover innovative ways to produce novel experiences that empower clients to "see" their problems differently in order to resolve them. In this quest to clarify issues, diagnosticians, psychological examiners, and intake workers are continually searching for distinctive clinical tools and techniques (such as drawings and other nonverbal procedures) to supply vibrancy to their everyday treatment regimen. This enthusiasm for introducing complementary methods to engage and communicate more effectively with clients has produced renewed attention among practitioners and researchers for finding simple and direct applications that can answer specific questions during the clinical interview and assessment process, as well as enhance dialogue and document progress during beginning therapy sessions (Linesch, 2000; Riley, 2001; Edwards, 2002; Safran, 2002; Gil, 2011).

The clinical uses of graphic images during diagnostic interviewing and psychological testing remain alluring to both clients and clinicians with their ability to illustrate concrete markers of the inner world. Through their many variations, drawing directives have provided a simplified but meaningful structure for the sharing of personal feelings and experiences; expressing conflicts and current concerns in a nonverbal language. Furthermore, these pictorial interventions furnish new and creative opportunities for promoting change and realizing treatment goals. These visual representations have endured in their popular use by demonstrating their primary value for generating hypotheses about intellectual, developmental, and emotional functioning during initial information gathering and broader evaluations (Hammer, 1997; Handler & Thomas, 2013).

Whether those involved in the unfolding diagnostic and beginning therapeutic process are children, adolescents, or adults, the action of creating paper-and-pencil drawings provides an expanded and insightful view of the self, and perception of their surrounding world. The visible productions serve as a tangible focus for discussion, interpretation, and review of problem areas for many clients who are hesitant to reveal their internal suffering. How individuals approach the task of drawing and the resulting product become an active experience with much "food for thought." Both the action of drawing and the resulting images and symbols make it easier for individuals, who are being assessed or beginning treatment, to express their present levels of functioning in a different manner. These methods also provide a unique framework for people in treatment to share their underlying struggles in a way that otherwise might not be communicated through verbal exchanges only (Killick & Schaveriaen, 1997). Through their many uses in clinical interviewing and assessment, drawings give clients an exciting opportunity to relate their thoughts and feelings in a broader fashion that truly examines the whole person. And the resulting images demonstrate once again that "a picture is worth more than a thousand words!"

CASE STUDY: Cheyenne R.

Cheyenne R. was a 14-year-old youth with an already long-standing history of acting out behaviors, including self-injurious and suicidal gestures. Abandoned at an early age and exposed to numerous drug-abusing caretakers, she certainly met the criteria for Reactive Attachment Disorder (a rare and serious condition whereby infants and young children do not establish healthy bonds with parents or caregivers due to years of neglect and mistreatment). There were already allegations of sexual and physical abuse, which was suspected through Cheyenne's extremely aggressive and impulsive conduct. By the time she was seen by a licensed professional counselor at a crisis center, she had already been hospitalized several times, as well as placed in a variety of foster homes and residential treatment centers. She had also participated in a sex offender program, but had continued to display provocative actions toward younger children.

Cheyenne was brought to the crisis center from a group home (her then current placement) with the need for evaluating her safety and the risk of harming others. She had become unmanageable and was making threats toward staff and peers. The individual conducting the clinical interview attempted to engage Cheyenne in conversation, but Cheyenne's annoyed and angry façade limited the interactions. At that time she was withdrawn, refused to talk, and was seething with fury for being brought for yet another evaluation! Needing to overcome Cheyenne's resistance and produce needed documentation to assist in treatment decisions, the examiner placed pencil and paper in front of Cheyenne and asked her to "draw your current mood." She quickly seized this alternative opportunity to express herself graphically rather than verbally, and created the following illustration (see Figure 1.2).

This challenging image certainly presented a substantial platform for enhancing further dialogue. The counselor was encouraged by Cheyenne's willingness to express herself in this fashion and seized the moment to address Cheyenne's frustrations and her overall sense of hopelessness. Although she had never hurt herself seriously in the past, the vexing nature of this drawing allowed Cheyenne to readily talk about her irritation with others in authority and how she usually dealt with her discomfort in such an impulsive and self-destructive fashion. She appreciated the interviewer's suggestion to utilize this creative method of relating to others, as it allowed Cheyenne the occasion to channel her annoyances in a safer and more appropriate manner.

To demonstrate her pleasure at the outcome, Cheyenne constructed other visual images to communicate her marked ambivalence about being examined and ultimately this process assisted through another of her rougher times. By introducing a simple intervention, this process of "sharing through images" allowed Cheyenne a chance to decompress and accept the need for a comprehensive evaluation within the context of a brief stay in a community hospital where she could carefully and more securely plan her future needs. This case example certainly underscored the point that the introduction of drawing techniques in difficult clinical situations can permit access to an otherwise unavailable emotional level (in this case Cheyenne's suffering, mistrust, and anger being blocked by her resistance and withdrawn behaviors).

1.2

DRAWINGS CAN BE REASSURING

When first introducing drawings into clinical interview formats and diagnostic evaluations, clinicians usually discover that the action of generating illustrations can be less threatening and can usually provide an enhanced sense of comfort that is sometimes not available during the more intimidating process of intake or providing psychological testing. For example, using drawings with traumatized clients provides one of the few ways to externalize emotions and events that may be too painful to disclose verbally during these initial sessions. When interviewing the abused child or adult; the resistant, angry, or oppositional child or adolescent; or the family in chaos, the introduction of drawings into this process allows an alternative action to express suppressed emotional pain or unspoken family secrets (Malchiodi, 1998, 2008, 2012).

When vulnerable individuals refuse to verbally reveal themselves and their secrets during interviews for intake or prolonged evaluations due to fear of receiving retaliation or rejection, clinical vehicles (such as initiating graphic images into the course of action) can become a highly valued avenue for "telling without really telling" (Peterson & Hardin, 1997). These visual descriptions oftentimes capture and describe a variety of emotional states and psychological processes. And they offer a different and unique pathway to present inner conflicts that may not be readily apparent through standardized interviews or captured on self-report questionnaires.

CASE STUDY: Paul K.

Ten-year-old Paul K. was brought to an outpatient therapist (a psychiatric social worker) for an initial intake session. His parents described his then current condition as: being easily angered, defensive, lacking in self-esteem, and expressing a variety of somatic complaints (including sleep problems and subsequent tiredness). They also noted a negative attitude towards school and learning struggles as coexisting problems. This appointment was the first time that the parents had ever reached out to behavioral health professionals, other than the school counselor.

For his part, Paul seemed very irritated with his parents and embarrassed that he was meeting with a stranger. Although grudgingly cooperative, he preferred not to talk much, but was willing to complete screening questionnaires and construct several drawings. On one form, he noted that he had "a quick temper and a short fuse," and made quick decisions without thinking through the potentially bad consequences. He also acknowledged several areas of Attention Deficit Hyperactivity Disorder (ADHD) symptoms; including being easily distracted, unfocused in his thoughts, and disorganized in his work pursuits. Furthermore, he indicated several emotional conflicts and interpersonal problems. He mentioned that he worried excessively about the future and perceived his peers as being much happier. In one notable drawing (from the directive "Draw-A-Person-In-The-Rain" that accesses perceptions of stress in the environment and how individuals may protect themselves from these sometimes perceived overwhelming elements) Paul constructed the following picture (Figure 1.3).

In this simple but remarkable drawing, Paul revealed how much he viewed himself as a helpless victim and how harshly he perceived his everyday world. Through this explicit image, he talked about his struggles in learning, how much he got "dumped upon" by teachers and his parents, how many times he had been targeted by his peers, and how helpless and inadequate he felt in resolving any of his problems. With all of these difficulties surfacing and being expressed, it was decided that a full battery of psychological tests would be more valuable not only for treatment direction, but for possible specialized services and classroom accommodations in the school. Without the utilization of drawing methods, many of these topics would have been overlooked during the intake session.

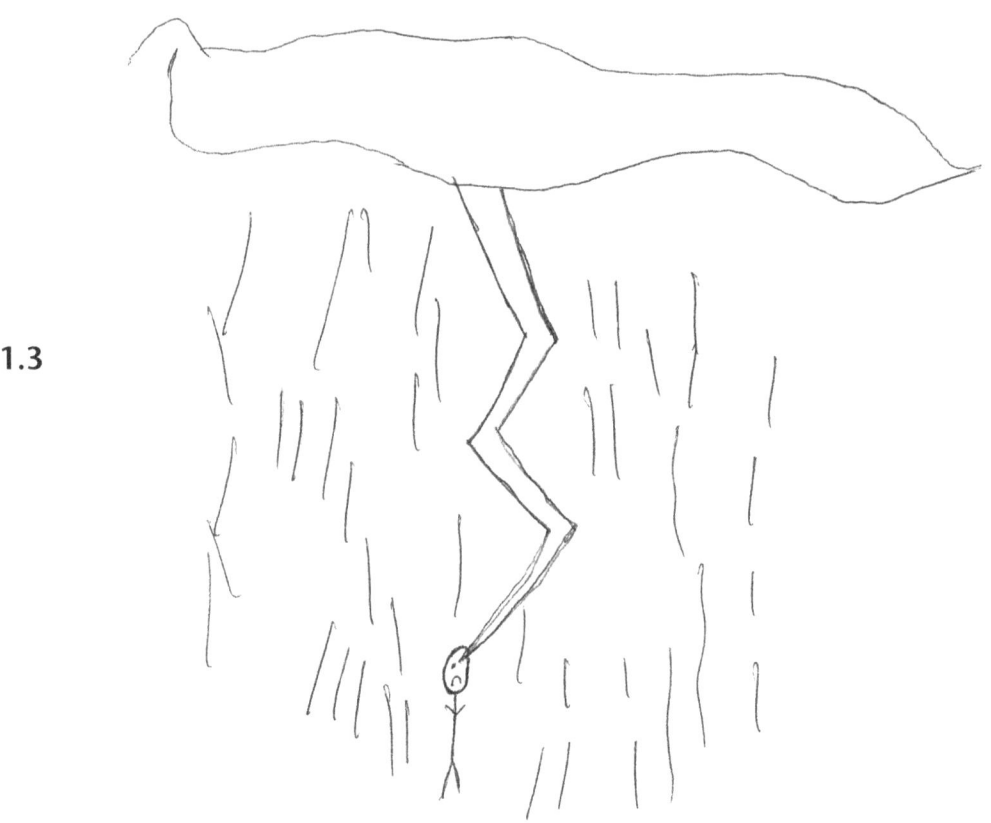

1.3

Incorporating drawing directives into initial interview sessions, or during psychological testing can enable many children, adolescents, and adults who may otherwise be unreceptive to discussing their issues or completing questionnaires the opportunity to view themselves more objectively within this expanded framework. Through the process of constructing images and possibly talking through them, individuals engaged in evaluations or beginning treatment can safely review their own productions and relate to their perceptions of the illustrations as opposed to answering questions from a new clinician who may inadvertently produce a less than inviting environment. The act of drawing and the subsequent products that are created allow a novel and curative approach for individuals who are being evaluated or have come for therapeutic assistance. They can graphically portray and view tangible representations of their emotions and ideas that otherwise would be hidden or not easily described verbally. And by asking people to reflect on their pictures, the experience can become an integral part of the evaluative process.

DRAWINGS IN EVERDAY PRACTICE 9

CASE STUDY: **Alice W.**

Alice was a nearly 18-year-old high school senior who was being screened at an outpatient behavioral health clinic after a traumatic car collision. Before her accident, she was described as popular, optimistic, and an active problem-solver. She participated on varsity school tennis and swimming teams, and had already been accepted into a prestigious university. Since the accident, however, she had come to perceive herself as being easily frightened of driving or even riding in cars. She also described herself as: always being "stressed out" and angry; continually distracted; and as no longer able to concentrate in classes or in sports. Because of these constant setbacks (combined with her pessimistic thoughts and overwhelming feelings), she was beginning to lose much of her confidence and motivation. Furthermore, she explained during the intake interview that she was eating more, had disturbing dreams, brooded and was usually sad, and did not feel that people really understood her inner fears. She also found herself being impatient with friends and had withdrawn from many social events.

When later scheduled for a more formal diagnostic evaluation to plan for further therapeutic interventions, Alice appeared moody, irritable, and was less willing to share more than she had already revealed. Seeing that the session was not starting off well, the clinician conducting the evaluation (an expressive therapist) decided that presenting the idea of drawing directives might provide an easier and novel path towards more meaningful exchanges. By offering a distinct and more structured approach, Alice was able to respond positively to this switch in diagnostic strategy and construct the following picture to more concretely portray her internal stressors (see Figure 1.4).

This portrait that she labeled a "tug of war" appeared to represent the considerable pressures that Alice had been struggling with since her accident. After she concurred about this possible interpretation, she became more accepting of the interactive process. At that point, it became much easier for her to elaborate on the tensions and insecurities that she was still experiencing. Through this informative exchange, she became more engaged during the encounter and a more willing participant in exploring her memories of the accident. She then began to accept the help that therapeutic interventions could provide. And it was revealed later that she even challenged her therapist to use drawings to provide visible markers of her progress, as well as illustrate possible solutions for her presenting problems.

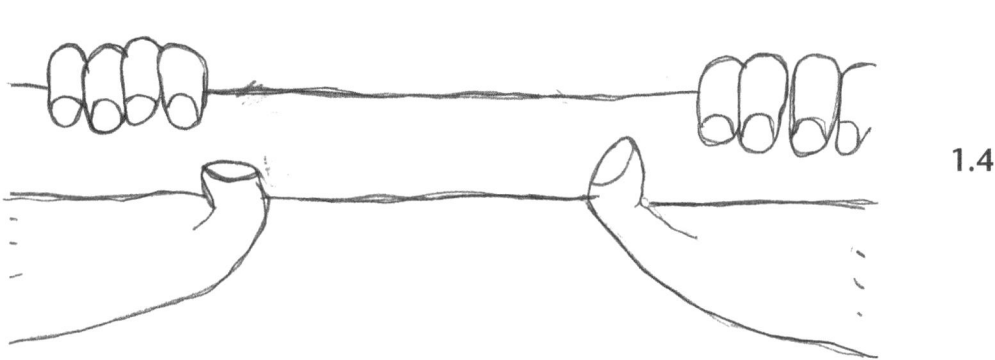

1.4

STRENGTHENING INSIGHT AND PROBLEM-SOLVING

Historically, drawings have been used extensively as an assessment technique by numerous clinicians to enhance insight into their clients' unconscious processes during diagnostic interviews and extended psychological evaluations (Groth-Marnat, 2009). While many practitioners and researchers have utilized graphic images to reveal personality characteristics through interpretation of certain indicators within the drawings (for example, the depth of a line employed may signify boldness or timidity) (Hammer, 1958, 1997), others have focused on providing alternative opportunities to increase the dialogue between client and clinician (Oster & Montgomery, 1996; Oster & Crone, 2004). Through their symbolic speech and the richness derived through revealing problem areas, clinical drawings offer a special language where much of the individual's inner world can be observed (perhaps for the first time!). Furthermore, they have the potential to highlight and introduce more relevant issues that are needed for diagnosis and treatment planning, including therapeutic opportunities for creative interventions (Malchiodi, 2011).

Because of the emotional defenses that most people are likely to employ in talking about their problems and issues, the clinical uses of drawings during assessment and interviewing provide a less invasive format to express painful affect, such as fear or anger. When introducing this possibly novel approach (for example, asking the client to construct a drawing of themselves at work or in school) during information gathering, individuals who seek treatment, or are in need of thorough evaluations, are more likely to share otherwise hidden thoughts through this one-step-removed method that drawings offer (Oster & Crone, 2004). With this enlarged avenue to express themselves, clients are more willing to disclose long-standing beliefs and feelings that heretofore had been held in check and not usually revealed to others. As many examiners and therapists have observed, this indirect approach of using drawings can quickly release salient information on current developmental, intellectual, and emotional functioning (Handler & Thomas, 2013). And the resulting graphic expressions have the advantage of being less threatening and provide the opportunity to uncover and portray presenting problems from the standpoint of a different type of assessment compared with conventional means of clinical interviews or formal psychological testing.

In today's behavioral health environment, where quick turnaround is required to describe relevant problem areas and limited sessions are the norm, drawings become even more strategic as a means of expediting assessment direction and treatment planning. Efficiency has become a necessary part of the duties of psychologists, social workers, professional counselors, and expressive therapists (as well as psychiatric nurses or other health staff) in a variety of clinical, rehabilitative, and school settings. Often, clients who are being evaluated lack the necessary skills to acknowledge or successfully process the conflicts or trauma being experienced. By communicating through images, people involved during structured interviews or engaged in assessment can successfully utilize these various pathways to more easily express themselves through these symbolic interactions. Nonverbal techniques allow opportunities for initial steps of processing and healing to occur. They also offer an alternative to self-expression that goes beyond completing behavioral or personality inventories and responding orally to structured or ambiguous situations that are the hallmark of psychological testing. For these reasons, the creation of visual images maintains the attention and enthusiasm of clinicians from all persuasions involved in the intake and diagnostic process, as well as in areas where additional interactive techniques are needed to enrich the recovery process (Kaplan, 1999).

DISCLOSING TEMPERAMENT

Whether using drawings as a projective technique (in this case, expressing thoughts and ideas as well as personality traits through graphic methods) or using the medium of pictorial productions to enhance communication and increase dialogue, it can safely be said that any action or gesture can bear aspects of one's character or temperament (Hammer, 1958, 1997). Graphic illustrations can take the form of relating one's ego strength, expressing uncertainty and mistrust of the environment, displaying a low frustration tolerance, or sharing inner conflicts (Handler & Thomas, 2013). Clues can also be gained from elements within the drawings regarding the client's self-concept under conditions symbolizing environmental stress (for instance, the previous example of "Draw-A-Person-In-The-Rain), or insight accessed about perceptions of familial relationships (see Chapters 3 and 4).

For the psychological examiner or clinical interviewer, the action of drawing and the drawings themselves begin the process of hypotheses generation pertaining to cognitive abilities, emotional resources, and personality characteristics that direct future inquiries or assist in the selection of other psychological tests or structured questioning. Quick and easy to administer, drawings can be used to corroborate clinical observations and help facilitate effective and personalized treatment planning. Clients' self-perceptions are readily revealed through the drawing productions, along with their personal view of their surroundings and interpersonal interactions. Constructing graphic images also help people heal from whatever crisis or trauma they have experienced (Malchiodi, 1998, 2012).

Assisting individuals to understand or think about their drawings, even at the assessment stage, can be a catalyst for additional insight and potential change. The symbols used in drawings sometimes can be very direct and easy to interpret, or they can be hidden in their true understanding, like in manifestations of dreams or myths. By adding visual thinking (or the ability to organize thoughts, feelings, and perceptions through graphic productions), and employing pictorial references to describe perceptions of people and things during the information-gathering process, the derived actions of drawing contribute to fresh experiences and innovative possibilities for positive adjustments to occur.

The utilization of drawings (similar to the format of unstructured psychotherapy) serves as a blank canvas, or clean slate, that can create glimpses of a hidden dimension where conflicts toil and are not always available to the individual for immediate expression. Especially when initially anxious or in marked distress, people involved in the evaluative process or who are seeking treatment will welcome the opportunity to be understood more readily and completely when multiple methods of assessment tools are used during beginning meetings. Often people who say that they cannot talk about a certain subject (or do not have the words to articulate their inner pain) are willing to graphically portray their mental struggles, or create signs and figures that represent their inner anguish. And every symbol created is always unique to each client! When opportunities are provided to communicate through a wider range of methods (as opposed to verbal means only), individuals being interviewed convey their worries and concerns more effectively and at a deeper and more meaningful level.

CASE STUDY: Sam K.

Sam K. was plagued by memories of fifth grade and middle school. Through those tumultuous years, he was keenly sensitive to slights and misunderstandings, and he often felt bullied. Now at the end of a successful freshman year in high school, this recently turned 15-year-old young man suddenly found himself being rejected again and these past feelings of disappointment and estrangement overwhelmed him. After descending into much emotional turmoil, Sam described his frustrations to a friend through a text message, with an attachment that showed him holding a gun. Although the gun was not real (a pellet gun), the picture was perceived as threatening when his friend's mother somehow discovered the image and forwarded it to their school's officials. Subsequently, the principal called Sam's parents and requested that he be seen for an evaluative session at a local crisis center before he could be allowed to return to school.

Initially, Sam was mortified, as well as suspicious and reticent to share his personal feelings with this new person (a clinical social worker). Sensitive to Sam's hesitant position and feeling somewhat stuck due to Sam's apparent oppositional stance, the clinician needed a unique way to break through this resistance. So, instead of the usual verbal give-and-take, the clinician asked Sam to construct a visual metaphor of the feelings behind his actions. Rather than enter the potential dilemma of whether to assess if Sam's acting out of his distress was real or not, the clinician decided that a novel approach that perhaps would visually demonstrate what was beneath the surface of the incident would allow Sam an easier path to self-disclosure. This basic directive allowed Sam to "speak" in a very different manner than he normally would have offered. The process also expanded the scope of the interactions between him and the intake clinician, which allowed him a freer and safer path to unburden his underlying conflicts.

For Sam, the initial attempts at establishing rapport were not enough to gain a full portrait of his true self and how he typically resolved problems. He seemed to require an alternative route to share his inner life. His thoughtful illustration (see Figure 1.5) provides yet another instance of the importance of expanding the "clinical toolbox" and emphasizes the shortcomings of language during the evaluative process (Andreas, 2013). And here was a prime example that once again exemplified how other interactive methods are needed to obtain a broader "picture" of what is really going on underneath a troubled client.

During beginning interviews or psychological assessments with clients, it always becomes easy to assume that the individual will respond to your words. However, words alone often cannot capture an insightful moment so dramatically! For Sam, it was this poignant drawing of early memories of being shamed that offered him a vivid reminder of how much he had matured over his freshman year, but also how those past memories still governed his present behaviors. Unfortunately, he still tended to act out his feelings, and usually in an immature and maladaptive manner. As his picture suggested, and as he elaborated upon during his review of the sketch, he would usually withdraw into himself and feel like "everyone" was taunting him when slights were perceived (except for his teachers, who were represented by the "light").

But now these regressive actions when under duress involved more thoughts and feelings of anger and retribution (as characterized by the original picture of him with a gun that he had texted to his friend). Without this outstanding drawing, the intake clinician would never have discovered these old memories in their first session and never would have had the opportunity to discuss them and allow Sam to express these early negative experiences so quickly. With this expanded information, the clinician was more relieved about the prognosis of the situation and could provide a positive treatment direction for the family and school by recommending outpatient therapy as opposed to a more secure setting for extended evaluations.

1.5

IDENTIFYING GOALS AND MOTIVATION

The primary goals of clinical interviewing and psychological evaluations are to gain a clear and comprehensive understanding of present functioning and underlying issues. Furthermore, these interventions are used to identify and gauge motivation for treatment and to expand the knowledge of both clinicians and clients to encourage more adaptive solutions to daily living. During these intake and assessment sessions, it is incumbent on all behavioral health professionals to provide outlines of possibilities that offer clearer therapeutic direction for active change.

By asking clients to graphically construct their "perceived worlds," "everyday feelings," "worst (or best) memories," or "problems," they can begin to enlarge their framework for communication and supply alternative symbolic meanings to their everyday experiences (Oster & Montgomery, 1996; Oster & Crone, 2004). Introducing self-expression through nonverbal techniques, such as drawings, also give clients a greater chance to lessen their inner tension and confusion and reduce their sense of isolation. These tangible illustrations can and do reveal ideas for improved ways to cope with perceived stressors and to actively begin to overcome problems.

Aditonally, the use of visual metaphors during the initial stages of rapport building or during more extended evaluations allows the clinician to demonstrate different and creative ways to access emotionally charged material. Providing feedback to the client, or by having the client respond to the symbolic images on the paper (instead of directly to the examiner), inspires individuals to seek broader possibilities in their pursuit of insight and personal change. These interactions are crucial for circumventing oppositional, or anxious, reactions that would normally prevent or inhibit clients from moving through the necessary stages for accepting therapeutic assistance. For instance, a client who would normally refrain from verbal exchanges might be more willing to construct pictures of their problem areas. Conceiving a symbolic space to express worries and concerns grants the client easier and more effective communication pathways, and focuses on future changes that need to take place. However, drawings may not be so easily accepted by all clients and in these cases talking through these images may suffice.

TALKING THROUGH IMAGES

Sometimes, the idea of introducing drawings into the diagnostic arena will meet with strong resistance. When this roadblock occurs, examiners or interviewers can offer an alternative opportunity; that is, asking clients to verbally describe their inner images or representations of the various drawing directives that are being requested, as opposed to expecting them to actually graphically portray their "problem" or "world" on paper. For instance, a man in his thirties was reticent to offer his vulnerabilities during an intake interview. As he was talking about past episodes of drinking and how frustrated he had become in previous attempts at stopping his alcohol consumption, he was asked to think of symbols that represented his feelings. He immediately took this cue and described himself in a "bubble" or "jail cell" to express his images of underlying fears, loneliness, and estrangement from friends and families.

This mid-30-year-old man continued to use these metaphors throughout the remainder of the session to expand his problem descriptions. This unconventional (for him) way of specifying difficulties by talking through his inner images relieved the pressure of verbally disclosing painful areas more directly. He then became more relaxed and free to discuss a broader range of personal and interpersonal difficulties than he initially had thought about before making this first appointment.

A second man, aged 58, became tearful during an initial therapy session and was unable to express the depths of his depression. Instead of continuing with the clinical interview, he was asked to verbally describe "his mood" through metaphors. His inner image and subsequent discussion of "a deep hole in the earth that bottoms out with lots of confusing emotions all together" allowed him to talk more completely about his frustrations, anger, and sadness ("full of tears"). For both of these men, the verbal sharing of "inside pictures" allowed them unique openings to divulge secrets, overcome fears to express their inner struggles out loud, and helped to establish a beginning rapport and trust that would ultimately assist in their treatment process.

The above case examples (in addition to many others that will be shared throughout this book) demonstrate the possible formats for constructing visual portraits during clinical interviews and the assessment process and how they expand opportunities for discussion through the symbolic representations that are created. And as just exemplified during the intake sessions with these men, it sometimes becomes possible to access hidden symbols by merely talking about them instead of placing them on paper! These unexpected requests for drawings (or producing verbal descriptions of what a client would place on a sheet of paper) begin the transition of building a "bridge" from the inside to the outside for sharing, learning, and growth.

The following examples also underscore this approach to overcoming resistance through unexpected and novel requests for information. Once during an evaluation in an emergency room, a young woman in her mid-twenties who was feeling overwhelmed, constricted in sharing her feelings, and apparently experiencing suicide ideation, was requested to visually portray her emotions when confronted by such confusing distress. Because she was reluctant to draw, she agreed instead to verbally describe her inner image—"like a house on fire and having only two buckets of water to douse the flames." Certainly, she was undergoing devastating fears and was unable to problem-solve effectively at that point in time. By offering a different path to describe her underlying angst, she was placed at ease and became more articulate in explaining her reasons for admitting herself into the evaluative unit of the hospital. For her, this alternate, one-step removed approach to describing her anxiety and feelings of helplessness allowed her freer access to her thoughts and feelings.

Another instance of using this "talking through images" approach occurred during an initial intake session for another client (who had also balked at constructing a drawing). Instead of graphically producing a portrait of her family members and her perceptions of problem areas, this 45-year-old woman described her relationship to her father by stating that she felt that they "lived on separate mountains and could not really hear or understand one other." Truly an insightful "picture" of her core problem areas that she could later elaborate upon throughout subsequent appointments.

VITAL POINTS

Whether by graphically portraying an "inside" image onto paper, or just talking about visual metaphors, these alternate reflections of underlying distress provide yet another and potentially exciting stage for sharing problem discussions, rather than addressing emotional difficulties in a straightforward, question-and-answer fashion. By expanding assessment approaches through the use of composing actual drawings, or by verbally describing figures that represent challenging areas of living, numerous opportunities are conceived to visually describe feelings and thoughts that come alive, instead of remaining elusive and hard to communicate. For example, reflections of self-loathing or personal inadequacies can more easily be discussed through verbal metaphors, or externalized onto a piece of paper. And possibly for the first time, these inner secrets have a chance of being articulated and heard by another person rather than remaining veiled through defensive posturing (Brooke, 2004). Asking clients to describe what they would see or construct in a drawing underscores two important aspects of the evaluative process—bringing to life the client's inner imprints and dialogue, while creating and increasing the external discourse between client and clinician (Dalley, Rifkind, & Terry, 2014).

As discussed thus far in the introduction to this book, drawings (or their verbal descriptions) can be used in a variety of ways to expedite intakes and the diagnostic process. This complementary way of talking has been shown as a facilitating technique to help overcome feelings of apathy, ambivalence, or helplessness (Oster & Crone, 2004). Children and adolescents, as well as adults and elderly clients, often experience a deep sense of disempowerment in their everyday worlds. They frequently perceive themselves as victims of a chaotic, unfair, or uncaring environment (Moon, 1994). Upon initially presenting for diagnostic evaluation or intake interview, it is not unusual to find these clients overly protected and mistrustful, as their rigid, emotional walls have surfaced and everyone around them are perceived as excessively distant. Even more threatening to them are the strangers in these novel settings, as all newcomers may be perceived as hostile and offering little value to them. To counteract this defeated and hopeless stance, clinicians must be willing and able to provide positive evaluative experiences within supportive interpersonal interactions that expand their clients' perception of their daily experiences.

EXPANSION OF INTERPERSONAL ENGAGEMENT

All clients who are entering behavioral health programs or counseling centers are experiencing acute symptoms of distress because they lack adequate coping skills or the ability to identify their usual coping resources (Willis, Joy, & Kaiser, 2010). These individuals, especially those who have been traumatized or victimized, must be transformed into actively engaged participants in the early stages of beginning interviews or assessment, and later during the establishment of a therapeutic partnership (Malchiodi, 1997; 2014). Few initial goals of treatment can be accomplished without a trusting relationship where feelings can be vented and new insights expressed.

Fresh meanings of conflicts must be discovered through an assessment process, which can later reinforce new interpretations of a possibly threatening world and expand the frame for future interventions. Discovering new means to express this inner confusion and hopeless feelings can serve as an effective path toward overcoming challenging hurdles and increasing personal ingenuity. Learning to identify the underlying stress triggers and improve adaptive abilities through the introduction of various clinical techniques (such as drawing directives) allows individuals being interviewed or assessed to view the process as a more effective and comprehensive means to increase their problem-solving skills in a relative safe and comfortable arrangement.

Engaging clients from a solely verbal approach is often not enough to uncover past trauma, or to reveal different possible reasons for maladaptive behaviors. By introducing directives, such as drawings (or even through verbally expressing these images) people who are being interviewed or assessed can: a) expand their frame of reference; b) gain new understandings by visualizing or concretely seeing their problems; and c) increase opportunities to discover alternative answers to their conflicts and concerns. To have clients construct a drawing about one of their problems on one sheet of paper, then draw a possible solution on another, for instance, offers new possibilities for overcoming their perceived helplessness (Oster & Crone, 2004). Through this unique pathway to visualizing areas of underlying conflict, clients who are being evaluated can now attain a new level of awareness through these nonverbal products or expressions and can immediately appreciate themselves and their own ideas more fully.

The act of drawing itself also enables clients to feel more hopeful and provides a tool for active engagement in later treatment by expanding additional possibilities for unique insights and productive change. Drawings used during intake sessions or psychological testing can stimulate inventiveness and support a unique approach to the problem-solving process, with an emphasis on specific treatment goals. When added to clinicians' already existing treatment techniques, drawings (and the use of "talking metaphors") can expand the prospects for: gathering new information about their clients, enhancing prescriptive remedies, and hastening the path toward recoveries.

STIMULATING INSPIRATION

As emphasized in the preceding sections, the act of constructing symbols (or even talking through metaphors) can stimulate inspiration, increase personal resourcefulness, as well as provide relevant, personal statements that represent both conscious and unconscious meaning. The drawings or reflections themselves allow the child, adolescent, or adult who is being assessed or interviewed to offer significant information through spontaneous imagery that may have been otherwise censored through their verbal psychological defenses. These graphic products or expressed images support opportunities for individuals to gain new insights and fresh, meaningful perspectives that are often not available to them through the usual modalities of verbal interventions.

When introduced early into the treatment process, drawings can highlight the important relationship that is being constructed between therapist and client, or what is termed the "therapeutic alliance" (Wadeson, 2010). And during interviews and testing, it increases the idea that different personal and interactive experiences are needed to understand the entire person. By using various drawing directives (such as "Draw Yourself in School," "Draw a Dream," or "Draw Yourself Before, During, and After" [a traumatic event]), expressive products or representations are created to be exchanged, discovered, and commented upon. The construction of graphic images helps to establish this working relationship which, in turn, enhances dialogue and spontaneity and expedites deeper levels of sharing insight during this new interpersonal relationship (Rubin, 2005).

The use of clinical drawings also provides a physical platform for the diagnostic process to occur and can expand deeper understanding as well as treatment possibilities. Through these visual or spoken symbolic markers, enhanced ways of self-expression are then channeled into productive interactions. From a simple picture, an expressed symbol, or a series of drawings that graphically portray problems or solutions, the resulting imagery can then be used to enhance meaningful communication. The drawings can become personal imprints or statements that define a point in time, a past fleeting thought, or a feeling that has been aroused. And, of course, drawings become a unique way to establish rapport. The initial task in assessment and interviewing is to launch this working relationship between the client and professional staff; otherwise meaningful data are difficult to obtain (Fischer, 1994). Drawings and verbal images offer this avenue toward interpersonal collaboration.

By observing the process of drawing, and what is shown and discussed upon completion, clinicians can more readily see vivid portraits of their clients' inner world or have a better understanding of their outer "public masks" that they may be presenting to the world (Oster & Caro, 1990). This revelation is especially poignant for teenagers or adults who might otherwise hide behind their interpersonal facade.

A case from a previous book, Clinical Uses of Drawings *(Oster & Montgomery, 1996) illuminated this point through the description of 34-year-old "George" who sought emotional support after being diagnosed with AIDS. Although he had known he was HIV-positive for several years, it was only recently that he had been hospitalized for AIDS-related pneumonia. While at intake he did not appear sick, he had just quit his high-level professional job and began seeking assistance to cope with his new reality. When asked to construct a picture of how others viewed him (his public mask) and how he viewed himself, "George" constructed two portraits—one reflecting an outwardly healthy and vigorous young man, and the other an illustration of a very sick-looking person who appeared emaciated and disheveled. By using this alternative format for self-disclosure, George was much more willing to reveal his deeply held fears and future concerns.*

While there is a fascination with attempting to provide meaning to these artistic creations within assessment and interview sessions, it is often best to just ask clients for their own interpretations (Malchiodi, 2012). By encouraging clients to express their personal meanings onto the drawings, those individuals involved in the evaluative and testing process can offer an exciting and unique direction that frequently enhances verbal interchanges and creates a better overall evaluative outcome.

For "George," the sketches allowed him to explore the shame and disappointment he was experiencing by examining how others would be questioning his lack of employment. Through the introduction of a different process e.g., drawing, clinicians have the opportunity to assist clients, like "George," to make more accurate self-judgments and to broaden objective views of themselves.

Another client, Marcia T. was also able to use this type of intervention to expand her ability to more openly express her inner tension and fears.

CASE STUDY: Marcia T.

Marcia T. was 17 years old and a high school senior when initially seen within a psychiatric hospital unit for a diagnostic evaluation. She had already been interviewed by other admissions personnel the previous day for expressed suicide ideation and gestures. Reportedly, Marcia had been feeling overwhelmed after experiencing multiple stressors over the past several months; including her grandmother's death, a break-up with her boyfriend, rejection from peers, and struggles in her school performance. There was also much perceived turmoil at home surrounding her inability to initiate college applications.

When first admitted, Marcia appeared tearful and depressed. Other reports by the admissions staff who assessed her in the emergency room to determine the need for inpatient status indicated that Marcia had experienced a loss of appetite and was socially withdrawn. Her insight and judgment were considered adequate and there was no evidence of psychosis or significant drug/alcohol usage. However, Marcia had stated that she felt rejected from peers at a neighbor's party and this rebuff led to superficial wrist cutting.

Once on the unit, Marcia was referred to a psychologist for an extended evaluation by the attending psychiatrist. Assessment questions pertained to what degree her mood experiences were interfering with her daily functioning, as well as her degree of suicide risk, and to assist in treatment directions and aftercare planning. There were also questions related to diagnoses and how her personality characteristics impacted her decision making.

Marcia appeared alert, oriented, and cooperative during initial contact. Her speech was clear and her expressed thoughts were relevant. However, she seemed somewhat subdued and inhibited in her affect. While she seemed intellectually bright and from all reports quite articulate, she was only grudgingly cooperative to sit through "yet another interview." Instead, the examiner thought it best to try another approach to broaden the possibility of greater spontaneity and interaction. After requesting Marcia to construct an image that would represent her problem areas, she produced the following "arrows" to visually describe and point to her conflicting issues (see Figure 1.6).

While Marcia did not produce an elaborate picture of her internal stress, this drawing exercise certainly allowed her the opportunity to discuss her areas of concern in an unexpected and less threatening way. By using this drawing directive to articulate her fears and conflicts, she became much more engaging and willing to talk about her everyday problems. This basic technique broke the barriers to her resistance in sharing her inner struggles. And through talking through this image she became more than willing to acknowledge her range of distress surrounding her feelings of worthlessness and perceived estrangement from peers and her family.

By overcoming her initial oppositional stance through drawings, it was much easier to introduce other psychological tests and questionnaires that would provide a broader picture of her cognitive and emotional strengths and weaknesses. For instance, on a depression scale Marcia noted many instances of worry, sadness, and loneliness. She further indicated that she never felt important and viewed other students as not liking her. She elaborated on her fragile self-esteem and her primary need to belong; even if it meant doing things that she really did not want, such as feeling forced to have sex or using drugs.

While she denied being a current suicidal risk, the past month had been particularly upsetting for her. In fact, she indicated on a suicide ideation scale (Reynolds' Suicide Ideation Scale, Reynolds, 1988) that on at least two occasions she was beset by thoughts of death and self-harm. During those occurrences, she thought about how and when she would kill herself and considered writing

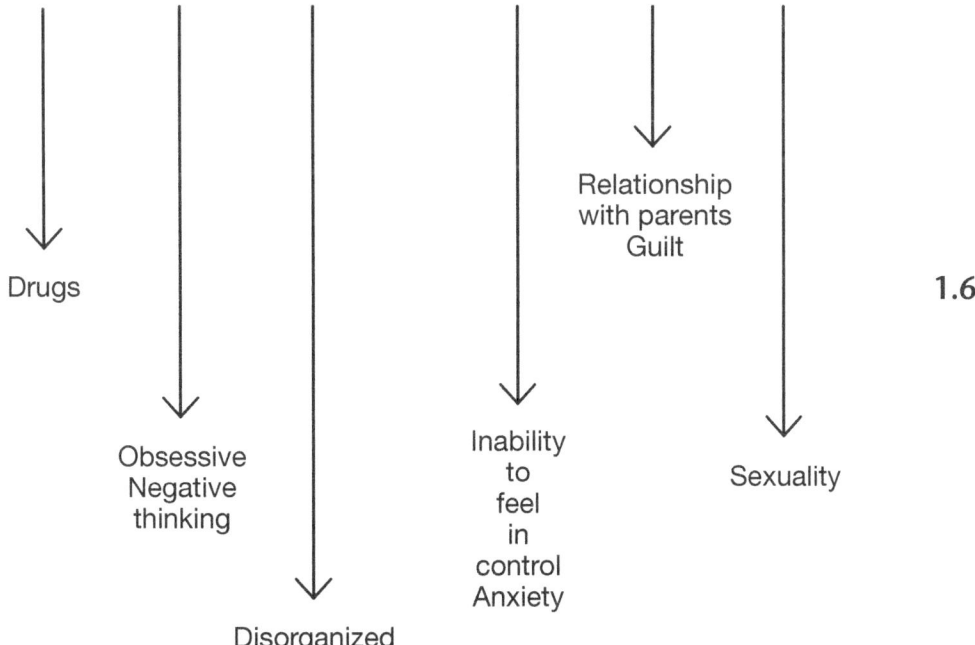

1.6

a suicide note. She also wondered whether she had the nerve to harm herself and reflected on whether her life was still worth continuing. Other data portrayed her as moody, distractible, worried, and very sad. She struggled with self-acceptance, appeared very self-critical, seemed dependent on others to solve problems, and of course felt exceedingly lonely.

Afterwards, Marcia commented on how much the drawing exercise helped her to focus and organize her thoughts and allowed her to relax with the examiner. If this activity had not been attempted, she concurred that she would have probably refused the other assessment material. With these primary areas of emotional anguish clearly displayed, she was much more willing to continue in the therapeutic process and accept help from the unit staff regarding her presenting and longer-term problems.

CONCLUDING REMARKS

In summary, adding drawings to clinical interviews and psychological evaluations can facilitate spontaneity among young children, help to understand what is behind troubled adolescents and assist them to move beyond personal developmental hurdles, and uncover underlying conflicts in adults that can lessen psychological pain. Constructing graphic images (or talking about them) also allows older adults to review their life's memorable events, as well as relive problems and past solutions (Oster & Crone, 1987; Oster & Montgomery, 1996; Oster & Gould, 2004). As the case examples in this chapter have illustrated, drawing directives offer the possibility to project one's inner life into a visual form that can later be used as a springboard for identifying initial conflicts, summarizing goals, and providing a baseline for later outcome measures. Introducing the opportunity to portray conflicts and worries into graphic images enlarges the framework and perspective for understanding the whole person, both verbally and nonverbally. And through these endeavors of creative expressions come powerful means of promoting personal and interpersonal change! Throughout this clinician's guidebook, there will be many practical demonstrations and case studies that will further underscore the value of introducing drawings to the clinical interview and psychological assessment process.

By producing concrete markers of acute distress or past trauma, these nonverbal representations have the power to elicit very meaningful responses and exchanges between clients and examiners that will create substantially more avenues for possible shifts in perceptions, feelings, and attitudes. And they do not inhibit discussion! Rather, drawings establish new and novel avenues toward enhanced communication styles that become vehicles for expression of fears, struggles, wish fulfilments, and fantasies. Drawings represent a symbolic speech that is not a substitute for talking, but instead can stimulate increased verbal dialogue in reviewing the products that are constructed either during the intake interview, diagnostic evaluative session, or the initial therapy hour. The clinical uses of drawings allow the individuals involved in assessment or interviewing the opportunity to reach beyond their surface concerns and explore deeper into their present struggles and past memories.

The remainder of this book will explore the history of drawings, their uses and interpretations during assessment and interviewing, and current research findings. There will also be sections on the basic administration and possible derivatives of common drawing directives. Additionally, numerous guidelines have been reviewed in other resources to enhance and interpret the visual language of drawings (Hammer, 1997;

Handler & Thomas, 2013), and these will be discussed in various chapters. And while there may or may not be universally agreed upon meanings to symbols or research-based hypotheses related to indicators of personality traits, there will be many case studies demonstrating that drawings are best used to establish rapport building, especially if not trained in psychological interpretation of images or art therapy. When used as icebreakers for getting people to relax and talk openly about how they feel about things occurring in their lives and how they perceive their current functioning in their interpersonal world are when drawings really become valuable tools during the clinical interview and assessment administrations.

Drawings are also very personalized, almost like a fingerprint. There are never identical drawings to be observed of a house, tree, person, or any other illustrations that have been requested of a client, though common themes abound in parts of the figures (see Figure 1.7). Furthermore, all clients bring their own unique background to the drawing process, including life experiences, cultural influences, and personal perspectives. It is with this increased understanding of combined interpretations and experience that clinicians can increase their awareness of the underlying and potentially self-defeating thoughts and self-destructive behaviors that have brought the person in distress to a particular office or setting.

Effective treatment can only occur when clinicians involved in intake interviews or psychological testing begin to understand the inner world of their clients. For this to happen, a shared language must be created through verbal and nonverbal means to promote movement and growth (Linesch, 2000). Nonverbal constructions can assist in the challenges to uncover expanded meanings of intrapsychic conflicts and of their resolution. Through the sharing of these images, clinicians gain glimpses of their clients' inner battles, as well as estimate their cognitive and emotional resources. The act of drawing and the drawings themselves offer a powerful and unique method of relaying information that can be actively explored during intake interviews, comprehensive testing, and beginning treatment. These completed graphic products (or speaking about them) offer a visual communication with richness, distinctiveness, complexity, and spontaneity that is not usually available through discussions alone.

Expressions through pictures are often more symbolic and less specific than words. These metaphors of tension, along with the sharing of experiences and perceptions, elicit visual images that are beyond ordinary awareness. Individuals engaged in the drawing process can then communicate through this symbolic language without having to acknowledge that their drawings are part of their real self. This protection from emotionally laden material makes the recounting of these thoughts and feelings less anxiety provoking and less likely to produce defensive posturing. What unfolds is crucial to insight and personal transformation.

Most clinicians and those in frontline decision-making positions will likely use drawings in addition to other materials, including behavioral observations, feedback from outside referrals, and self-report questionnaires, to access enough information to decide on a starting diagnosis and initial treatment plan. Psychologists, or other clinicians involved in the evaluation process, who expand their testing "toolbox" by including drawing directives in their broader-based assessments, will also gain a helpful companion in their discovery of cognitive and emotional functioning. The clinical uses of drawings provide important supplemental hypotheses that may readily support this data-gathering process. These graphic productions can then provide a unique and exciting way for the client to participate in the intake or testing process through creative and growth-oriented tasks that are bound to spark interest and greater understanding of their situation.

1.7

REFERENCES

Andreas, S. (2013). Breaking the spell. *Psychotherapy Networker* (May/June).

Bivans, S. (2013). *The use of projective drawings as interpreted through self psychology to activate stages of change in the treatment of substance abuse.* Pacific Graduate Institute: Dissertations and Thesis.

Brooke, S. L. (2004). *A therapist's guide to* art *therapy assessments: Tools of the trade* (2nd ed.). Springfield, IL: Charles C. Thomas.

Dalley, T., Rifkind, G., & Terry, K. (2014). *Three voices of art therapy: Image, client, therapist* (2nd ed.). London: Routledge.

Edwards, D. (2002). *Art therapy.* Thousand Oaks, CA: Sage.

Fischer, C. (1994). *Individualizing psychological assessment.* Northvale, NJ: Lawrence Erlbaum Associates.

Gil, E. (2011). *Helping abused and traumatized children: Integrating directive and nondirective approaches.* New York: Guilford Press.

Groth-Marnat, G. (2009). *Handbook of psychological assessment* (5th ed.). New York: Wiley.

Hammer, E. F. (Ed.). (1958). *The clinical applications of projective drawings.* Springfield, IL: Charles C. Thomas.

Hammer, E. F. (1997). *Advances in projective drawing interpretation.* Springfield, IL: Charles C. Thomas.

Handler, L. & Thomas, A. D. (Eds.) (2013). *Drawings in assessment and psychotherapy: Research and application.* New York: Routledge.

Kaplan, F. F. (1999). *Art, science, and art therapy.* London: Jessica Kingsley.

Killick, K. & Schaveriaen, J. (Eds.). (1997). *Art, psychotherapy, and psychosis.* London: Routledge.

Linesch, D. G. (2000). *Celebrating family milestones: By making art together.* Toronto, ON: Firefly.

Malchiodi, C. A. (1997). *Breaking the silence: Art therapy with children from violent homes* (2nd ed.). New York: Brunner/Mazel.

Malchiodi, C. A. (1998). *Understanding children's drawings.* New York: Guilford Press.

Malchiodi, C. A. (2006). *Art therapy sourcebook.* New York: McGraw-Hill.

Malchiodi, C. A. (2008). *Creative interventions with traumatized children.* New York: Guilford Press.

Malchiodi, C.A. (Ed.) (2011). *Handbook of Art Therapy* (2nd ed.). New York: Guilford Press.

Malchiodi, C. A. (Ed.). (2012). *Art therapy and health care.* New York: Guilford Press.

Malchiodi, C. A. (2014). *Creative interventions with traumatized children* (2nd ed.). New York: Guilford Press.

Moon, B. L. (1994). *Introduction to art therapy: Faith in the product.* Springfield, IL: Charles C. Thomas.

Oster, G. D. & Caro, J. (1990). *Understanding and treating depressed adolescents and their families.* New York: Wiley.

Oster, G. D. & Crone, P. (2004). *Using drawings in assessment and therapy* (2nd ed.). New York: Taylor & Francis.

Oster, G. D. & Gould, P. (1987). *Using drawings in assessment and therapy.* New York: Brunner/Mazel.

Oster, G. D. & Montgomery, S. S. (1996). *Clinical uses of drawings.* Northvale, NJ: Jason Aronson.

Peterson, L. W. & Hardin, M. E. (1997). *Children in distress: A guide for screening children's art.* New York: W. W. Norton & Company.

Reynolds, W. M. (1988). *Suicidal ideation questionnaire: Professional manual.* Odessa, FL: Psychological Assessment Resources.

Riley, S. (2001). *Group process made visible: The use of art in group therapy.* New York: Routledge.

Rubin, J. A. (Ed.). (2001). *Approaches to art therapy: Theory and techniques.* New York: Psychology Press.

Rubin, J. A. (2005). *Child art therapy: Understanding and helping children grow through art* (25th Anniversary Edition). New York: Wiley.

Safran, D. S. (2002). *Art therapy and AD/HD: Diagnostic and therapeutic approaches.* London: Jessica Kingsley.

Steele, W. & Malchiodi, C. A. (2011). *Trauma-informed practices with children and adolescents.* New York: Routledge.

Wadeson, H. (2010). *Art psychotherapy.* New York: Wiley.

Willis, L. R., Joy, S. P., and Kaiser, D. H. (2010). Draw-a-person-in-the-rain as an assessment of stress and coping resources. *The Arts in Psychotherapy, 37*(3), 233–239.

2 Foundations of Clinical Drawings

> To the extent that I managed to translate the emotions into images—that is to say, to find the images which were concealed in the emotions—I was inwardly calmed and reassured.
>
> Had I left those images hidden in the emotions, I might have been torn to pieces by them.
>
> There is a chance that I might have succeeded in splitting them off; but in that case I would inexorably have fallen into a neurosis and so been ultimately destroyed by them.
>
> As a result of my experiment I learned how helpful it can be, from the therapeutic point of view, to find the particular images which lie behind the emotions.
>
> *Memories, Dreams, Reflections* (1965), Carl Jung, p. 177

HISTORICAL ASPECTS OF CLINICAL DRAWINGS

Throughout the centuries, drawings, as well as other artistic creations, have been perceived as significant extensions of personal and interpersonal communication. In ancient times, evidence revealed that people etched and carved on stone and underground walls to depict their feelings and actions. These unknown individuals entered dark caves to paint and sculpt images on the rock walls, which portrayed rituals or significant events of the time. These earliest known sketches and "artwork" were constructed about 20,000 years ago, during the last stage of the Paleolithic period and were mainly discovered in Spain and southern France (Janson, 1991).

What little is known throughout this early history has been further enhanced through symbols based on pictographs (pictures that resemble real life) and ideograms (symbols that represent ideas). Ancient Sumerian, Egyptian, and Chinese civilizations began to use such figures before refining them into more elaborate writing systems. Pictographs can also be considered as forms of expressive art. They are designated as such in scenes from pre-Columbian and Native American art; Ancient Mesopotamia handiwork; and paintings throughout the United States before colonial times. From the caves of New Mexico to rocks on the beaches of Rangell, Alaska (personal observations), these creative expressions have provided hints to unknown explorers and mysteries without clear historical passages.

These early drawings have been cataloged in scientific investigations as examples of how early individuals attempted to generate their ideas and emotions. These basic, but expressive, notations were viewed as the essence of beginning language and have been studied by numerous disciplines, most notably archaeologists and art historians. During the past century, even the fields of neuropsychiatry and neuropsychology were studying

26 FOUNDATIONS OF CLINICAL DRAWINGS

the symbolic meanings of these indigenous pictograms and petroglyphs; aiming to create new ways of exchanging ideas between native people and modern scientists to safeguard and value their cultural diversity (Meyer, 1985).

IMAGES OF PSYCHOLOGICAL MATURATION

Transitioning from these past explorations into visual language, behavioral health practitioners have also been studying and using similar types of drawings throughout the past two centuries. This interest was especially observed in the discipline of developmental psychology, where it was shown that simple constructions of shapes and figures (like in early pictographs) and how they change in their complexity over time seemed to follow an orderly sequence in a child's maturation (cited in Oster & Crone, 1987; Oster & Montgomery, 1996; Oster & Gould, 2004). In a process that is comparable to their prehistoric ancestors, young children soon discover that they have the capacity to produce images as a means of self-expression. Although they might first find pleasure in creating just meaningless scribbles, these activities soon give way to orderly shapes and integrated objects. And like primitive people, children consistently draw elements that they consider essential and eliminate others that are not important to them (Hammer, 1967, 1997).

Even by age three, children appear to gain a greater mastery of their fine motor coordination and their emotional control, as well as derive considerable satisfaction in recreating visual descriptions of what they perceive around them. As Howard Gardner

2.1

(1982) mentioned in his book, *Artful scribbles: The significance of children's drawings*, children become quite engrossed in their illustrations. These constructions then become their first attempts to make sense of the world around them, as well as their thoughts and feelings about the events they perceive.

The earliest defined shapes formed by children appear to be circles or ovals and are viewed as the simplest patterns that are depicted in most cultures (see Figure 2.1). Through these early stages in human development, these figures become the main forms for representing heads, eyes, or mouths (DiLeo, 1973). These elementary outlines, which are the easiest to draw, tend to be a function of basic eye–hand coordination that results from the growth and development of the nervous system.

However, these early exploratory attempts at nonverbal creations seem to be representations of ideas rather than a direct image of an object itself. Through experimentation in producing graphic images, children begin to visually construct what they think exists, rather than what they actually see. And across nationalities, whether with pencil or crayon on paper, or sticks in the sand, children continue the process of graphically sharing their perceptions of the world around them more accurately (Peterson & Hardin, 1997). In trying to add meaning to these drawings as they mature, images of important concepts are often produced; for example, children initially attempt to construct human figures, then they later begin to create drawings of animals, houses, and trees (see Figures 2.2 and 2.3).

DEVELOPMENTAL SEQUENCES

Even more than a century ago, writers described their observations of children's drawings, and through their artistic expressions evolving stages and age-related levels were revealed (Cooke, 1885; Ricci, 1887). One of the more comprehensive descriptions of children's maturational drawings was completed by Cyril Burt (1921). Based on personal observations and systematic studies, Burt classified sequences in children's graphic abilities by distinct stages. He indicated that children between ages two and three begin to construct scribbles. He regarded these activities as purposeless expressions that become more refined and differentiated over time.

Other developmental researchers, such as Luquet and Piaget (cited in Thomas and Silk, 1990), regarded the early scribbles as a form of play and exercise. Thereafter, pictures appear to form or be interpreted with basic meanings attached. By age four, children begin using single lines to replace their unorganized scribbles. Around age five, a stage of "intellectual realism" usually appears and children typically draw what they know; therefore, such drawings as a house or tree are often observed (cited in Krampen, 1991). Over subsequent years, children begin to sketch crude rudimentary shapes that are structured and more complex. Thus, when confronted by an older child who can only scribble when requested to construct a person or other figures, it is likely that this youth is developmentally delayed, has few controls over his motor skills and emotional expressions, or has a specific learning disability.

During the latency years from age six to ten, Burt (1921) classified children's attempts at drawing as "concrete and detailed" to parallel Piaget's (1959) stage of "concrete operations." The scaling and details of pictures become more realistic. Among these years, children draw less of a "tadpole" body and are more likely to add a head, a separate trunk, attached arms, and legs. Later, hands, fingers, and clothing are added to human figure drawings (Thomas & Silk, 1990). They also begin using perspective and begin to develop rules for color, such as brown for a tree trunk or green for leaves. As Malchiodi

2.2

(1998) pointed out, however, unusual color at this later age during the latency stage may signify more significance in the child's maturation than at earlier years.

Burt (1921) also observed that children at age 11 preferred to copy and trace the works of others, as opposed to creating original art work. He believed that drawings by 11- to 14-year-olds often display an acute deterioration in quality due to advances in their cognitive abilities, enhanced use of language, and emotional sensitivity. The inclination for this age group is to draw geometrical forms and decorations, rather than human forms. Burt (1921) additionally noticed that an artistic revival occurred again during the middle adolescent years when they start demonstrating more interest in color and form (see Figure 2.4).

Later investigators (most prominently Elizabeth Koppitz (1984), who constructed developmental scoring systems for children's drawings) came to similar conclusions that early teenagers' drawings are inferior to those by latency-age children. However, she hypothesized that youngsters who reach puberty become excessively self-conscious and critical of their drawings. They begin drawing rapidly and carelessly, making sketches with little effort or producing stereotyped figures or cartoons.

Although there have been some criticisms of all stage theories of development, most investigators of child psychology have acknowledged discernible differences in standard figure drawings during key maturational periods. Mainly, the majority of researchers and theorists over the years refined each of the phases of development that were espoused by earlier workers in the field. For example, DiLeo (1973), in his review of earlier studies in the 1800s, spoke of the discovery of stages or sequences in graphic expression of children that have been repeatedly confirmed throughout present-day research.

2.4

FOUNDATIONS OF CLINICAL DRAWINGS   31

These previous researchers suggested six sequential stages to artistic development. First is scribbling, which appeared similarly related to an infant's babbling speech. Next is the emergence of a tadpole stage, in which drawings resemble a circular head with appendages. For instance, three-year-olds usually construct people mainly with a head and one-dimensional arms and legs (see Figure 2.1). A transitional phase follows, whereby a trunk appears (usually an elongated tear drop beneath the head) with some details of a human figure. In this case, four-year-olds are likely to shift from larger heads to create a person with arms and legs attached to a smaller head and stretched resemblance of a body (see Figure 2.5). A succeeding phase usually displays a full-face drawing of a person with added details of the face (eyebrows, ears) and more defined body parts (e.g., fingers, feet) as the child ages. Another transitional step may be observed in this pathway, in which attempts at profiles are made. Finally, an accurate profile orientation is completed, which is considered an introduction to movement (see Figure 2.6).

Later, Dale Harris (1963) highlighted the progression of children's drawings that included three general stages of development. The beginning period demonstrated the child as focusing on the pleasure and satisfaction experiencing by gaining motor control and just generating marks or scribbles. Over that time, these creations began to form character and structure. The subsequent juncture in development of graphic productions was mainly imitative, whereby children began to show details and organization within their drawings. Finally, Harris (1963) suggested that the final phase in development was learned. He noted uses in the consistent rules of design and balance. He also suggested that the later development was defined by internal satisfaction and added communication within a structured format.

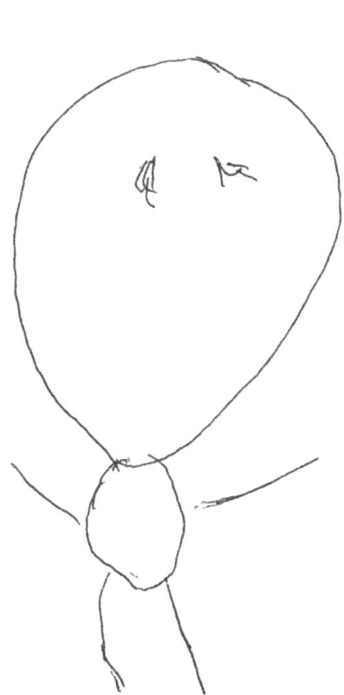
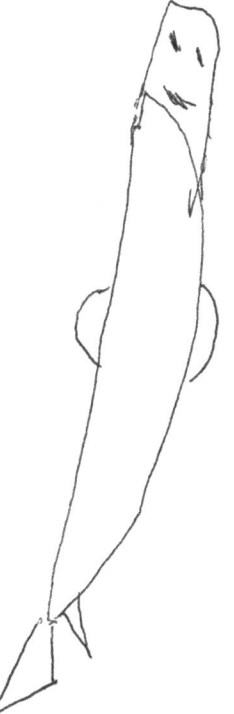

2.5

2.6

Rhoda Kellogg (1969), who attempted to integrate the fields of child development and anthropology, collected and examined nearly a million drawings from children, as she looked for common images and structures. She also verified that drawings mature in an orderly fashion from certain basic scribbles toward a consistency of shapes. Through her enormously detailed work, she emphasized that meaningless scribbling by infants turns into specific forms and symbols. She noted that by age two, children's drawings can be differentiated into 20 different types of markings and appear to be the foundation of graphic expression. These dots, lines, and circles apparently display various muscular movements without perceptual guidance. Every child, Kellogg believed, can make these markings and those who cannot are somehow disabled. Other investigators shared their thoughts that there are actual neurobiological reasons for art making, and these connections seem to have an influence on the drawings of children (Morris, 1962; Dissanayake, 1989).

COGNITIVE MATURATION

Early studies during the twentieth century also provided behavioral health professionals with an abundant and varied understanding of the psychological aspects of children's drawings. Initially, children's illustrations were the subject of much speculation in describing intellectual development (Goodenough, 1926). Along with the rapid rise of standard intellectual testing at that time period (e.g., Stanford–Binet, Wechsler Scales), drawings were soon discovered to be useful by-products of clinical interviews and diagnostic assessments that uncovered developmental disorders and were later included in more comprehensive psychological testing batteries.

What was important for the clinician using drawings as diagnostic tools for interpretive value was to recognize that what appeared to be abnormal features drawn or omitted on a particular figure might be quite the standard for a specific age group. This concept of developmental normality was especially emphasized by Elizabeth Koppitz (1984), who highlighted the need for clinicians and researchers to carefully differentiate their sample populations in age groupings when discussing any childhood phenomenon. She described six important steps to consider when interpreting completed drawings in children and young adolescents. She noted that the individuals studying childhood drawings should consider:

- observing behavioral attitudes during the constructions;
- acquiring a global impression of the images;
- viewing the drawings through a developmental perspective;
- judging the quality of the illustrations;
- analyzing the content within each figure; and
- assessing signs of visual–motor integration impairment.

Up to that point, the scoring systems were primarily based on the assumption that as children grew older, their drawings reflected accurate changes in their level of cognitive maturation.

CASE STUDY: Greg B.

Greg B, a nearly 8-year-old youngster, presented for an initial screening by a psychologist at an outpatient behavioral health clinic. His parents were concerned about his struggles in school, which included being poorly organized and exhibiting poor fine motor coordination that made it difficult for him to copy and write efficiently. Although described as a "wonderful and nice boy," Greg was extremely sensitive and tended to pout and sulk when upset. He was also viewed as being easily frustrated, fearful of being placed in new situations, and needing extra help to remain focused and complete assignments. Additionally, there were expressed concerns about his social anxiety, apparent sadness, and not being accepted by peers.

During a brief evaluation, it was apparent that Greg was quite bright. He was extremely articulate (an estimated Verbal IQ score of 134 [Very Superior range]) and was also able to reason effectively, even on nonverbal tasks presented to him. However, weaknesses were reflected in areas associated with sustained attention, visual–motor integration, and copying proficiency. These vulnerabilities certainly had the potential to undermine his work output and lead to many frustrations.

As part of the screening, Greg was requested to produce illustrations that would corroborate his seemingly immature fine motor coordination. His basic drawings of a house, tree, and later a family illustration were quite basic and appeared several years delayed. In particular, his human figure drawings were reminiscent of 5-year-old constructions (see Figure 2.7). With this evidence, Greg was referred for an extended evaluation with an occupational therapist specializing in these types of disparities in development, especially those children struggling with fine motor problems. Later, he was placed in a specialized program in his school ("Handwriting without Tears") that offered him better ways to hold a pen and pencil, and as a result he became more effective in copying and writing his assignments.

Observing how children normally express themselves at various stages through their drawings is primary to understanding part of their basic development. As children appear to follow similar and progressive changes in their drawings, shifts are seen that are usually characteristic of each age group. However, more than distinct stages were needed in these descriptions to fully detail a child's nonverbal maturation.

34 FOUNDATIONS OF CLINICAL DRAWINGS

2.7

Later, comprehensive studies completed by Gardner (1982) and Golomb (1990) provided broader and more thoroughly researched concepts for understanding children's drawings by adding their research to various perspectives from the fields of developmental psychology, art, and anthropology (cited in Malchiodi, 1998). These educators and researchers demonstrated that young children from cultures in different parts of the world also transitioned through similar stages of artistic expression that included scribbling, basic forms, human figures, schematic representations, realism, preadolescent caricatures, and adolescent artistic abilities. It has been these descriptive studies of children's drawings that have provided a newer and more elaborate framework for detailing stages of nonverbal development and have laid the basis for using drawings in current ways to estimate intelligence and even later to gauge personality traits (Handler & Thomas, 2013).

EMOTIONAL INDICATORS

Health and mental health professionals have also made attempts at understanding the aesthetic experience, explaining the process involved in producing art, analyzing the genius of certain artists, and exploring the meaning of particular creations. For instance, during the past century, there was a burgeoning interest in the interpretation and utilization of drawings to describe the emotional and psychological aspects of the nonverbal expression of individuals in treatment (Betensky, 1995; Hammer, 1997; Leibowitz, 1999). These graphic images were believed to reflect the inner worlds of clients; depicting their thoughts and feelings, as well as relaying information concerning their psychological status and inner struggles through these alternative avenues of expression.

It was Ernst Kris (1952), though, known for his psychoanalytic studies of visual constructions and for combining psychoanalysis and direct observations of infants, who depicted the psychological process of drawing as "the placing of an inner experience into the outside world (that is, the mechanism of projection)." In a similar vein, Zygmunt Pietrowski, one of the clinical pioneers to devise a scoring system for the Rorschach Inkblot Test, observed that art creations were one of the first methods to be regarded as a "projective" technique of both conscious and unconscious personality traits (Pietrowski & Abrahamsen, 1952). Drawings used in these formats during diagnostic interviewing and beginning psychotherapy provided a unique opportunity to: explore conflicts and concerns, view alternative problem-solving possibilities, and make uniquely personal statements that represented both conscious and unconscious wishes from a very distinctive perspective (Riley, 1997). And within the projective battery of psychological tests, drawing directives served a special function by providing a minimally threatening and maximally absorbing introduction to the various assessment procedures (Hammer, 1997). In this capacity, Hammer stated, the "drawing page" provides an introductory "canvas" that captures glimpses of personality traits and attitudes, behavioral characteristics, in addition to the person's strengths and liabilities.

CASE STUDY: James D.

James D. was an 8 years, 4-month-old third grade student when referred for a psychological assessment by his parents and school. He had transferred from one elementary school to another at the request of his parents due to a continuation of conflicts with both teachers and peers. After three weeks in his new placement, the parents described the move as satisfactory with only minor adjustment issues. In discussing the problem areas with the parents, they noted that James was "like two different persons—one a very likeable, bright and engaging child; the other a very demanding, argumentative, and defiant youngster."

The parents then remarked on his sudden mood changes and his need to control everyone around him. They viewed him as immature and not able to control his impulses once confronted by emotionally laden situations. They also had concerns about his inability to focus and attend to his school work. Furthermore, they noted that his learning style consisted of completing his work rapidly, then becoming distractible and disruptive to the other students.

During the testing portion of the evaluation, James was alert and cooperative. He was able to demonstrate excellent abilities on a variety of cognitive and educational measures. In fact, on an IQ test, his overall score of 131 placed him within the Very Superior range. On this intellectual instrument, he displayed outstanding scores in his verbal fluency skills, especially in areas of abstract reasoning and in his fund of general knowledge. As expected, his weaker areas were reflected in his concentration and attention to detail. Thus, complaints about his impulsivity and over reactions seemed to be a consequence of these latter liabilities.

Despite his many scholarly assets, his emotional experiences appeared much less developed. On projective measures, his responses were narrow and constricted, suggesting that he would become easily overwhelmed when confronted by even minor demands and stressors that were not familiar to him. He also seemed to rely primarily on his emotions to resolve problems situations. This limited reasoning approach was bound to create much inner tension, which he obviously could not express in an adaptive manner.

As part of the assessment battery, James was asked to construct several drawings that would highlight his emotional turmoil. One drawing, in particular, appeared to characterize his marked irritability. In this illustration (see Figure 2.8), James seemed to express his anger and frustrations. In talking about the picture, he became visibly upset and expressed how much he wanted to seek revenge on his previous school setting and those people that had caused him "so much grief." More than any other of the psychological instruments, this portrait of his rage allowed him to view the session as a positive experience (a way for him to channel his aggression and possibly talk about it to a person outside his family and school). From this session, he requested continuing appointments to assist in resolving his old grudges.

2.8

SYMBOLS OF MENTAL ILLNESS

Even before these discoveries of "projective" drawings, interest grew in the art productions of the mentally ill throughout Europe in the late 1800s and early 1900s. A pioneer in this field to initially notice symbolism in sketches by the "insane" was Max Simon (1888), who apparently was shocked by these "obscene drawings" and actually ordered the termination of such activity. Despite this cessation of patient art, the subsequent years yielded considerable interest and insight into the possibilities that drawings could provide for the psychological examiner, intake clinician, or therapist, as a pathway into the internal thoughts of clients in turmoil. Many practitioners of that time believed that artistic expressions could confirm a diagnosis, especially of the more severe forms of mental illness, such as schizophrenia. For example, Tardieu's (1872) *Etude medico-legale sur la folie* included patient art productions as legal criteria for the diagnosis of emotional disturbance. Also, Lombroso (1895) attempted to demonstrate that drawings and paintings of the mentally ill could offer numerous insights into their inner emotional state and disturbed ways of thinking (cited by Malchiodi, 1998).

Later, during the 1920s, Hans Prinzhorn, an art historian and psychiatrist, was able to collect 5,000 pieces of artwork created by patients being treated for mental illness throughout Europe. His 1972 publication, *Artistry of the Mentally Ill*, gathered much attention to the possibilities that art expression held for diagnostic value and rehabilitation. Even before these observations, Ebenezer Cooke (1885) detailed changes typical of normative drawing differences in how children construct visual images. Thus, the focus of drawings of individuals who were beset by cognitive challenges and emotional disturbance had been observed and discussed for very many years.

FREUD AND JUNG

Much of the early clinical uses of drawings were centered in psychoanalytic thought. For his part, Sigmund Freud (1933) dedicated an abundance of attention on masterpieces and their creators. He assumed that universal human conflicts and neuroses could motivate artists to create their inner experiences on canvas. He began studying the works of famous artists, like Michelangelo, and posited that there were signs in the paintings that demonstrated inner struggles and worry. Freud later alluded to the fact that the pursuit of art was in itself "cathartic" and the act of painting and the symbols within them represented their anxiety. It was their actions of painting, sculpting, or drawing that assisted these masters to overcome their intrapsychic struggles. For both artists and patients, their completed products were perceived by Freud as a unique way of reflecting inner, personal confusion and in making sense of their lives.

Freud (1958) also hypothesized that symbols represented forgotten memories and were likely to emerge through dreams or art expressions. He surmised that these representations were primarily a disguise for anxiety-laden content and safeguarded individuals in treatment from feeling overwhelmed by their underlying tension. In his writings, he explained how images presented in dreams could be illustrated through drawings and how some patients could more easily express themselves through this means than by trying to describe them in words. With the advent and appreciation of Freud's writings and the ensuing psychoanalytic movement, trained professionals began to grasp the symbolism of art products completed by their emotionally disturbed patients and were more accepting and able to use them readily in their everyday work (cited in Kris, 1952).

Soon afterwards, Carl Jung (1971) asserted that symbols embodied parts of personal experiences that could be enhanced through psychoanalysis. His emphasis on creativity as a primary component of the treatment process placed special importance on personalized images in the form of archetypes with universal meanings. Although Freud was never particularly fond of asking his patients to draw in sessions, Jung often encouraged his clients to create images on paper. He concluded that this use of expressing fantasy through symbol production was a highly effective way to evolve and heal (Jung, 1956). With both of these major psychoanalytic figures explicating their views on symbols and artistic expression, the clinical uses of drawings quickly became a popular issue for discussion within the behavioral health community.

Through these major contributions, drawings and other art activities within sessions became appreciated in terms of nonverbal expression that gave access to unconscious material and treatment direction (Case & Dalley, 1992). Due to Freud and Jung's explorations of the mind's unconscious processes, clinicians who valued the interpretive possibilities of graphic illustrations established a groundwork for diagnostic questioning, clinical interviewing, and therapeutic interventions that paralleled and incorporated the ongoing work in psychoanalysis and other modalities of healing.

CREATIVE PURSUITS IN PSYCHOTHERAPY

The psychotherapists who followed the pioneers in psychoanalysis soon realized, like Jung, that verbal language alone was not adequate for revealing the entirety of unconscious experiences.

They too emphasized that the active use of graphic metaphors in sessions (as well as other art media) would provide an additional dimension of unique images that could not otherwise be described in merely verbal terms. During this transition, Judith Rubin (2005), an analytically trained psychotherapist and early proponent of art therapy, stated that drawings could assist in establishing a strong working relationship between the clinician and client. The productions created during these sessions could then stimulate and promote interactions and spontaneity, as well as expedite deeper levels of sharing insight into the struggles that had not as yet been expressed.

Those clinicians who envisioned the benefits of the creative process in assessment and psychotherapy began to utilize these visual images as "bridges to the unconscious," rather than relying on possibly well-defended verbalizations of thoughts and feelings. Furthermore, many clients who were being seen for assessment or during beginning therapy sessions soon discovered that it was much easier to construct pictures of disturbing dreams, or conflicted feelings, than attempt to verbally describe them through spoken words, with its many limitations. The clinical uses of drawings soon became a "hot topic" and framework for discussion among those practitioners pursuing not only alternative channels for insight, but also diagnostic criteria for various forms of psychopathology (MacGregor, 1989).

CASE STUDY: Elizabeth G.

Elizabeth G. was 16 years old when first administered psychological testing. Her parents' main concerns were displayed on a behavioral checklist indicating that Elizabeth appeared apathetic and distractible, felt like a failure, and lacked self-esteem. She was also displaying sleep problems and experienced frequent tiredness throughout the day. Consequently, her grades had declined and she no longer viewed school in positive terms. In the past, she had been diagnosed with Attention Deficit Disorder (ADD) due to being unfocused and disorganized, and was treated with stimulant medication, albeit with only mixed results.

At this point in her life, she was falling asleep late at night and would refuse to get up in the mornings for school. Although intelligent and creative, she tended to be "passively stubborn." She reported that she tended to avoid conflicts, especially with her teachers, and refused to turn in her homework rather than receive criticisms. She maintained that she could be accomplished on assignments when motivated, but these productive occurrences were decreasing. Now, she no longer wanted to care or exert any effort towards school.

After meeting with her parents, Elizabeth was seen alone in the psychologist's office. She presented as sad and distant with little incentive to reveal her personal problems or sit for an extended evaluation. She grudgingly completed several questionnaires related to her mood that all pointed to a severity of depressed symptoms with thoughts of suicide. Instead of coaxing her to offer additional information, she was asked to construct a set of drawings that would symbolize her mood and physical experiences. She immediately accepted this novel approach at self-expression with excitement. Instead of resistance, she exhibited a broadening of affect and a more cooperative stance.

Elizabeth's first drawing was that of a closed fist (see Figure 2.9). After completing the image, she stated that the curled, tightened hand represented her discomfort when she felt nervous or angry. She mentioned that this coping strategy was not a conscious response; rather she noticed that she performed this action repeatedly instead of confronting a demanding issue. This beginning illustration led to substantially more discussions about her various temperaments and coping mechanisms.

2.9

2.10

As the interpersonal dialogue continued, Elizabeth spontaneously drew another of the requested drawings (see Figure 2.10). In this illustration, a "person in the rain," Elizabeth was attempting to share her feelings of being overwhelmed and alone. She suggested that the person in the picture felt sad and helpless to resolve any of her problems. In this example, it appeared that her environment was perceived as very harsh and threatening, and that she tended to over-generalize her lack of emotional resources. Through this drawing and other questionnaires, she began to expand her story. She disclosed the depths of her depressed symptoms ("I feel sad and worried most of the time") and relayed statements about her suicide thoughts ("I thought about what to write in a suicide note"; "I thought that no one cared if I lived or died").

Responses to other aspects of projective testing underscored her inability to cope with stressors, and emphasized a high degree of tension and anxiety that could lead to feelings of alienation. With this information, a shared discussion with Elizabeth and her parents provided more active therapeutic interventions that included a brief hospitalization and follow-up appointments with a psychiatrist and outpatient therapist. She seemed relieved to have divulged all these feelings to an objective professional and was appreciative of the nonverbal approach to self-revelations. Certainly, the introduction of drawings allowed a freer and safer space for Elizabeth to share a more accurate portrait of her inner experiences.

ART THERAPY AS A DISCIPLINE

Art therapy (as a separate field of study) was also being developed in this exciting backdrop to the twentieth century. Margaret Naumburg (1966), one of the original pioneers in this new professional discipline, relocated to the United States from Europe as psychoanalytically trained. With this type of depth psychology background, she emphasized the use of free associations and interpretations with spontaneous artwork in her treatment approach. Later, Edith Kramer (1971) advanced the idea that the process of creating artwork in itself was a separate path towards recovery that did not even require verbalization. During those years, clinicians using these methods were viewed more as educators or artists rather than professional mental health workers. By the 1960s and 1970s, however, art therapy was establishing itself as a distinct field of academic pursuit and an independent discipline for practitioners that studied human possibilities.

Another major influence of this new theoretical and professional discipline, Hanna Kwiatkowska (1978) introduced the idea of expanding art therapy into the clinical arena of family evaluations and family therapy. Through her career at the National Institute of Mental Health (NIMH) that focused on families of schizophrenic children, she developed a semi-structured interview to reveal relationships and dynamics among members prior to any treatment. Around the same time, Jane Rhyne (1973) advanced certain aspects of art therapy as part of the humanistic movement (an active direction for mental health professionals during that historical period). She emphasized the use of art activities that allowed for broader aspects of self-expression and the enhancement of group interactions.

In today's behavioral health climate, Cathy Malchiodi (2001, 2006) is at the forefront of art therapy advocacy. Currently, she is clarifying the value of expressive methods in the treatment of trauma-based suffering (Malchiodi, 2014). And she, with many other contributors, has expanded the realm of art therapy into the medical fields, including the support of patients beset with such illnesses as cancer, epilepsy, asthma, and Alzheimer's, along with the subsequent grief that follows the patients and families (Malchiodi, 2012).

Additionally, other art therapists (as well as many other treating professionals) have focused their efforts on trauma survival and treatment. For example, art therapist Linda Gantt and her psychiatric collaborator have trained hundreds of clinicians in their trauma therapy methods (Tinnin & Gantt, 2013). Their brain-based understanding of traumatic memory and dissociation inspired the development of numerous techniques for rapid and comprehensive treatment of Posttraumatic Stress Disorder (PTSD). For her part, Eliana Gil (a psychologist and art therapist) has concentrated her energies on a well-selected repertoire of approaches in assessment and treatment procedures that have been adapted to facilitate successful interventions of traumatized children (Gil, 2011, 2013). She has also established training institutes for trauma recovery and education, as well as for child and family play therapy. And even more recently, Linda Chapman has expanded her style of art therapy to the treatment of acute and chronic relational trauma in toddler populations, in addition to children and adolescents (Chapman, 2014). Her creation of a neurodevelopmental art therapy (NDAT) approach is viewed as a long-term intervention for the treatment of childhood disorders associated with the enduring negative impact of early and ongoing interpersonal trauma on brain development.

Through their ongoing work and persistence, art therapists are now employed in a wide variety of clinical settings using drawings and other creative media with individual, group, and family treatment, as well as aiding in the assessment and diagnostic process. When acknowledging that words may not be enough to fully describe the human condition, these professionals turn to images and symbols to elaborate the "visual narratives" of their clients. In telling their stories through graphic expression, clients in assessment and psychotherapy can find alternative journeys to wellness and transformation.

INTERACTION OF ART THERAPY AND PSYCHOLOGY

The fields of psychiatry, psychology, and education provided the basis for the emergence of art therapy as a separate professional discipline (Junge & Asawa, 1994). Additionally, it was psychologist Bernard Levy and art therapist Elinor Ulman who envisioned and collaborated in developing the first art therapy journal and the first art therapy training program in the United States (cited in Junge, 2010). Since test administration had been an integral part of becoming a psychologist for nearly a century and its uses of human and object drawings a field for systematic utilization and research, it was only natural that the clinical interviewing and assessment structure that were integral to the teaching of psychology practitioners would also be considered a core component in art therapy training programs.

During much of the twentieth century, psychologists developed assessment batteries that incorporated drawing tests to estimate intelligence and gauge cognitive disorders, and later to draw inferences regarding personality characteristics (cited in Betts & Groth-Marnat, 2013). One of the first psychologists to use drawings as a potential intellectual scale, Florence Goodenough (1926), also discovered the value of discerning certain personality characteristics from these same creations. Other clinicians of the time, such as Loretta Bender (1938), who devised a brief neurological test of copying shapes to assess brain impairment (Bender Gestalt Test), also studied drawings by children who were rated by their teacher as "oversensitive," "timid," "worriers," or "absent-minded." And many practitioners, such as Hanvik (1953), utilized the construction of human figures to differentiate emotionally disturbed children from those without significant conflicts.

Emanuel F. Hammer (1958) later observed in his pioneering work *The Clinical Applications of Projective Drawings*, that more salient qualitative clues were being ignored from drawings that were given the same quantitative IQ scores. He set out to articulate the differences in personality traits among the parts of human figure drawings (for example, arms that might be crossed defiantly versus those hanging passively at the side or placed timidly behind the back). Similarly, he documented differences in human drawings that displayed wide ranges of facial expression, size, and placement on the paper. Thus, considerable groundwork was being established for investigating the drawing indicators of emotional characteristics and the criteria that would be used and researched to provide keys to personality traits beyond brief estimates of intelligence.

Other innovators of drawing techniques conceived their own modifications from Goodenough's attempt at a drawing IQ test in this burgeoning field of observing and appraising emotional constructs. These methods included Machover's figure-drawing technique (1952) and Buck's House–Tree–Person version (1948), where commonly constructed objects were added to the basic design of an individual person. At that time, interpretive data was being derived from these drawing methods through various sources. This cumulative evidence was gathered by: background history of clients, free associations to their illustrations, common symbols derived from historical and analytical writings, comparisons among drawing products, and correlational relationships between indicators and other tests of personality (such as the TAT and Rorschach).

For example, it was demonstrated that problems in spatial organization, difficulties in forming angles, and omission of normal parts were more readily observed on pictures of trees and houses compared with assessment instruments that requested only the copying of particular shapes, such as the Bender Gestalt (cited in Hammer, 1997). And it was noted that the differences between schizophrenics and persons with brain injury and dysfunction could best be exemplified by their respective drawing performances (Wolman, 1978). One study described by Wolman that compared significantly mentally ill patients with lower-functioning individuals revealed that schizophrenics tended to construct houses with obvious anthropomorphic qualities such as wide-mouth doors, eyelike-placed windows, and curlicue-of-hair chimneys; embellished even further by tie-like pathways that seemed to look more like a face or a "classic" split tree (that is, side-by-side trees that potentially reflect the disintegration of the self). By contrast, persons with intellectual disabilities or specific brain trauma did not display these signs in their illustrations.

CASE STUDY: Lakandra E.

Lakandra was a 17-year-old young woman residing in a residential treatment facility. Displaying serious emotional disturbance since she was 8 years old, her functioning had declined to where she could not exist satisfactorily in her local community. She required several inpatient admissions due to psychotic-like indicators and aggressive behaviors. Symptoms included racing thoughts, difficulties controlling generalized worries, and marked swings in her moods. As a consequence of these problem areas, her self-esteem was quite fragile and her impulsivity dominated her actions. Signs of hypervigilance, frequent nightmares, intrusive thoughts and images, and behavioral avoidance were also documented.

During an updated evaluation, Lakandra's construction of a house certainly contained anthropomorphic qualities that corroborated her history of psychosis (see Figure 2.11). The drawing (and other very unusual ones of a tree and person) seemed to underscore the intensity of her symptoms. Serious impairments were also reflected on measures of social and adaptive functioning, in addition to her executive operations (ability to regulate attention and behavior).

2.11

Furthermore, she was portrayed as highly anxious, impulsive and emotionally immature on aspects of projective testing. Overall, it was determined that she still needed the security of a highly structured environment to promote her growth through adolescence and early adulthood.

Because questions pertaining to intellectual disabilities are often important referral questions to psychologists, it became useful to show examples of drawings that display the problems that an individual might be experiencing due to perceptual deficits or damage caused by specific trauma to the head. In general, it was determined that lower-functioning individuals often constructed a drawing with excessive pressure (or took an extra amount of time compared to same-aged peers) to complete a particular task. These individuals were often distinguished as displaying feelings of inadequacy through their inability to improve a drawing through erasure and redoing. Additionally, their illustrations seemed likely to omit important parts of a house or person, or provided indicators of perseveration (the inability to stop markings once started). Other factors observed in drawings of intellectually disabled individuals included oversimplified, unidimensional figures, or stark, skeletal representations of trees (Wolman, 1978).

FOUNDATIONS OF CLINICAL DRAWINGS 45

CASE STUDY: **Charlotte P.**

Nineteen-year-old Charlotte P.'s history was characterized by cognitive impairments, aggressive behaviors, and psychotic-like symptoms. Her academic, emotional, and behavioral difficulties led to many specialized educational settings even before entering first grade. At that time, she was diagnosed with Pervasive Developmental Disorder (a condition of profound immaturities in all spheres of maturation). She then began demonstrating extreme outbursts at home that necessitated residential placement by age nine. By the time of this evaluation she had been hospitalized approximately 20 times due to continued instability and aggression.

Charlotte demonstrated marked deficits on an administration of intellectual testing that was referred by her therapist. All scores were well below average, suggesting a diagnosis of intellectual disability (IQ = 48–55). She displayed substantial impairments in sustained attention, perceptual tracking, copying efficiency, and her ability to work within time constraints. She also had little capacity to reason abstractly, or express herself verbally. Her drawings also provided evidence of marked developmental delays. This lack of cognitive maturity was especially noted on her house and tree drawings (see Figures 2.12 and 2.13). Her house was very unsophisticated and childlike. Her construction of a tree also exposed signs of personal inadequacy and aggressive, ineffective defenses, in addition to inner confusion and tension that would make her susceptible to being overwhelmed easily by even slight stressors.

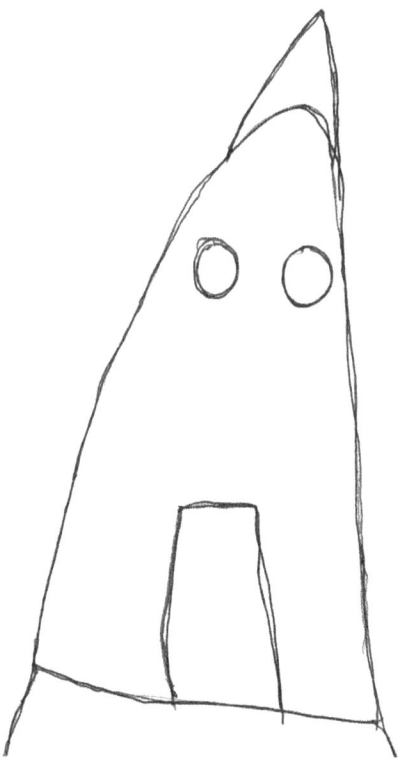

2.12

46 FOUNDATIONS OF CLINICAL DRAWINGS

2.13

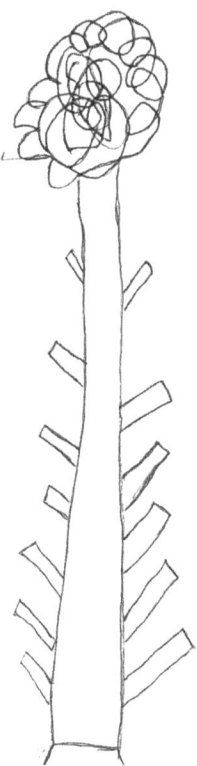

CONTROVERSIES IN DRAWING INTERPRETATION

Also over the last century, a focus of controversy emerged regarding whether the utilization of drawings during evaluations could even be useful in assessing emotional problems and intellectual development (Anastasi & Urbina, 1997; Bandeira, Costa, & Arteche, 2008). Considerable research began to reveal that the reliability and validity of potential signs within drawings were quite variable across studies (Lilienfeld, Wood, & Garb, 2000). Moreover, there was little evidence regarding acceptable inter-rater reliabilities of clinicians' interpretations of figure-drawing characteristics (Thomas & Jolley, 1998). These reservations in validity and reliability remain divided among many experienced clinicians and researchers (Laak, De Goede, Aleva, & Van Rijswijk, 2005). Mainly, it was pointed out that global scoring methods, such as the one developed by Elizabeth Koppitz, rather than the one-to-one relationships between single items in a drawing and particular character traits, were best able to distinguish psychopathological individuals from normal groups of people (Tharinger & Stark, 1990).

While many of these critiques were aimed at the use and interpretive value of drawings in psychological assessment, Klopfer and Taulbee (1976) rightly concluded that drawings would continue to be used in assessing general development and estimating intelligence, in addition to their application as a projective instrument as long as an interest was maintained in depth psychology. Their usage within assessment batteries has continued to produce substantial research in behavioral science journals and has resulted in numerous presentations at annual psychological and art therapy conventions. Even with this ongoing debate, survey results provide evidence that these procedures continue to be among the most popular among a large number of psychologists and other clinicians involved in the assessment and interview process (Bekhit, Thomas, & Jolley, 2005), with usage rates varying from one third to one half of all those surveyed.

Since previous literature mostly focused on figure drawing tests, such as the House–Tree–Person (Buck, 1947) and the Goodenough–Harris Draw-A-Person (D-A-P) techniques (Harris, 1963), these research articles were explored thoroughly by graduate students and clinical practitioners who were interested in the introduction of drawing activity in the diagnostic work with children (Yedidia & Lipschitz-Elchawi, 2012), adolescents (Koppitz & Casullo, 1983), and adults (Hammer, 1997). And with so much attention paid to this area of graphic expression, students in both psychology and art therapy immersed themselves in this burgeoning literature that combined both disciplines. Because the early investigators were primarily psychologists and had developed many of these drawing-based intelligence and projective methods, art therapists were able to incorporate these techniques into their own discipline and create expanded tools into their unique assessment and interview styles.

FROM PSYCHOLOGY TO ART THERAPY ASSESSMENTS

The basics of psychological procedures naturally influenced the beginnings of art therapy assessments. In this manner, art therapy pioneer Margaret Naumburg (through her book chapter in Hammer's *Clinical Application of Projective Drawings* [1967]) was credited with providing a connection between psychologically–based to art-based therapy assessments. Since that time, there has been a plethora of art therapy assessments developed throughout the field's history. Some art therapists borrowed elements of previously designed procedures, others invented their own personal styles, and some fell somewhere in between.

In a survey conducted by the American Art Therapy Association (Mills & Goodwin, 1991), it was revealed that many art therapists either modified existing procedures or created new ones, rarely relying on published tools. Some art therapists developed their art-based assessments through their own experiences—what they felt provided them valuable information about their own clients. Some of these art therapy assessments were loosely administered, whereas others were highly structured. Additionally, a few focused on particular populations, whereas others had more general application. (For a comprehensive overview of art therapy assessments refer to Donna Betts' website www.arttherapy.us/assessment.htm and Brooke's *Tools of the Trade* [2004].)

Two of the more popular art therapy assessment approaches, the Silver Drawing Test of Cognition and Emotion (Silver, 1996, 2002) and the Draw-a-Story (DAS) procedure (Silver, 1990, 2002) provided semi-structured techniques for the examiner and became an influential procedure for art therapists. Additionally, Barry Cohen's "Diagnostic Drawing Series" (1990) was one of the best systems at the time to demonstrate solid research reliability in the diagnosis of psychosis. And another art therapy drawing directive, constructing a "Person Picking an Apple from a Tree" (Gantt & Tabone, 1998), produced much data on validity and reliability with diverse populations (see Bucciarelli, 2007). As a historical reference, Myra Levick et al. (1989–1999), "The Levick Emotional and Cognitive Art Therapy Assessment" (LECATA) was an integral part of evaluation for high-risk children in the Miami-Dade County School system in Florida. A series of five drawing tasks were scored according to specific concrete criteria for intellectual (Piaget) and developmental defense mechanisms (Freud). It was based on Levick's text *They Could Not Talk and So They Drew* (1983).

Silver Drawing Tests

Through her work with deaf children in therapy during the 1960s and later with learning disabled and adult stroke victims, art therapist and educator Rawley Silver developed structured tasks that assessed the cognitive skills and emotional needs of her clients. In her compiled works (Silver, 1990, 1991, 1996), she demonstrated how to use structured methods of stimulus drawings to prompt responses that solved problems or represented concepts and elicited stories related to mood. Her art tasks displayed how drawings could measure cognitive development related to height, width, and depth that were not previously addressed in earlier drawing techniques. She also used modifications of these procedures in later studies to investigate childhood depression, and cross cultural and gender differences (Silver, 2002, 2003).

Silver regarded art as a language that paralleled the spoken or written word and, therefore, could assist in the assessment of cognitive skills and discovering emotional resources. Her goals in providing these techniques were to a) bypass language in evaluating abilities to solve conceptual problems; b) provide more accurate evaluations of personal strengths, which are often overlooked by verbal measures; c) facilitate early identification of emotional problems, such as depression; and d) provide a pre–post instrument to assess individual progress, or the effectiveness of educational or therapeutic intervention. Her initial hypothesis was that children who have poor language skills are often restricted in traditional tests of intelligence. She noted that drawing and other art activities could produce a more accurate picture of a child's cognitive resources.

The Silver Drawing Tests (SDT) consist of three tasks or subtests that measure a client's ability to solve conceptual problems graphically. These tasks include a predictive or sequential drawing, a drawing from observation, and a drawing from imagination. In constructing these measures, Silver produced activities that were broader than other drawing tests, such as the D-A-P, and involved a series of appealing tasks that allowed clients to adapt various images in their drawing constructions. There is no time limit, though most examinees take 3 to 5 minutes to complete the first two tasks that are structured protocols and 5 to 10 minutes to finish the last subtest (drawing from imagination by choosing from a series of images and combining them in a drawing that has a title and related story). The tests can be administered individually or to groups. The Silver manuals are highly structured and well illustrated, providing health and mental health practitioners with clear methods for their uses.

Silver (1996) also did extensive research on the DAS in studying children's images associated with depression, as well as investigating cognitive and creative skills. She developed a drawing protocol of the DAS to screen for depression by using a set of simple line drawings that stimulated children to develop stories about their drawings. She selected graphic illustrations that appeared to prompt negative fantasies and requested children to choose two of the images to combine in a drawing. Her research viewed depression as a continuum from moderate sadness to suicidal and self-destructive thinking and she suggested that these states of depressed affect would be revealed through the drawings and stories.

Diagnostic Drawing Series

The Diagnostic Drawing Series (DDS) is a drawing interview developed by art therapists to provide a reliable and valid assessment tool that was originally linked to diagnostic nomenclature in the revised *Diagnostic and Statistical Manuals* (Johnson, 1988). This drawing task was created because of the clinical imprecision of other art assessment procedures and the need for establishing a foundation of data for research and clinical purposes. The protocol for the three-drawing test incorporates instructions for unstructured, structured, and semi-structured tasks (Cohen, 1990).

Norms were developed for control and various diagnostic groupings, such as samples of individuals with major depression, dysthymia, and schizophrenia. Non-psychiatric groups were also included in subsequent studies of sexually abused children and head-injured persons. The main advantage noted for using the DDS over other art techniques was its ease of administration combined with media that foster self-expression (Mills, Cohen, & Menses, 1993).

In the manual developed for scoring the DDS, 23 categories were listed with 183 decisions demanded of a rater. Despite the seeming complexity, there appeared to be an extremely high inter-rater reliability. Thus, the drawing series offered both researchers and clinicians something that was missing from many of the above-mentioned directives: that is, the confidence to use a reliable and valid tool for assessment purposes.

The Person Picking an Apple from a Tree

The Person Picking an Apple from a Tree (PPAT) (Gantt, 1990, 2000, 2004) drawing-based art therapy assessment instrument is used to determine the correlation of mental health symptoms with specific variables in client drawings. Participants are directed to use the standardized materials, a set of 12 Mr. Sketch(™) scented markers and a 12" ×18" piece of white paper, and asked to "draw a picture of a person picking an apple from a tree." The drawing is evaluated using 14 equal-appearing interval measurement scales in the Formal Elements Art Therapy Scale (FEATS) Rating Manual (Gantt & Tabone, 1998). The formal elements, or global variables, were tied to symptoms of specific DSM-IV TR Axis-I mental disorders and will be integrated into the newest revision of the DSM (DSM-5).

The PPAT and its corresponding rating system (FEATS) have been widely researched with a variety of patient cohorts with improvements reflected in the validity and reliability of the PPAT (e.g., Gussak, 2009). Making current results widely available via an ongoing database will ultimately facilitate convenient access to the information to aid art therapists and other clinicians interested in the process of evaluation, treatment planning, therapy and research. Normative data will be added to the database, serving as a foundation upon which later records (normative and patient cohorts) can be compared (Bucciarelli, 2007).

In this assessment technique, the client is asked to draw a person picking an apple from a tree in any way they want—using shape, line, and color (the client is provided with a drawing medium like markers, pastels, or colored pencils). The drawing can then be assessed for prominence of color and color choice, developmental level, line quality, realism, logic, detail, and problem-solving. For example, someone with depression might have low prominence of color and detail and may show some difficulty with problem-solving to pick the apple. According to Gantt and Tabone (2003), the significance of the assessment is how the client draws the components of the image (the formal elements), not what the client draws (the content). Once the drawing is complete, the formal elements in the image can be evaluated with the FEATS Rating Manual.

What also emerged was the importance of the *formal elements* of the drawing: that is *how* the drawing was completed, not the symbolic content. Briefly, a shaky or sketchy line quality may indicate anxiety; a dense, pressured line may indicate frustration or aggression; faintly drawn lines may indicate loss of energy. The space used on the page may also be meaningful. The smaller the image and the greater the space left on the page, the more likely the person was depressed, sad, or un-invested. Once color was introduced, it added a whole new dimension: while some subscribe symbolic importance to colors, what is more significant is the number of colors used (color prominence) and the use of colors for accurate representation (color fit).

Specifically, the PPAT assessment can purportedly assist in the diagnosis of clients with: major depression; bipolar disorder; schizophrenia; and dementia, amnesic, and other cognitive disorders. The assessment was originally developed to use with psychiatric patients for the diagnosis, treatment planning, and evaluation of symptomatic change over time (Gantt & Tabone, 1998). However, the PPAT assessment has also been used as a tool to indicate client changes in response to medication or treatment, degrees of depression, and long-term substance abuse (Rockwell & Dunham, 2006).

ENHANCEMENTS TO ASSESSMENT

Because many aspects of the art therapy approach differ from the psychological projective approach, the art-based method is a promising and novel one. For example, the PPAT is good at determining state (as opposed to trait) emotional characteristics and as such it is an easy assessment to administer multiple times (and the assessment time needed is short). In this way, the PPAT has benefits over other assessments that take longer to administer and score. If PPAT data is correlated with another assessment that is longer, then the PPAT becomes a useful short-cut with little sacrifice of information. So, the PPAT is particularly useful for monitoring therapy and ensuring treatment progress.

While the advances in these clinical tools continue among academics and practitioners, the focus has been to discover the distinctiveness of various clinical instruments within each of the two disciplines, that is, psychology and art therapy (Neale and Rosal, 1993). While art therapists have benefitted from the psychological literature, they now consider that their novel perspective and extensive knowledge of art materials can make a strong contribution to mental health research (cited in Betts & Groth-Marnat, 2013). And through their academic and clinical journey, they have attempted to establish the usefulness of drawings in clinical practice to assess such disparate avenues as marital conflict (Groth-Marnot & Roberts, 1998), in addition to demonstrating diagnostic indicators of ADHD (Safran, 2002), headaches (Stafstrom, Rostasy, & Minster, 2002), and eating disorders (Thomas, Getz, Smith, & Rivas, 2013).

CAUTIONARY TALES

While the primary emphasis of these first two chapters has focused on the benefits derived from introducing drawings into the assessment and clinical interview process, there are many instances where exceptions must be considered. For example, some clients may be overly fearful or mistrustful of how their drawing constructions will be perceived or who will have access to them. Other individuals may just be too anxious about personal revelations and balk at the idea of placing their thoughts and feelings onto paper, or even talk about them honestly. Furthermore, those individuals who may be especially vulnerable to stress when unusual demands are placed on them, no matter how minor, may be overwhelmed and resistant at the idea of performing or talking about artwork. These otherwise innocuous requests for constructing drawings may be viewed by psychotic or defenseless individuals, for example, as affronts to their personal integrity and may cause much internal and outward agitation, and therefore, detriments to information gathering (cited in Oster & Crone, 2004).

Also, through the interview and assessment process, it becomes especially crucial for clinicians to listen to the clients' explanations of the drawings before providing interpretations or alternative meanings. The illustrations that are produced are more than merely a static indicator of psychopathology; rather the images can become rich landscapes of ideas, past associations and experiences, individual meanings, and expressed feelings. A nonjudgmental stance throughout the drawing administrations provides a solid foundation that supports clients' own initiatives for a positive experience to occur with insight gained and sets the path for the acceptance of professional help. Through this dynamic process, emphasis should be placed on the client's strengths, and the use of drawings thereby becomes a springboard to enhance participation through the remainder of the evaluation.

Of course, it is possible that even a simple request for a drawing will exacerbate an already difficult situation. Clients may hesitate at the instructions, become highly upset, or begin a senseless power struggle. In these instances, it may be prudent to not emphasize the drawing directives and introduce them again later if the opportunity warrants. It is better to provide clear expectations that the creating of drawings is important to the deeper understanding of their inner selves. And sometimes it is even helpful to request drawings without expectations of observing or talking. This non-demanding approach creates a more relaxed environment that can increase the sense of privacy and spontaneity.

Even this more relaxed approach, however, may be too threatening for some clients. They may not want to perform in such novel and revealing situations. Other diagnostic instruments can replace the requests for drawings, but opportunities will be missed to see this nonverbal and creative side of the clients' internal struggles. It truly can be an important and enlightening part of the interactive process.

CONCLUDING COMMENTS

This chapter established the foundations for the introduction of graphic images into the diagnostic and therapeutic milieu. Through descriptions of developmental sequences, estimates of intelligence, and emotional indicators, the historical pathway of the many uses of drawing activities and other nonverbal techniques within the interview and assessment process was introduced. A long-standing history of behavioral health treatment has demonstrated that clients in distress need alternative ways to "speak" about their inner experiences. Because drawings add flexibility, imagination, and a novel experience to the initial encounter, it has been easily incorporated into the clinician's "toolbox" as a way to build comfort and trust for clients of all persuasions. By requesting visual illustrations, or metaphors, to express past conflicts or hopes for the future, clinicians over the years have come to appreciate their unique value for rapport building as well as gaining insight and enhancing the "therapeutic alliance."

The rapid increase of the clinical uses of drawings has expanded the framework of psychologists and other behavioral health practitioners in both assessment and therapy and has allowed the discipline of art therapy to increase its standing among behavioural health professionals. Through their novel approaches to evaluations and treatment interventions, the addition of drawing directives has established tangible markers revealing hidden trauma, reviewing acute problems and concerns, and enhancing the direction of treatment goals. Salient conflicts and struggles can be observed within the illustrations and discussed through the visual images that have been constructed during these early sessions. From the historical connection of artistic expression to the niches discovered within behavioral health research and treatment, the value of presenting the chance to "draw" one's problems and solutions has made the interpersonal world of client and clinician that more enriching and exciting.

The remainder of the book will provide the basic drawing directives that have been utilized during intake evaluations, as well as their uses during clinical interviews and psychological testing. Standard drawing instructions will be presented, in addition to possible interpretations. Additionally, variations of these traditional directives will be offered to expand the scope of the clinician and formulate new pathways for clients to uncover their "hidden voices." Numerous case examples throughout the remainder of the book will highlight these introductions to the broad array of requested drawings.

Through these images and case studies, clinicians will gain an appreciation of the depth of the human condition. The concluding chapters on clinical interviewing and psychological testing will substantiate the valuable addition of graphic images during the evaluative process. At the conclusion, clinicians will have had the opportunity to glimpse the many possibilities that drawings can contribute to the general interviewing and assessment process. Adding graphic expression to verbal interactions can only broaden the understanding of the evaluative experience for both clients and clinicians. Capturing these visual metaphors onto paper allows a vivid world of much-needed exploration during these initial sessions.

REFERENCES

Anastasi, A. & Urbina, S. (1997). *Psychological testing* (7th ed.). Bloomington, MN: Pearson.

Bandeira, D. R., Costa, A., & Arteche, A. (2008). The Draw-a-Person test as a valid measure of children's cognitive development. *Psicologia: Reflexão e Crítica*, 21(2), 332–337.

Bekhit, N. S., Thomas, G. V., & Jolley, R. P. (2005). The use of drawing for psychological assessment in Britain: Survey findings. *Psychology and Psychotherapy: Theory, Research and Practice*, 78(2), 205–217.

Bender, L. (1938). A *visual motor gestalt test and its clinical use*. New York: The American Orthopsychiatric Association.

Betensky, M. G. (1995). *What do you see?: Phenomenology of therapeutic art expression*. London: Jessica Kingsley.

Betts, D. & Groth-Marnat, G. (2013). The intersection of art therapy and psychological assessment. In L. Handler & A. D. Thomas (2013), *Drawings in assessment and psychotherapy: Research and application*. New York: Routledge.

Brooke, S. L. (2004). A *therapist's guide to* art *therapy assessments: Tools of the trade*. (2nd ed.). Springfield, IL: Charles C. Thomas.

Bucciarelli, M. (2007). How the construction of mental models improves learning. *Mind & Society*, 6(1), 67–89.

Buck, J. N. (1948). The H-T-P test. *Journal of Clinical Psychology*, 4, 151–159.

Burt, C. (1921). *Mental and scholastic tests*. London: P. S. King & Son.

Case, C. & Dalley, T. (1992). *The handbook of art therapy*. London: Tavistock/Routledge.

Chapman, L. (2014). *Neurobiologically informed trauma therapy with children and adolescents: Understanding mechanisms of change*. New York: W.W. Norton.

Cohen, B. M. (Ed.). (1986). *The diagnostic drawing series handbook*. (Available from Barry M. Cohen, PO Box 9853, Alexandria, VA 22304.)

Cohen, B. M. (1990). Diagnostic drawing series. In I. Jakab (Ed.), *Stress management through art: Proceedings of the internal congress of psychopathology of expression*. Boston, MA: ASPE.

Cooke, E. (1885). *Art teaching and child nature*. Boston, MA: Houghton Mifflin.

DiLeo, J. H. (1973). *Children's drawings as diagnostic aids*. New York: Brunner/Mazel.

DiLeo, J. H. (1983). *Interpreting children's drawings*. New York: Brunner/Mazel.

Dissanayake, E. (1989). *What is art for?* Seattle, WA: University of Washington Press.

Freud, S. (1933). *New introductory lectures on psychoanalysis.* New York: W. W. Norton.
Freud, S. (1958) [1900]. *The interpretation of dreams.* New York: Basic Books.
Gantt, L. (1990). A validity study of the Formal Elements Art Therapy Scale (FEATS) for diagnostic information in patients' drawings. Unpublished doctoral dissertation, University of Pittsburgh, Pittsburgh, PA.
Gantt, L. (2000). Assessments in the creative arts therapies: Learning from each other. *Music Therapy Perspectives*, 18(1), 41–46.
Gantt, L. (2004). The case for formal art therapy assessments. *Art Therapy*, 21(1), 18–29.
Gantt, L. & Tabone, C. (1998). *Formal arts therapy scale. The rating manual.* Morgantown, WV: Gargoyle Press.
Gantt, L. & Tabone, C. (2003). The Formal Elements Art Therapy Scale and "draw a person picking an apple from a tree." *Handbook of Art Therapy*, 420–427.
Gardner, H. (1982). *Artful scribbles.* New York: Basic Books.
Gil, E. (2011). *Helping abused and traumatized children: Integrating directives and nondirectives.* New York: Guilford Press.
Gil, E. (Ed.). (2013). *Working with children to heal interpersonal trauma. The power of play.* New York: Guilford Press.
Golomb, C. (1990). *The child's creation of a pictorial world.* Berkeley, CA: University of California Press.
Goodenough, F. L. (1926). *Measurement of intelligence by drawings.* New York: Harcourt, Brace & World.
Grother-Marnat, G. & Roberts, L. (1998). Human figure drawings and house tree person drawings as indicators of self-esteem. A quantitative approach. *Journal of Clinical Psychology*, 54(2), 219–222.
Gussak, D. (2009). Comparing the effectiveness of art therapy on depression and locus of control of male and female inmates. *The Arts in Psychotherapy*, 36(4), 202–207.
Hammer, E. F. (Ed.). (1958). *The clinical applications of projective drawings.* Springfield, IL: Charles C. Thomas.
Hammer, E. F. (Ed.). (1967). *Clinical applications of projective drawings* (2nd ed.). Springfield, IL: Charles C. Thomas.
Hammer, E. F. (1997). *Advances in projective drawing interpretation.* Springfield, IL: Charles C. Thomas.
Handler, L. & Thomas, A.D. (2013). *Drawings in assessment and psychotherapy: Research and application.* New York: Routledge.
Hanvik, L. J. (1953). The Goodenough Test as a measure of intelligence in child psychiatric patients. *Journal of Clinical Psychology*, 9, 71–72.
Harris, D. B. (1963). *Children's drawings as measures of intellectual maturity.* New York: Harcourt, Brace, & World.
Janson, H.W. (1991). *History of art* (Vol. 1, 4th ed.) [expanded by Anthony F. Jason, Harry Abrams, Inc.]. New York: Prentice Hall.
Johnson, D. R. (Ed.). (1988). Assessment in the creative arts therapies (Special Issue). *The Arts in Psychotherapy*, 15(1).
Joiner, T. E. & Schmidt, K. L. (1997). Drawing conclusions—or not—from drawings. *Journal of Personality Assessment*, 69, 476–481.
Jung, C. G. (1956). *The collected works of C. G. Jung, volume 5: Symbols of transformation* (G. Adler & R. F. C. Hull, Eds. and Trans.). Princeton, NJ: Princeton University Press.
Jung, C. G. (1965). *Memories, Dreams, Reflections* (A. Jaffe, E. R. Winston, & C. Winston, Trans.). New York: Random House.
Jung, C. G. (1971). *The portable Jung* (J. Campbell, Ed., R. F. C. Hull, Trans.). New York: Viking Press.
Junge, M. B. (2010). *The modern history of art therapy in the United States.* Springfield, IL: Charles C. Thomas.
Junge, M. B. & Asawa, P. P. (1994). *A history of art therapy in the United States.* American Art Therapy Association.

Kellogg, R. (1969). *Analyzing children's art*. Palo Alto, CA: Mayfield.
Klopfer, W. G. & Taulbee, E. S. (1976). Projective tests. *Annual Review of Psychology*, 27(1), 543–567.
Koppitz, E. M. (1984). *Psychological evaluation of human figure drawings by middle school pupils*. Orlando, FL: Grune & Stratton.
Koppitz, E. M. & Casullo, M. M. (1983). Exploring cultural influences on human figure drawings of young adolescents. *Perceptual and Motor Skills*, 57(2), 479–483.
Kramer, E. (1971). *Art as therapy with children*. New York: Schocken.
Krampen, G. (1991). *Fragebogen zu Kompetenz-und Kontrollüberzeugungen: (FKK)*. Hogrefe: Verlag für Psychologie.
Kris, E. (1952). *Psychoanalytic exploration in art*. New York: International Universities Press.
Kwiatkowska, H. Y. (1978). *Family therapy and evaluation through art*. Springfield, IL: Charles C. Thomas.
Laak, J. T., De Goede, M., Aleva, A., & Rijswijk, P. V. (2005). The Draw-A-Person Test: An indicator of children's cognitive and socioemotional adaptation? *The Journal of Genetic Psychology*, 166 (1), 77–93.
Leibowitz, M. (1999). *Interpreting projective drawings: A self psychological approach*. New York: Brunner/Mazel.
Levick, M. et al. (1989–1999). "The Levick Emotional and Cognitive Art Therapy Assessment" with J. Bush (Miami-Dade Art Therapy Program). (Taken from M. Levick [1983]. *They could not talk so they drew*. Springfield, IL: Charles C. Thomas.)
Lilienfeld, S. O., Wood, J. M., & Garb, H. N. (2000). The scientific status of projective techniques. *American Psychological Society*, 1, 2.
Lombroso, C. (1895). *The man of genius*. London: Scott.
MacGregor, J. (1989). *The discovery of the art of the insane*. Lawrenceville, NJ: Princeton University Press.
Machover, K. (1952). *Personality projection in the drawing of the* human *figure*. Springfield, IL: Charles C. Thomas.
Malchiodi, C. A. (1998). *Understanding children's drawings*. New York: Guilford Press.
Malchiodi, C. A. (2006). *Art therapy sourcebook*. (2nd ed.). New York: McGraw-Hill.
Malchiodi, C. A. (Ed.). (2011). *Handbook of Art Therapy*. (2nd ed.). New York: Guilford Press.
Malchiodi, C. A. (Ed.). (2012). *Art therapy and health care*. New York: Guilford Press.
Malchiodi, C. A. (2014). *Creative interventions with traumatized children*. (2nd ed.). New York: Guilford Press.
Meyer, M. (1985). *Apprentissage de la lange maternaelle ecrite*. Paris: UNESCO.
Mills, A., Cohen, B. M., & Menses, J. Z. (1993). Reliability and validity tests of the Diagnostic Drawing Series. *The Arts in Psychotherapy*, 20, 83–88.
Mills, A. & Goodwin, R. (1991). An informal survey of assessment use in child art therapy. *Art Therapy*, 8(2), 10–13.
Morris, D. (1962). *The biology of art*. London: Methuen.
Naumburg, M. (1966). *Dynamically oriented art therapy: Its principles and practice, illustrated with three case studies*. New York: Grune & Stratton.
Neale, E. L., & Rosal, M. L. (1993). What can art therapists learn from the research on projective drawing techniques for children? A review of the literature. *The Arts in Psychotherapy*, 20, 37–49.
Oster, G. D. & Crone, P. (2004). *Using drawings in assessment and therapy*. (2nd ed). New York: Taylor & Francis.
Oster, G. D. & Gould, P. (1987). *Using drawings in assessment and therapy*. New York: Brunner/Mazel.
Oster, G. D. & Montgomery, S. S. (1996). *Clinical uses of drawings*. Northvale, NJ: Jason Aronson.
Peterson, L. W. & Hardin, M. E. (1997). *Children in distress: A guide for screening children's art*. New York: W. W. Norton.
Piaget, J. (1959). *Judgment and reasoning in the child*. Paterson, NJ: Littlefield, Adams.
Pietrowski, Z. A. & Abrahamsen, D. (1952). Sexual crime, alcohol, and the Rorschach Test. *Psychiatry Quarterly (supplement)*, 26, 248–260.

Prinzhorn, H. (1972). *Artistry of the mentally ill.* New York: Springer.

Rhyne, J. (1973). *The gestalt art experience.* Monterey, CA: Brooks/Cole.

Ricci, C. (1887). *The art of children.* Pedagogical Seminary. Bologna, Italy.

Riethmiller, R. J. & Handler, L. (1997). The great figure drawing controversy: The integration of research and clinical practice. *Journal of Personality Assessment*, 69, 488–496.

Riley, S. (1997). Children's art and narratives: An opportunity to enhance therapy and a supervisory challenge. *The Supervision Bulletin*, 9(3), 2–3.

Rockwell, P. & Dunham, M. (2006). The utility of the Formal Elements Art Therapy Scale in assessment for substance use disorder. *Art therapy*, 23(3), 104–111.

Rubin, J. A. (2005). *Child art therapy (25th Anniversary Edition edition).* New York: Wiley.

Safran, D. S. (2002). *Art therapy and AD/HD: Diagnostic and therapeutic approaches.* London: Jessica Kingsley.

Silver, R. A. (1990). *Silver drawing test of cognitive skills and adjustment.* Sarasota, FL: Ablin Press.

Silver, R. A. (1991). *Stimulus drawings and techniques.* Sarasota, FL: Ablin Press.

Silver, R. A. (1996). *Silver drawing test of cognition and emotion.* Sarasota, FL: Ablin Press.

Silver, R. A. (2002). *Three art assessments: The silver drawing test, draw a story, and stimulus drawings & techniques.* New York: Brunner-Routledge.

Silver, R. A. (2003). The silver drawing test of cognition and emotion. In C. Malchiodi, *Handbook of art therapy.* New York: The Guilford Press, 410–419.

Simon, D. P. M. (1888). *Les Écrits et les dessins des aliénés, par le Dr P.-Max Simon, . . .* G. Steinheil.

Stafstrom, C. E., Rostasy, K., & Minster, A. (2002). The usefulness of children's drawings in the diagnosis of headache. *Pediatrics*, 109(3), 460–472.

Tardieu, L. (1872). *Etude medico-legale sur las folie.* Paris: Baillière.

Tharinger, D. J. & Stark, K. (1990). A qualitative versus quantitative approach to evaluating the draw-a-person and kinetic family drawing: A study of mood- and anxiety-disorder children. *Psychological Assessment: A Journal of Consulting and Clinical Psychology*, 2(4), 365–375.

Thomas, A. D., Getz, J. W., Smith, J. D., & Rivas, E. (2013). Anorexic house-tree-person drawings: Profile and reliability. In L. Handler & A. D. Thomas, *Drawings in assessment and psychotherapy: Research and application.* New York: Routledge.

Thomas, G. V. & Jolley, R. P. (1998). Drawing conclusions: A re-examination of empirical and conceptual bases for psychological evaluation of children from their drawings. *British Journal of Clinical Psychology*, 37(2), 127–139.

Thomas, G. V. & Silk, A. M. J. (1990). *An introduction to children's drawings.* New York: New York University Press.

Tinnin, L. & Gantt, L. (2013). *The instinctual trauma response and dual-brain dynamics: A guide for trauma therapy.* Morgantown, WV: Linda Gantt.

Wolman, B. B. (1978). *Handbook of treatment of mental disorders in childhood and adolescence.* New York: Prentice-Hall.

Yedidia, T. & Lipschitz-Elchawi, R. (2012). Examining social perceptions between Arab and Jewish children through Human Figure Drawings. *Art Therapy*, 29(3), 104–112.

3 House–Tree–Person and Variations

HUMAN FIGURES AND EVERYDAY OBJECTS

The House–Tree–Person (H-T-P) drawing method and its variations within clinical interviews and behavioral health assessments have been used to investigate different aspects of cognitive and personality functioning, in addition to being incorporated in the treatment of mental disorders since the early part of the twentieth century (Milne, Greenway, & Best, 2005). H-T-P specifically has been utilized historically to measure brain dysfunction and emotional indicators of conflicts and past trauma. A number of variations have also been devised to enhance the value of these types of drawing directive as a clinical tool, and to increase their predictability within other personality measures of a comprehensive evaluation (Lichtenberg, 2013).

These nonverbal techniques have assisted psychologists and other clinical practitioners, as well as educators and employers, to differentiate various populations in order to intervene effectively with appropriate accommodations. Generally, the H-T-P and its variations are administered as part of an interview or a broader test battery that allows for an integration of multiple responses on assorted cognitive and projective instruments. The examiner then has the opportunity to assess mental capacities, as well as view the inner world of clients and their interpersonal perspectives through the construction of graphic images of common human figures and everyday objects perceived in their world.

The purpose of this chapter is to provide clinicians who use drawings during assessment and interviews a chance to review the historical and standard directions of drawing formats, as well as provide alternative instructions that expand the scope of information gathering. The utilization of clinical drawings offers an entry point into the personal world of clients beyond their verbal presentation. Using paper-and-pencil sketches to enhance diagnostic and beginning therapy sessions permits nonintrusive and minimally threatening methods of sharing and gathering subjective experiences from the client that might not have been revealed so readily due to discomfort or resistance. Through this evaluative framework, a simple request to draw can provide a maximally absorbing and unique introduction into the interview or testing situation.

The process of requesting drawings also serves as a comfortable bridge to the total examination and offers time for the client to get used to the new surroundings and the person on the other side of the table. Placing a picture onto a piece of paper provides an opportunity for clients to share their perspectives of themselves, their surroundings, and the places where they reside. For the clinicians interpreting these drawings, or the clients who verbally share their own insights of the constructions, these interactions initiate an important process of communication that offers the opportunity to investigate the conflicts, worries, and anxieties that have brought these experiences to occur.

Projective drawings, mostly of the human figure (but later adding other objects familiar to clients), have been used to formally assess intellectual functioning and personality traits since the 1920s (Goodenough, 1926). These graphic expressions were ultimately integrated into comprehensive psychological assessment batteries, as well as clinical interview sessions, to establish rapport and to generate hypotheses toward diagnostic impressions. While Machover (1949) initiated a beginning monograph to expand personality characteristics to "person" drawings in both symbolic meaning and structural factors, it was Buck (1948) who extended these emotional indicators within the illustrations of a house and tree. With this foundation of drawing interpretation established, other researchers began to expand this symbolism into diagnostic and therapeutic research (Hammer, 1958, 1997). And even later, the H-T-P spawned many varying uses in clinical practices and in research to establish its value as a rich source for interpretive and theoretical discussion (Handler & Thomas, 2013). The H-T-P series of drawings is one of the most used methods to gather data regarding an individual's degree of cognitive maturity, personality integration, and interpersonal connectedness. Their use is especially valuable when individual signs are not used out of context or measured by artistic ability (Riethmiller & Handler, 1997).

HOUSE–TREE–PERSON

These three objects—a house, a tree, and a person—were chosen because of their common familiarity to very young children, their acceptance by people of all ages, and their ability to stimulate an enhanced fund of free associations. Besides their use in psychological assessment and clinical interviewing, drawings of these entities have been shown to be useful as: a) a screening device for detecting maladjustment; b) an evaluative aid for children entering school; c) an appraisal device in screening applicants for employment; and d) a research instrument to locate common factors in an identified group of people (cited in Oster & Gould, 1987; Oster & Montgomery, 1996; Oster & Crone, 2004). Other interpretative evidence derived from the construction of these figures has instigated research in areas of eating disorders (Thomas, Getz, Smith, & Revas, 2013) as well as child sexual abuse (Thomas & Engram, 2013).

Instructions for this drawing test specify that the examinee draw a house, a tree, and then a person on separate sheets of paper, without additional comments as to type, size, or condition. (A variation on this instruction that places these three objects on one sheet of paper will be discussed later in this chapter.) Clients are expected to draw these three forms in any manner from among the many they have personally experienced. Furthermore, they are encouraged to make their best attempts at the figures (for example, for the house and tree, instructions may include "I want you to draw the best house (or tree) that you can; you may draw any kind you wish; it's entirely up to you"). For the person, the client is encouraged to draw a "whole person, not just a stick figure."

The ordering of asking to construct the H-T-P always remains the same. This sequence is viewed as gradually more psychologically difficult, with the tree drawing and the human figure appearing the most likely to produce personal responses (Hammer, 1958, 1997). Additionally, it is not enough to merely translate emotional indicators derived from the drawings; rather, it behooves the examiner to ask questions about the illustrations (for example, "What types of activities occur in the house?" "What are the weakest and strongest parts of the tree?") to gain further insight from the client (Buck, 1992; Handler, 1996). Also, it becomes salient for the examiner or interviewer to consider the client's developmental level, his or her artistic background, and the common interpretive elements (Malchiodi, Kim, & Choi, 2003).

HOUSE DRAWINGS

The drawing of a house is thought to elicit connections regarding a person's home life and the interpersonal dynamics that are experienced within the family setting. The house, it has been theorized, symbolizes the main place wherein affection and security are sought. Drawings of a house seem to represent sources of nurturance and support, as well as conflict and tension. Thus, the house reflects the family drama, encompassing the interactions among the significant members (Leibowitz, 1999).

After the house's construction, the relevant features seem to include:

- the door and walkway—signs of accessibility;
- the chimney and smoke—whether it signifies warmth within the home;
- windows and shades—indicators of openness or mistrust;
- the baseline and surroundings—displays of emotional security or possible anxiety.

(Buck, 1992; Handler, 1996)

Evaluation of these variables involves the core aspect of interpretation and the gathering of much-needed information about personality characteristics, emotional defenses, and interpersonal conflicts based on their presence, absence, or emphasis that provide differential meanings. The overall impression of the house drawing can usually dictate a sense of emotional richness or bareness, cognitive growth or immaturity, and/or questions pertaining to interpersonal attachment.

Illustrations of the house may also encompass significant figures associated with the residence (most likely family members), in terms of their accessibility, approachability, and stability (Leibowitz, 1999). The occupants allow the examiner to gain a glimpse of the client's perception of interpersonal comfort and meanings that can derive from a shared dwelling. Pictures of houses also offer hints toward a type of environmental drawing, in that there is an opportunity to explore what is happening outside the house (Malchiodi, 1998). This extended view invites stories about the neighborhood and its location, or about other social support outside the family system.

Some interpretations of house drawings have also implicated certain details as related to sexual conflicts. For instance, when the chimney is overemphasized, there may be conflicts surrounding phallic issues of power or dominance (Hammer, 1958, 1997). Additionally, certain elaborations of the window fixtures suggest concerns with oral issues of dependence while an emphasis on curtains usually connotes a general mistrust of the environment. And while an omission of a door may evoke resistance to letting others in or isolating the self, regular walkways usually connote accessibility (Leibowitz, 1999).

Furthermore, developmental differences and progressions may be expressed through house drawings. From a maturational perspective, children under the age of 8 most often draw a chimney perpendicular to the slant of the roof (appearing at a 45° angle), whereas an upright chimney demonstrates that they have surmounted an important cognitive hurdle in their development (DiLeo, 1983). Therefore, older children who continue to construct a chimney at an angle are usually delayed in their perceptual maturation.

CASE STUDY: Kelli R.

Kelli R., an 18-year-old woman was referred for a comprehensive psychological evaluation by her therapist at a residential treatment center to ascertain current diagnostic impressions and assist in treatment and aftercare planning. At the time of the assessment, Kelli had been participating in individual and group psychotherapies to improve her social and coping skills. Through these interventions, she had been attempting to process her feelings regarding past trauma and sexual offending histories. Academically, she had been afforded special education services for many years, but due to her family conflicts and acting out behaviors had missed much of the educational and cultural process. Past testing indicated intellectual functioning within the "Borderline" range (Full Scale IQ 70 to 79).

As part of the assessment, Kelli was asked to construct a H-T-P among other drawing directives. Her creation of a house was significant in many areas. First, the slanted chimney was a sign of cognitive immaturity (see Figure 3.1). The chimney also expressed sexual connotations (which appeared relevant to her past trauma that occurred within her household, as well as her overly sexualized behaviors reported in previous placements). Other emotional indicators within the "house" drawing emphasized the cross-hatched roof (inner tension that was corroborated in discussing her intense fears), the basic drawing itself (signs of impulsive and blunt interpersonal expressions), and the use of the bottom of the paper as a ground line (another example of cognitive immaturity). These latter signs of developmental delays were apparent in other illustrations and were highlighted in her diagnoses that included specific learning disabilities.

According to DiLeo (1983), one emotional indicator that may appear in a house drawing is a chimney emitting a moderate degree of smoke, which is often associated with feelings of warmth and affection. Conversely, an overemphasis on the smoke could allude to a greater degree of household tension. Most often, when a request is made to draw a house, the observed result is usually a house-like structure that illustrates only the exterior. Even

3.1

with this type of drawing, much can be surmised concerning emotional accessibility, need for external structure, impulsivity, and personal defensiveness, to name only a few signs of personality makeup.

To obtain a more complete drawing that encompasses the interior, a direct request from the examiner has to be made. For example, clinicians can ask the following questions to increase the flow of communication. Such queries as: "Who lives there?" "What usually goes on inside the house?" "Do people visit here?" or "What is the general feeling inside?" can elicit a myriad of narratives and added insights into the perceptions of a particular house illustration. Again, the idea of introducing drawings into clinical interviews or psychological testing is to enhance interpersonal exchanges and gain important facets about the individuals being assessed and the world they inhabit. Their responses may not have been so readily available without the addition of this nonverbal and unique approach towards information gathering.

The following emotional indicators or signs within house drawings provide a limited interpretive guideline for the numerous variations that may be observed (adapted from Jolles, 1971; Burns, 1987). Specific interpretations should only be offered in the context of all factors within the combined H-T-P, in addition to confirmation gained from the clinical history, presenting problems, and other assessment data. Again, since these drawings are typically requested at the beginning phase of an interview or psychological evaluations, they set the stage for generating hypotheses towards eventual test selection and diagnostic possibilities (adapted from Oster & Crone, 2004).

1. Details:
   - *essential* (at least one door, one window, one wall, roof, chimney);
   - *irrelevant*, such as shrubs, flowers, walkway (needing to structure environment more completely, (associated with feelings of insecurity or needing to exercise control over surroundings).

2. Chimney (symbol of warm, intimate relations; often associated with symbol of dominance):
   - *absence* (lacking psychological warmth, conflicts with significant male figures, passivity);
   - *overly large* (overemphasis on sexual and dominance concerns, possible exhibitionistic tendencies);
   - *excessive smoke* (inner tension, anger).

3. Door:
   - *above baseline, without steps* (interpersonal inaccessibility);
   - *absence of door* (extreme difficulty in allowing accessibility to others);
   - *very small* (shyness or reluctant accessibility);
   - *open* (strong need to receive warmth from external world);
   - *very large* (overly dependent on others);
   - *with lock or hinges* (defensiveness).

4. Fence around house (need for emotional protection).
5. Gutters (suspiciousness).
6. Perspective.
   - *from below* (feelings of an unattainable desirable home life);
   - *from above* (rejection of home situation, feelings of alienation).

7. **Roof:**
    - *Unidimensional—single line connecting two walls* (unimaginative or emotionally constricted);
    - *Overly large* (seeking satisfaction in fantasy);
    - *Significant* crosshatching (strong conscience and guilt feelings.

8. **Shutters:**
    - *Closed* (extreme defensiveness and withdrawal);
    - *Open* (ability to make sensitive interpersonal adjustment.

9. **Walkway:**
    - *Very long* (lessened accessibility);
    - *Narrow* at house, broad at end (superficially friendly).

10. **Wall adequacy** (directly associated to degree of ego strength):
    - *Strong walls* (sturdy self-concept);
    - *Thin walls* (weak or vulnerable sense of self).

11. **Window(s):**
    - *Absence of windows* (hostile or withdrawing);
    - *Many* (indiscriminately open, desire for outside contact);
    - *Present on ground*, absent from upper story (gap between reality and fantasy);
    - *With curtains* (reserved, controlled);
    - *Bare* (behavior is mostly blunt and direct).

CASE STUDY: **Karl C.**

Twelve years old and entering the seventh grade, Karl C. arrived on time for an initial screening interview at an outpatient group practice. At that time in the family life cycle, Karl had become out of his parents' control. They viewed him as being moody, irritable, and expressing much anger. They also indicated that he was seemingly becoming more apathetic and lacked the self-esteem to attempt any new activities. A behavioral checklist completed by the parents also portrayed Karl as "highly" impulsive and disruptive. From their perspective, he was unpredictable in his moods ("either happy or sad"), conveyed a "bad" attitude, lacked interpersonal boundaries, and had become increasingly aggressive (especially towards his brother).

Because Karl was reluctant to talk, the examiner requested a series of drawings to promote his cooperation and provide a different approach to the interview. In his illustration of a house, it was apparent how much rage and frustration Karl was experiencing (see Figure 3.2). His "house" was split apart and on fire! Through the completion of this simple, one-step-removed technique, Karl was able to share some of his more sensitive thoughts and feelings. He believed that no one truly understood him and he was unsure of parental expectations. He also mentioned the need for more "freedom" and how frustrated he felt by family restrictions. Furthermore, he indicated that he no longer talked to his family members.

The introduction of drawing directives seemed to reduce Karl's resistance to the evaluative process. He appeared more willing to cooperate with other sources of assessment (computerized questionnaires). His responses seemed forthright and characterized him as being very depressed, withdrawn, and isolated. A meeting afterwards with the entire family assisted Karl in accepting help in treatment and he was referred to a clinician experienced in early adolescence and family therapy.

3.2

THE TREE

Perhaps the most universal symbol for depicting human development is the tree. It is used as a metaphor in most religions, and in myths, rituals, art, and poetry (Burns, 1987), and has come to symbolize life and growth (Hammer, 1958). The tree also appears to reflect long-standing, unconscious feelings toward the self—that is, one's self-image. These emotions tend to reside at a more primitive level of functioning and are personified by the various parts of the tree. For example, a large tree may represent an externalizing personality, or perhaps someone who is overcompensating for their inner anxiety, whereas a tiny tree may evoke a sense of passivity or inhibition (Leibowitz, 1999).

Of the three H-T-P drawings, the tree seems easiest to project one's own self perceptions —just think of standing up and visualizing your chest, arms, and head—that is, your body being a metaphor for the tree in this case. According to Hammer (1997), the tree is the one drawing of the H-T-P to convey an individual's "emotional" image, or who you are and the intactness of your personality. Positive or negative feelings toward the self are easier projected onto a tree illustration because this object is less connected to the home life or to directly viewing one's person.

Buck (1992) stated that the trunk signifies the person's basic power (or ego strength). Sometimes, the trunk is large to overly emphasize bodily concerns, or a physical presentation compared to its surroundings (ego strength—whether overly inflated or inadequate). Heavy lines or shading to represent the trunk are often viewed as forms of anxiety and inner tension. When the trunk is bent, slanted, or leaning, one gets the sense of a damaged self-concept, as the person seems to be weighted down (Leibowitz, 1999).

On rare occasions, the tree may be split in the middle, as hit by lightning, or constructed as two separate parts (signifying a very fragile ego or even a serious mental illness). For instance, in our book Clinical Uses of Drawings *(Oster & Montgomery, 1996), an example of a tree drawing was described in an illustration by a 17-year-old female who had been admitted to an acute hospital unit after a psychotic episode precipitated by a combination of alcohol abuse and an adverse reaction to an antidepressant medication. In the case study, this young woman constructed two parts of a tree—one as a stump with an ax that had leveled it (connoting her lack of integration) and another that was seemingly more complete but alluded to recent trauma; both appearing to display her intense anxiety and extremely fragile and vulnerable sense of self. Through the interactive process of constructing and sharing her tree drawing she was able to more readily reveal her secrets surrounding neglect and disappointment.*

Other parts of the tree, such as the limbs, seem to represent connections to the world, such that detached or small limbs could allude to problems in reaching out for assistance. By contrast, large branches might suggest an overbearing personality, while club-shaped or very pointy branches may reveal harsh and rigid defenses and underlying aggression. The roots of the tree may refer to grounding and reality testing (for example, thin roots may evoke feelings of struggling connectedness), whereas the appearance of fruit usually indicates a need of nurturing. When knotholes occur, they may reveal a past trauma with the height representing how long ago it may have happened. Also, reinforcement within the knothole is often considered how much healing has transpired.

64 HOUSE–TREE–PERSON AND VARIATIONS

CASE STUDY: Sakura R.

Fifteen-year-old Sakura R. had a long-standing history of behavioral and emotional difficulties that had been identified since she was two years old. Since that time, she had sustained several psychiatric hospitalizations and residential placements. When initially seen for a comprehensive psychological evaluation, she was presenting with intense anxiety that was marked by low self-esteem, a poor self-concept, and social inadequacies. She was also displaying inconsistencies in her coping strategies, which had led to impulsive and inappropriate actions. Additionally, she exhibited poor judgment, inattention, and felt helpless to overcome her difficulties.

As the beginning of the assessment process, Sakura was requested to construct a tree drawing that would potentially reflect her self-image. As illustrated in Figure 3.3, her image appeared quite fragile. With no roots and a narrow trunk, the tree, it seemed, could easily have toppled over. It seemed more of a wistful plant than a substantial tree drawing. And with the scribbled crown, it certainly alluded to her underlying anxiety, impulsivity when feeling stressed, and uncertainty in her life.

3.3

Overall, tree drawings are usually viewed as being related to one's life role and one's capacity to obtain perceived reinforcement from the environment. Generally, the drawing of a tree has been considered especially fertile in providing insights to life content. Interpretations from these drawings describe accurate biographical situations, as well as offer personal characteristics of the client. For instance, branches can represent "the feeling to derive satisfaction from the environment" (Leibowitz, 1999), while an overabundance of roots above ground may warn the examiner about possible distortions in reality testing (Hammer, 1958).

Whereas validity studies of the H-T-P only suggested that the technique was at best a "rough and non-specific measure of psychopathology" (Handler, Campbell, & Martin, 2004), the tree test alone has succeeded in differentiating psychiatric patients from controls, and has been shown to distinguish various psychopathological states (cited in Corff, Tivendell, & LeBlanc, 2013). In these researchers' views, the tree is believed to better reflect a client's emotional history and tap a deeper level of one's personality than signs from a person drawing.

There have also been studies suggesting that connections exist between reported trauma and the number of scars, knotholes, and broken branches of the tree drawing (Torem, Gilbertson, & Light, 2006). These investigators demonstrated that these indicators correlated with the duration of physical abuse in both psychiatric and non-psychiatric individuals. Thus, adding questions after a tree drawing can be pertinent to the gathering of added knowledge about the client's perception of self and perceptions of his or her surroundings. Inquiries such as: "Is the tree healthy?" "Who waters the tree?" or "Has anyone tried to cut it down?" can access needed evidence towards a client's self-view. These questions can also augment the beginning of rapport and overcome initial resistance.

Besides Buck's (1948) early descriptions and elucidations of tree drawings in his H-T-P manual, two other systems have been developed that focus solely on the tree as an independent diagnostic entity. These abundantly illustrated books offer lengthy descriptions and details regarding its explanatory value (Koch, 1952; Bolander, 1977). Clinicians should refer to these two elaborate books for a more comprehensive understanding of using tree drawings as projective instruments.

The following signs or marks that may appear on a tree drawing are just a small fraction of possible interpretations. However, they do give therapists and diagnosticians a beginning guide for exploring personality characteristics related to their clients (adapted from Oster & Gould, 1987; Oster & Crone, 2004). Identification of these personality markers in the tree drawing assists the clinician in exploring issues that may be overlooked during initial interviews or later in more traditional psychological testing.

1. **Extremely large tree** (aggressive tendencies).
2. **Tiny tree** (expressions of inferiority and insignificance).
3. **Faint lines** (feelings of inadequacy, indecisiveness).
4. **Two lines for trunk and looped crown** (impulsive, variable).
5. **Exaggerated emphasis on trunk** (emotional immaturity).
6. **Overstated crown** (inhibited, analytical).
7. **Emphasis on roots** (emotionally shallow, reasoning limited).
8. **No ground line** (vulnerable to stress).
9. **Ground line present, no roots** (repressed emotions).
10. **Fine, broken lines** (overt anxiety).
11. **Shading** (dark or reinforced) (hostile defenses, aggressive).
12. **Scar, knothole, broken branch** (associated with trauma, e.g., accident, illness, rape).

13. Knotholes
   - *Outline reinforced* (shock impact greater);
   - *Blackened inside* (shame associated with experience);
   - *Circles inside* (experience in past and healing);
   - *In relation to trunk* (higher, more recent);
   - *Large* (worried about procreation);
   - *Small animal inside* (ambivalence over childbearing).

CASE STUDY: **Sierra A.**

Sierra A. was 14 years old when admitted to an inpatient treatment center with an extensive history of severe physical and sexual abuse, as well as parental neglect, that resulted in the removal from her biological parents' home when a young girl. She had already been involved in many therapeutic interventions through the concerns of her adoptive parents, but her behaviors continued to be "out of control." In the past, she had run away and had exhibited many antisocial behaviors with subsequent arrests and hospitalizations.

Her requested drawing of a tree appeared to underscore many of her background themes (see Figure 3.4). The wide trunk and smaller crown appeared to signify her impulsivity and emotional immaturity, as she tended to act out her frustrations physically compared with talking through her conflicts and concerns. The emphasized knothole could certainly represent her significant trauma history, and the inside shading seemed to reveal both her shame associated with the abuse and the attempts at healing through therapeutic interventions surrounding her unresolved issues.

HUMAN FIGURES

Wide agreement exists that human figure drawings are primarily a manifestation of clients' perceptions of themselves or who they wish to be (Wenck, 1986). The drawing of a person apparently stimulates conscious awareness of bodily image and self-concept, both physically and psychologically. For instance, a person represented by tiny drawings or dangling arms may suggest inner experiences of inadequacy. By contrast, the drawing of an outsized person may arouse emotions regarding an ideal self.

Human figure drawings were the first constructed illustrations considered for clinical work and ensuing research. The Goodenough–Harris Drawing Test (Harris, 1963) was primarily used as a screening device by practitioners to quickly assess and estimate the cognitive ability of a school-age child. These early uses of drawing a person (Draw-A-Man) investigated normative development from childhood through adolescence and related this visual–motor maturation to intellectual growth. Of all intellectual screening measures created over the years, it still continues to be the briefest and most convenient to use. Scoring systems were associated with developmental and intellectual abilities exhibited in large samples of children's drawings. Besides its general use in estimating intelligence, this drawing test was extended to evaluate children with auditory handicaps, suspected neurological weaknesses, adjustment problems, and character defects (cited in Oster & Crone, 2004).

This drawing technique was based on Florence Goodenough's original conjectures suggesting that fairly accurate judgments of intellectual maturation could be specified from observing a school-age child's attempts at drawing a man (Goodenough, 1926). Her scoring system became popular with child and school psychologists, as well as

3.4

pediatricians, and was used without modification from its original standardization until Dale Harris's revision in 1963. At that time, drawings of a woman and a self-portrait were added to the instructions.

Their research and scoring methods established a solid foundation for many of the succeeding procedures for drawing methodology and interpretation. Cognitive functioning, such as intellectual quotients (IQ scores), was estimated by inclusion of such features on the human figure as individual body parts, clothing details, proportion, and perspective. The test manual included 73 scored items based on age differentiation, relation to total score on the test, and relation to group intelligence scores (Harris, 1963).

Once established, this scoring technique corresponded relatively well with the original standardized tests of intelligence that were being created at that time, such as the Stanford–Binet Tests, and even more closely with the Wechsler Scales for children. However, over the years, research studies discovered that the estimated IQs derived from the drawings were generally lower than overall IQs from these more comprehensive batteries of intelligence (Palmer, 1983). Consequently, the illustration of a person should never be used as a substitute for more complete scales of intelligence; neither should it (or any other drawing directive) be the sole basis for determining academic or social placement. Results of this screening measure should only be used to select those children who may need more comprehensive evaluations.

Drawings completed by younger children are usually very basic, consisting of a head with few facial characteristics, with arms and legs protruding from the head. As seen in Chapter 2, the young child constructs the head and body together as one circular shape. If a child's figure is purposeless or seems like uncontrolled scribbles, the resulting score is given a zero credit, which is equivalent to 3 years, 0 months in this scoring system. Any drawing that appears to have direction is scored as one credit and is equivalent to 3 years, 3 months. Each subsequent credit adds a 3-month interval. With ongoing development, the normal child produces drawings that are increasingly heterogeneous and more accurate.

The overall picture of this scoring method gives credits regarding whether a) such body segments as the head, trunk, arms, and legs are included; b) the arms and legs are attached properly; c) there are eyes, a nose, a mouth, and hair; d) there are details of fingers; and e) proportions of the features are accurate. Tables are provided in the test manual that convert raw scores to standard scores (IQ equivalents) and percentile ranks (Harris, 1963).

CASE STUDY: Joseph S.

Joseph S. was only 6 years old and in kindergarten when his parents and pediatrician referred him for a psychological evaluation. Premature at birth, Joseph still exhibited signs of developmental lags and learning delays. Previously diagnosed with ADHD and dyslexia, he was struggling in school. Teacher reports indicated that he had trouble "remembering things," such as letters of the alphabet, bringing things to school, and words to a rhyme. He also had difficulty listening attentively. Other concerns expressed by the mother included Joseph being: restless and fidgety, disruptive in class, and in need of extra instruction. Despite these vulnerabilities, he was portrayed as "pleasant and tries to learn."

Joseph presented as an engaging youngster who was easily focused during structured activities. He sat through an intellectual evaluation without too many problems, with resulting scores in the average range (90 to 109). However, his drawings were markedly immature. This difficulty in fine motor coordination and perceptual development was especially poignant during his construction

3.5

of a person (see Figure 3.5). The picture was out of proportion and at an expected chronological age of approximately 4½. His other drawings of a house and tree were equally delayed. With this crucial information, in addition to other facets of the testing pointing to attention deficits undermining his potential, his school and pediatrician were more understanding of his specific strengths and relative weaknesses. They were then able to compose an Individual Educational Plan (IEP) that provided Joseph with the specialized services that he required to become better adjusted to the expected academic demands.

Goodenough, along with other clinicians, soon realized that the Draw-A-Man test also provided possible indicators of personality dynamics, in addition to intellectual aptitude. With this new perspective, the D-A-P test was adapted for personality description and interpretation by Karen Machover (1952). She hypothesized that certain graphic expressions within the drawings reflected specific personality characteristics. These traits derived from the D-A-P test were believed to reflect the person's self-concept, portraying unconscious projections of conflicts and concerns. For example, she viewed the construction of body parts (such as the head) as containing suggestions of social balance and control of bodily impulses, while the arms and legs were perceived as symbols of social adaptation.

Further research of the human figure asserted that intense emotions (e.g., hostility) appeared to be commonly projected onto drawings through the creation of glaring eyes, bared teeth, sneering lips, or even placing weapons in the hand of the drawn person (Hammer, 1967, 1997). Poor reality testing could also be assessed in drawings by a) manifestations of bizarre facial features (for instance, animal faces on human figures); b) nonhuman, robot-like characters; c) religious or mysterious symbols on the drawings; or d) depersonalized, empty facial expressions. Other personality aspects commonly seen in human figure drawings included a) aggressiveness, as seen in the use of claw-like hands; b) concerns regarding sexual identification; c) portrayals of dominant and inferior persons; and d) impulses toward rebelliousness and seductiveness.

CASE STUDY: Melissa B.

Melissa B., a 16-year-old female, was referred for an extended assessment due to school underachievement and to promote more realistic goals for her treatment and educational teams. Previous evaluations had displayed inconsistent functioning, with solid skills exhibited on straightforward tasks but with little capacity to solve abstract reasoning problems. Melissa also had a significant behavioral health history that included indices of ADD, symptoms of emotional dysregulation, eating disorders, fire-setting behaviors, and self-injurious actions. There was also suspected sexual abuse that had not been documented.

During a series of drawing directives, Melissa created a person that was developmentally appropriate but seemed exaggerated in its sexuality (see Figure 3.6). Emotional indicators of mistrust and impulsivity were additionally reflected in the human figure. These characteristics corroborated other findings within the testing battery and were discussed within the report and relayed to the various professionals involved in her care.

3.6

Of the three H-T-P drawings, the person is the most difficult to construct and the one drawing most likely to be refused by individuals who are sensitive to their shortcomings or who fear failure. Therefore, a request to complete the drawing (more than a stick figure) often needs the most encouragement from the examiner. During the drawings, clinicians should observe the sequence in which different body parts are drawn, and other important procedural details, in order to start generating clinical hypotheses about the examinee's personality dimensions. At times, it is helpful for the clinician to instruct the client to make up a story about each drawn figure to elicit specific characteristics, such as age or personal feelings. Questions like: "Who is the person?" "How old is she?" "Who looks out for him/her?" and "What is she thinking (and feeling)?" all lead to an easier discourse between clients and examiners.

Proponents of the human figure drawing test mostly agree that there is not always a one-to-one relationship between a specific sign or emotional indicator and a definite personality or trait (Machover, 1952; Hammer, 1967, 1997; Koppitz, 1968). However, research studies of these variables have shown that anxieties, conflicts, or attitudes are often communicated in the drawings by unique signs and symbols and vary according to client and time frame. At best, there may be several characteristics that consistently indicate emotional problems (Malchiodi, 1998). Therefore, meaningful diagnoses cannot and should not be made from a single sign; rather, the total drawing, as well as combinations of other indicators, must always be included when analyzing the drawing.

Additionally, drawings must be interpreted on the basis of chronological age, developmental maturation, emotional status, social and cultural background, and other relevant history of the individual. For instance, sketchiness in the line quality has heretofore been viewed as an emotional indicator of anxiety. Yet, this sketchiness appears to increase with age and is normal for most adolescents, who tend to demonstrate some degree of anxiety when producing figure drawings (Koppitz, 1968).

To overcome these difficulties in supporting the original studies, refinement in scoring rules and increased objectivity were required. In this regard, Naglieri, McNeish, and Bardos (1991) established a newer methodology. Their system, the Draw-A-Person: Screening Procedure for Emotional Disturbance (D-A-P: SPED), now seems to be the standard for recording protocols. They suggested the number of items present rather than the presence of any particular item (or sign) more effectively differentiates normal pictures from maladjusted ones. They also noted that drawing interpretation should be based on these global aspects of drawings and used primarily as gross screening measures, rather as specific indicators of a certain conflict or diagnosis.

However, there has remained renewed exploration of using drawings in clinical interviews and for their diagnostic value. Numerous studies and clinical usage of the D-A-P Test have indicated rich and informative signs within the drawn human figure that consistently differentiate populations. For example, not drawing shoulders on the male or female may convey a sense of avoidance from responsibility with implications of inadequate feelings (Leibowitz, 1999). The following list of these emotional indicators offers a guideline for observing specific indicators within the graphic image. Mainly, theorists and researchers in the field of drawing analysis have concurred on the interpretation for each particular sign (adapted from Jolles, 1971; Mitchell, Trent, & McArthur, 1993).

1. **Poor integration of body parts** (impulsivity/low frustration tolerance).
2. **Shading** (anxiety—excessive shading, greater the degree of anxiety);
    shaded face (seriously disturbed, damaged self-concept);
    shaded arms (aggressive impulses).

3. **Line quality:**
   sketched (insecure, uncertainty);
   light (low self-esteem);
   reinforced (anger, vulnerable emotional defenses).
4. **Figure slanting more than 15 degrees** (instability, mental imbalance).
5. **Small size** (insecure, withdrawn, depressed, feelings of inadequacy).
6. **Large size** (expansiveness, positive mood).
7. **Transparencies** (seeing through the clothing—immaturity).
8. **Head:**
   large (preoccupation with fantasy life, focus on mental life);
   small (obsessive-compulsive, intellectual inadequacy);
   back to viewer (paranoid or schizoid tendencies).
9. **Mouth:**
   overly emphasized (immaturity, oral-aggressive);
   very large (orally erotic);
   exaggerated teeth (orally aggressive, sarcastic).
10. **Shoulders:**
    unequal (emotionally unstable);
    large (preoccupied with the perceived need for strength);
    squared (overly defended, hostile toward others).
11. **Arms:**
    folded over chest (hostile or suspicious)
    held behind back (wanting to control anger, interpersonal reluctance)
    omitted (inadequacy, helplessness)
    short (withdrawal, inhibiting impulses)
    long (ambitious, reaching out toward others)
12. **Hands:**
    large (acting out behaviors);
    cut off (feelings of inadequacy).
13. **Fingers:**
    long and spike line (aggressive, hostile);
    enclosed by single loop (wish to suppress aggressive impulse).
14. **Legs:**
    absent (constricted, possible castration anxiety);
    size difference (mixed feelings regarding independence);
    long (striving for autonomy);
    short (emotional immobility).
15. **Feet:**
    long (striving for security or virility);
    tiny (dependency, blunted feelings);
    omitted (lack of independence).
16. **Profile of person** (evasive, excessively withdrawn, possibly paranoid).
17. **Disheveled hair** (possible sexual concerns, underlying confusion).
18. **Elaborate belt, emphasis around waist area** (sexual conflicts, tension).

CASE STUDY: Monique W.

Monique was a second grade, 8-year-old youngster who, according to her parents, was inattentive and inconsistent in her learning performance. In the past, she had received speech and language services for delayed comprehension. Adopted from a South American country at age 3 by a single mother, she seemed to be thriving in many physical activities (biking, roller skating, jump roping). However, school work was a strain. She had difficulty completing assignments, talked too much, and was behind her peers in understanding math concepts.

During the course of an evaluation for school, Monique demonstrated mostly grade-appropriate abilities. Educational tests were at grade level (though at the lower end) and her intellectual functioning was considered within the low average range (scores from 76 to 92 reflected significant disparities among specific ability realms). She mainly exhibited difficulties on items associated with fine motor coordination, visual integration, and puzzle solving.

These liabilities in her nonverbal learning skills were also observed on her drawings. These weaknesses were especially noted on the request for "Draw A Person." On this illustration (see Figure 3.7), Monique's figure was somewhat immature. Indicators of delays were reflected by transparencies, differences in arm constructions, and the stick legs. Emotionally, the figure was accurate in its presentation as a "happy-go-lucky" child. Recommendations from the assessment focused on her need for occupational therapy interventions that converged on her visual–motor integration weaknesses.

3.7

KINETIC–HOUSE–TREE–PERSON

Robert Burns (1987) expanded the use of the H-T-P by assuming that drawings with action could reflect a client's underlying well-being more profoundly than static illustrations. By adding a slightly different instruction "Draw a house, a tree, and a person on this paper with some kind of action" (K-H-T-P), he provided new insights and varied perceptions not previously realized from individual drawings. The actions, styles, and symbols derived from this novel direction seemed richer in their interpretive value compared with standard drawing directives. For Burns, though an active proponent of the original H-T-P, this variation on a theme demonstrated how this unique directive of adding action to standard pictures produced a novel experience between examiner and examinee.

Through his research, Burns (1987) showed that the personality dynamics disclosed through the K-H-T-P was enhanced when incorporating all three figures onto one sheet of paper. He also revealed (through this more action-oriented drawing) that clinicians could generate salient hypotheses associated with a) the feelings or impressions surrounding the entire picture; b) the perceived warmth or hostility of the house; c) the activity level of the drawn person; d) the strength of the tree; and e) the relationship between tree and house (e.g., how close are the two objects, or how sheltering or protective is the tree?). Letting clients talk about the interactions, he determined, could also underscore the examiner's notions about the figures in the drawing and provided a more secure platform to discuss their world. Again, these added instructions stimulate conversations and interactions during assessments and interviews and offer clinicians more possibilities for uncovering conflicts and concerns in a briefer time period.

Furthermore, Burns (1987) emphasized the advantages of action drawings (as opposed to static pictures) as a way to offer supplemental significance to personality dimensions in many difficult clinical situations. He suggested that this novel drawing approach actually initiated a beginning to the therapeutic healing process.

Through numerous illustrations (in combination with his substantial clinical insight gained through many years collecting and analyzing drawings), his book on this action perspective to the H-T-P provided an enriched understanding to this newer, unified approach that was not always apparent during the construction and analysis of separate drawings.

CASE STUDY: Mandy S.

Sixteen-year-old Mandy S. was brought to an outpatient group practice by her single mother for an extended evaluation. She had been experiencing adjustment problems to her new neighborhood for several years and her academic performance had suffered. She had also displayed behavioral difficulties, including being disrespectful to teachers, spray painting a wall, and being mean to a classmate. On a behavioral checklist, the mother described Mandy as defensive, easily embarrassed, lacking in self-esteem, and feeling like a failure. Mandy concurred that she felt "stupid and dumb." Other acknowledged symptoms included increased feelings of depression, social isolation, and disturbances in sleeping and eating.

Mandy had been attending sessions with the school counselor on a regular basis and attempted several individual visits with an outside therapist, with little success. She was also being prescribed an antidepressant by her family physician. None of the interventions had made much of an impact and she and her mother were concerned about her ongoing moodiness and daily inconsistencies. As an example, Mandy described one week as skipping school one day then sleeping the entire next day, failing an English exam, believing that she was always behind in her coursework, and having volatile relationships with peers. On a scale of 1 to 10 (with 10 being the best), most of her days were less than 4. At that point in eleventh grade, Mandy's Grade Point Average (GPA) was 1.5, and plans were being discussed for her to enter an alternative technical program.

Despite her vulnerabilities and missed educational opportunities, Mandy appeared quite bright and articulate. On an intellectual measure, she scored within the superior range (Full Scale IQ = 125). Her only below average scores occurred in functional areas of sustained attention and copying speed, signifying the possibility of ADD symptoms that might impact her daily functioning. In fact, an ADD screening form that she completed indicated many symptoms related to this disorder. Also, she seemed to suggest that she was easily angered, displayed a low frustration tolerance, daydreamed constantly, and was quite moody. She also discussed that she had difficulty organizing her assignments and completing them.

Emotionally, Mandy did not view herself in significant distress. She mainly pointed to problems in anger and hostility. She perceived life as unfair, was mad about "everything," and thought her peers did not like her. Much of her focus emphasized feelings of frustration and helplessness. However, she denied significant signs of sadness. And it appeared that much of her presentation was somewhat naïve and lacked interpersonal quality. With all of her problems, she attempted to put forth a positive light. This posture was mainly seen in her drawings that displayed happy, peaceful, and optimistic themes. In one of these drawings, a K-H-T-P seemed to reflect this carefree attitude (see Figure 3.8). Her comment regarding the illustration was "just enjoying the day." Through this construction and other sketches, she seemed to indicate that she was enjoying the attention and that her mood was "good for a change."

DRAW-A-PERSON-IN-THE-RAIN

Over many years, numerous clinicians and researchers have developed alternative drawing directives that help to identify personality characteristics and emotional resources when conducting psychological evaluations and clinical interviews. One particularly intriguing modification of the original D-A-P instruction was to extend an added dimension (i.e., rain) to the standard instruction. The creators of this concept designed a procedure that attempted to elicit an impression of emotional vulnerability from clients when placed within a symbol of a minor environmental stressor (i.e., rain) (cited in Verinis, Lichtenberg, & Henrich, 1974; Lichtenberg, 2013).

The rationale behind the Draw-A-Person-In-The-Rain (D-A-P-R) stemmed from the need of examiners to have an efficient method to determine whether individuals were highly vulnerable to stressful circumstances and to discover how best they coped with the situation. With this novel directive, clinicians could also address the appropriate treatment direction, including the degree of suicidal risk. In this context, the amount and intensity of rain in the drawing (for example, dark clouds, heavy rain, and lightning) seemed to represent the degree of perceived external stress being experienced by the individual. By comparison, the individual's protection (i.e., raincoat, boots, and umbrella) signified his or her defensive structure to deal with this perceived stressful event. For example, a highly anxious individual purportedly would construct a drawing with an intense amount of rain, but still be wearing some type of outer protection. Someone who feels vulnerable and overwhelmed by their environment would be more likely to draw a figure without an umbrella or rain coat, often looking sad, and helpless to overcome the circumstances. This unique directive has displayed extremely impressive results and

3.8

frequently correlates with other measures of the assessment battery (like the Rorschach) that might reflect ineffective emotional capacities (see examples in Oster & Gould, 1987; Oster & Montgomery, 1996; Oster & Crone, 2004).

CASE STUDY: Toni N.

Toni N., a 15-year-old female was placed into foster care after being abandoned by her mother at 6 years of age. Since that time, Toni had become aggressive and self-destructive, with homicidal and suicidal ideation that culminated in several hospitalizations. At one point, she turned on a gas stove and returned to her room in the hope that her adoptive mother would light a match or cigarette and blow up the house with both of them being killed.

Despite her usual provocative manner, Toni was very cooperative during an evaluation ordered by an attending psychiatrist. She seemed challenged by cognitive measures and her intellectual quotient of 92 (lower average) suggested notable strengths as well as substantial weaknesses. While displaying solid skills in her language dexterity and abstract reasoning, she appeared constricted in her fund of knowledge (she had missed many educational opportunities over the years) and was limited in her ability to retain and process information during multi-task operations. This latter vulnerability seemed a by-product of increased anxiety when confronted by new learning situations.

Her picture of a person-in-the-rain was quite striking on several levels. During previous drawings of people, she had constructed images of confident and confrontational young ladies (see Figure 3.9); yet when the direction placed her within the context of a seemingly minor stressor (the rain) she appeared overwhelmed, sad, and defenseless (see Figure 3.10). As other test material pointed to similar conclusions—that is, she possessed traits of an avoidant coping style that on the surface made her seem immature and aggressive but underneath she was very shy, withdrawn, and fragile. With this added insight, it was easier to provide more accurate feedback to the psychiatrist in order to construct appropriate medical and therapeutic interventions.

Clinicians who conduct assessments and interviews use this technique (the D-A-P-R) to assess the amount of internal tension that people are experiencing, as well as perceived threats within their environments (i.e., viewing their world as unusually harsh), and how well their coping capacities are being sustained when added pressures are confronted. When outer garments are not displayed for protection, clients appear to be portraying their inability to manage even minor stress with subsequent feelings of helplessness and inner regression being expressed. Thus, a highly passive individual who has few emotional resources would tend to construct a figure that seemed defenseless. On the other hand, individuals who utilize denial as their main defense mechanisms are more likely to illustrate people who do not look upset and perhaps even enjoy the stressful confrontation (e.g., a smile on their face; see Figure 3.11).

This drawing technique offers useful information to the diagnostician or examiner when the referral source has expressed concerns about the person's vulnerability to external pressure. Such referral questions as: a) How well does this person respond to stressful circumstances? b) What kind of emotional resources does this individual possess to deal with anxiety-provoking environments? c) Is this person able to plan effectively in situations that might be considered anxiety-provoking? Or d) What kinds of defense mechanisms (e.g., denial, avoidance) does this person employ when confronted with

3.9

3.10

3.11

unpleasant situations? can all be answered when this procedure is used in conjunction with other available cognitive and personality test information measuring similar constructs.

Emotionally immature individuals given this directive during evaluations will often project their own perceived helplessness of being dumped upon in their drawing by illustrating a disheveled person without protective covering or holding a broken umbrella. These portrayals appear to represent low self-esteem, an inability to cope with daily stressors, and unresolved dependency issues. It has been shown that individuals who construct these types of drawings have neither the motivation to leave their undesirable circumstances, nor are they prepared to face the challenges of protecting themselves from even minor stress when left to their own initiative.

Persons who are not easily overwhelmed when confronted with stress will generally add protective clothing or devices and have contented faces in their drawings. These individuals are at least demonstrating that their basic emotional defenses are intact, even if they use denial as their primary mechanism to avoid unpleasant thoughts and feelings. By contrast, people who react unfavorably to the slightest degree of tension will likely picture themselves as panic-stricken without a means of escape.

It is best for the clinician to make comparisons between this isolated drawing directive and other human figure drawings completed during a comprehensive evaluation, in additon to other assessment instruments within the test battery. For example, suggestions from a D-A-P-R drawing reflecting withdrawal tendencies may coincide with similar personality responses to the Rorschach Inkblots or Thematic Apperception Test (TAT) and may further substantiate a passive style of interpersonal functioning. Additionally, other drawings in the D-A-P series may all seem fairly normal. Only when a novel introduction of a stressing symbol is required (i.e., the rain) does a more accurate illustration occur that is directly related to underlying conflicts. In this case, only when faced with potentially stressful external circumstances does the person's compensatory abilities falter, revealing weak emotional resources and vulnerabilities (e.g., a frown on the face, a broken umbrella, standing in a puddle).

By providing this variation of the D-A-P along with other drawing directives, clinicians obtain a glimpse of the examinee in both normal and stressful conditions. Many times, a person's disposition toward abnormal reactions is not visible through standard drawing directions. Only when an unusual request is made during a series of drawings is the existence of pathological signs discovered, which is the main purpose for administering projective techniques.

FAMILY DRAWING PROCEDURES

Draw-a-Family

Another enhancement on using human figure drawings as projective indicators of personality is the Draw-A-Family or family drawing technique. This informative technique was originally suggested by Appel (1931) and later expanded by Wolff (1942). Its tremendous popularity among drawing procedures most likely paralleled the therapeutic emphasis on understanding family structure and implementing family interventions during the 1970s and 1980s. The wealth of information gathered when broadening the focus to the family constellation is enormous and advances the drawings arsenal of clinical tools used by behavioral health professionals.

This directive allows clinicians to view and broaden their understanding of the client's context within their expressed symptoms. When used during the evaluative or beginning phase of treatment, it widens the scope of awareness into interpersonal struggles and helps paint a clearer picture of the client's world. The additional knowledge becomes invaluable when discussing future intervention plans. It is also instrumental when discovering the inter-relationships among blended families, as clients can clearly indicate in a drawing the various subgroups (dyads and triads) to whom they are involved.

The instructions for this drawing procedure are minimal. The examiner provides clients with pencil and paper and asks them to merely "Draw a picture of your whole family" (Harris, 1963). If they do not spontaneously offer the names of their family members, they are asked to identify them afterward to elicit additional associations. When completed, the family drawing tends to reveal attitudes toward family members and perceptions of family roles. These interpersonal relationships are often expressed by the relative size and placement of the figures and by substitutions or exaggerations of distinct family members. For example, clients may omit themselves from the family drawings, suggesting feelings of rejection, especially during separation or divorce. This underlying reaction towards disapproval is occasionally seen in family drawings by adopted children, especially during their adolescent years when identity concerns are brought to the forefront (DiLeo, 1983).

CASE STUDY: **Marla B.**

Marla B. was struggling. Her single mother was in a new relationship and Marla was uncertain about this new person in her life. Her brother was a student outside of the home and his being away at college left a vacuum and put more pressure on her. However, she was no longer accepting this new responsibility and was mostly acting out through school absences and failure. Certainly, she was "crying for help."

3.12

When her mother brought her for an evaluation at the recommendation of a physician, Marla was reticent to engage in conversation or complete the requested inventories and questionnaires. Her mother, though, indicated on a checklist that Marla was easily angered, defensive, felt like a failure, had become socially withdrawn, and lacked self-esteem. Certainly, Marla's initial stance corroborated these characteristics.

At that point, requests were made to construct a series of drawings in the hope that Marla would respond more positively to this one-step-removed approach. And in fact she was more receptive to this idea and sketched the drawing of her family (see Figure 3.12). With this portrait, Marla seemed comfortable to discuss what had been occurring over the past year. She remarked about her ambivalent feelings towards her mother's boyfriend and the closeness she used to experience with her mother. She mentioned feeling lonely about her mother's absence since she had been going out quite a bit. Marla also acknowledged her distress and the inappropriate manner in which she had been coping with her feelings.

When Marla presented the picture to her mother at the end of the session and spoke about her hurt, the mother was surprised but understanding. She suggested that an extra session was needed to discuss these matters before a more comprehensive evaluation was scheduled. Marla cheerfully agreed to this idea and promised to be cooperative in the future.

Kinetic-Family-Drawing

A particularly useful alternative to the standard family drawing is explored through the Kinetic-Family-Drawing (K-F-D) (Burns & Kaufman, 1970), which added the instruction of "doing something (an activity) together." This alteration of the original Draw-A-Family also directly requested individuals to include themselves in the picture. It is usually given after the first family drawing, so as not to contaminate the possibility that clients will omit themselves or other family members.

The K-F-D's special contribution lies in the principle that how clients view themselves in their family system may be different than how they see themselves outside the household. This modification thus provides alternative views of interpersonal perceptions for ongoing assessments at the beginning and during individual and family therapy. It can be used for such practical concerns as decision making during custody disputes, determining whether a child should be removed from a parental home, or demonstrating to parents how their turmoil and differences may be impacting their children (Hammer, 1997). Also through this method, clinicians have observed clients attempting to represent boundaries within their drawings as protective coping skills when there are suggestions of inappropriate behaviors (for instance, physical or sexual abuse) occurring in their families (Malchiodi, 1998).

Additionally, this adaptive drawing technique sometimes produces a strong reaction like, "We don't do anything together" (a key revelation to initial hypotheses regarding familial interaction). Although this directive is pertinent when used with children, it stimulates memories of childhood when used with adults. It could produce recollections of past positive or negative family experiences and interrelationships, which are fruitful in relating previous occurrences to current history and symptoms.

From this drawing directive of a family in action, it is common to observe clients illustrating their families in a passive posture (e.g., watching television or a movie), which may suggest a possible lack of direct communication or with further probing, an enjoyment of just being together. Another common response when using these kinetic family drawings is a picture reflecting dinner table scenes. In these portrayals, clients may place the parents at opposite ends of a long table (representing their emotional distance from one another) or place themselves at one end (attesting to the perceived competition that they may experience). Whether the dinner table is full with food or bare may address the examinee's worries about living in an environment that is lacking in enriched stimulation or concerns regarding the amount of emotional nurturance that is experienced (Oster & Crone, 2004).

Other features discovered from family drawings include compelling interpersonal dynamics between parents and children or among siblings. For instance, dramatic results may reflect a child's panic during interactions with an alcoholic father, feelings of isolation in a stepfamily, or withdrawing from perceived threats within a dysfunctional household (Hammer, 1997). Clues to these personality traits may consider whether a) clients draw themselves in proximity to the parents (as a way to demonstrate increased status over their siblings or to express feelings of acceptance or rejection); b) they omit siblings as a symbolic gesture toward eliminating competition; c) they include themselves in the drawing (displaying personal feelings of not belonging); or d) the family is drawn in accurate proportions (making a child or adult much taller demonstrates perceived dominance or ineffectiveness).

Clinicians may also observe the parents' facial expressions in the drawings for valuable clues to uncover hidden thoughts and feelings. Such features as whether clients perceive one parent to be harsh, one to be gentle, or one to be more supportive are all vital areas to pursue during further interviews and testing that may provide clearer direction to therapeutic planning and intervention.

CASE STUDY: Arlene G.

Arlene G., a 17-year-old, twelfth grade student was referred for a comprehensive evaluation by her parents and prescribing physician to clarify whether attention weaknesses, learning style delays, or emotional factors might be hindering her academic potential and interpersonal maturation. According to her mother, who brought her to the sessions, Arlene tended to be inattentive and disorganized in her work habits. Arlene was also described as exhibiting symptoms of anxiety and panic, as well as displaying impulse control problems. She had received treatment in the past for ADHD and mood variability.

On a behavior scale related to school functioning, the mother suggested that Arlene "very often" had difficulty organizing tasks and activities. She also noted that Arlene "often" failed to give attention to details, made careless mistakes, had problems sustaining her attention during longer assignments, was forgetful during daily activities, and tended to blame herself for her problems and felt excessively guilty.

Arlene had missed much school during the past year due to several illnesses. Furthermore, she only attended a few days the following year due to a third surgery on her knee from another meniscus tear. Her mother detailed Arlene's condition as anxious, defensive, and irritable. She additionally noted that at home Arlene seemed sad, and displayed tiredness and poor concentration due to sleep problems. She also mentioned that Arlene appeared to have lost interest in many activities, lacked self-esteem, and felt disappointed in her work.

In the past, Arlene had been very social and active. She was apparently an outstanding softball player before her injuries and had been the captain of a debate team. She had also participated in journalism, the school's track team, and various service clubs.

Arlene presented for the two-day evaluation as alert and oriented, but seemed very tired during the first session and somewhat guarded and defensive. Her affect was constricted and she did not offer much spontaneity in speech or mannerisms. Since there was a need to complete this extended assessment in a timely manner, it was felt that offering Arlene the opportunity to illustrate her background and problems would be more efficient and provide a safer environment to engage her on more demanding tests.

Arlene readily agreed to this approach. When requested to portray herself with her family doing something together, she portrayed the four of them at a bowling alley. She said that her family attempted to get together on a weekly basis with rotating preferences, where each individual got to choose the activity. This "getting together time" was an attempt to provide an outlet for Arlene to extend herself outside the home and begin to assimilate back into her community.

After this technique, she seemed to relax and was more willing to discuss her situation, the problems that were occurring, and the need for this evaluation to provide her a basis for accommodations when she entered college. Although the drawing was fairly innocuous (see Figure 3.13), it offered Arlene the opportunity to relax and accept the direction for continued testing.

3.13

The drawing was interesting, though, in that it appeared Arlene had taken a step in front of the family, possibly as a way of showing her initial attempt at independence. Because she perceived the offer of drawing instead of talking at the beginning of the evaluation as positive, rapport was more easliy established and she was more willing to begin the series of intellectual and personality tests that were required.

Family-Centered-Circle-Drawing

Another variation in family drawings developed by Robert Burns (1990) is a procedure known as the Family-Centered-Circle-Drawing (F-C-C-D). This drawing directive assists individuals to more clearly perceive the relationships between themselves and their parents. Burns proposed that by making a series of family drawings within a structured circle and centering the figures, clients have easier access to unconscious material and reveal more of their internal versions of their parents.

The directions for this technique are relatively simple. Standard paper is used with a circle already drawn measuring 7 1/2 to 9 inches in diameter (or you can ask the examinee to draw a large circle on the paper). The instructions for obtaining an F-C-C-D are to: "Draw your mother in the center of a circle. Visually free associate with drawn symbols around the periphery of the circle. Try to draw a whole person, not a stick or cartoon figure." With less sophisticated clients, you can say, "Make symbols or pictures that represent your parent, and make pictures that make you think of (or describe) your parent around them." The instructions are then repeated, twice substituting father and the person doing the drawing for the original mother figure. Another drawing is then constructed of the parents with the client in a circle-centered drawing.

Once the drawings have been completed, observations are made pertaining to a) what types of symbols are used; b) what possible barriers in communication are constructed; c) how close the parents and individual are to one another; and d) whether caring is being expressed among the family members. As in all drawing directives mentioned throughout this book, it is incumbent upon the clinician to be cognizant of other diagnostic possibilities within the images. Aspects of the completed drawings, such as relative size of the figures, omission or overemphasis on bodily parts, facial expressions, and the types of symbols (whether loving or hateful, expressions of anger, positive or negative), are all essential factors in creating initial hypotheses about diagnostic criteria and for later treatment direction.

In his book, Burns (1990) described several features to examine in the final drawings. These observations included:

1. What symbols are directly above or below each figure and are these positive or negative?
2. Relative sizes of the drawings. Is the client smaller or larger?
3. Who is in the center (possibly the controlling member of the family)?
4. Are there clear alliances within the family structure?

Burns' (1990) work with these techniques is a culmination of his attempts at combining Eastern philosophies (such as the use of Mandalas) with Western techniques, such as the Rorschach (Rorschach, 1942). His book on Family-Centered-Circle-Drawings provides many examples with extensive clinical interpretations to describe his methods and to supply a foundation for future research and clinical usage. By having clients place the family and separate members at the center of a circle surrounded by visual and freely associated symbols, Burns truly demonstrated a stimulating model for obtaining expressive material to promote clinical insights and discussions.

CASE STUDY: Eddie C.

Eddie C. was an 18-year-old man entering community college after a long-standing history of ADHD and mood instability that had seriously impacted his school performance. Ultimately, as a high school senior, he spent most of his time playing video games and neglected his studies and preparation for college applications. According to his father (who attended the initial assessment session), Eddie's behavior had declined over the past two years and his grades and efforts were viewed as inconsistent. He described Eddie's then current condition as being easily angered, defensive, irritable, and tending to be oppositional and defiant. He also noted that Eddie lacked self-esteem, felt like a failure, exhibited poor concentration, and seemed to have lost interest in most activities. He was especially concerned that Eddie had become "addicted to video games," causing him to withdraw socially and avoid academic challenges.

Despite his problems in school, Eddie appeared bright and was optimistic about his future (he wanted to attend engineering school). He had made good grades in the past when classroom accommodations were provided and scored at a high level on the SAT (around 2000) and the ACT. Although he admitted to spending much time online and playing video games, he mentioned that he also taught tennis at a country club and helped elderly people in the use of computers and cell phones. Furthermore, he said that he enjoyed "hanging out" with friends and used to like fishing.

While Eddie's performance on various parts of the evaluation was inconsistent (IQ scores from low average to very superior with similar educational testing ranges), he denied many of his serious emotional problems and attempted to place himself in a positive light. However, Eddie did perceive himself as shy and avoidant. He preferred being alone to socializing and was reluctant to initiate conversations. He seemed to experience interpersonal discomfort and was likely withdrawing from social engagement. He believed that he was getting a "raw deal" from life and that no one cared about or understood him. He also had difficulty self-disclosing and reported feeling awkward when talking in a group.

While Eddie had trouble self-disclosing, he did acknowledge problems within his family environment on personality inventories. In this arena, he complained about limited communication, anger outbursts, disagreements, and lack of understanding. He believed that he was punished with little justification, was being treated as younger than his chronological age, and longed for the day that he would leave home. He did not think that his parents were sympathetic to his plight and that they blocked attempts at his success.

Because Eddie had spoken somewhat of family issues, it was thought that introducing drawings would provide a safer platform to speak openly through the images. One such directive, a family-centered-drawing that focused on his father, served to open this pathway for expanded communication (see Figure 3.14). In this illustration, Eddie constructed a picture of his father with various symbols surrounding him that represented Eddie's perception of him. Despite the conflicts, Eddie seemed proud to emulate his father (his father was a working professional) who had "started with nothing, worked hard, and provided a substantial and comfortable home" for the family (this was symbolized by a shovel turning into a house). In the drawing, Eddie also noted that his father was "spiritual and nice" (the parents were active church members). The other sketches symbolized such characteristics as being strong, sociable, and as someone who never quits (the portrait of the bull on the left side).

3.14

Through this drawing exercise and others that were presented to him, Eddie became less defensive and was able to disclose some of his vulnerabilities. He acknowledged his anxiety, frustration in his academic inconsistencies, and ineffective problem-solving methods. He also seemed more willing to admit needing extra help, especially with someone who would listen to him and "be on his side." Upon completion of the evaluation, he was willing to plan subsequent therapy appointments.

Mother-and-Child

Another variation to instructions for graphic expression focuses on family dynamics, and in particular the dyadic relationship between mother and child. This drawing directive is based on Object Relations Theory and hypothesizes that mother-and-child drawings yield unique portraits of the interpersonal self that is not always revealed in static human drawing pictures. The illustration of a parent and child (it could also be the father) encourages clients to indicate how they perceive their most important relationships, especially a primary one such as that between mother and child.

The developer, Jacqueline Gillespie (1994, 1997), perceived this visual image as more than merely an indicator of the social self. She believed that the picture represented an inner emotional bond between a mother and child in the earliest days and months of their combined lives. Object Relations Theory defines these early interactions as the source of self-perceptions within interpersonal relations that become primary segments of the maturing personality.

Gillespie (1994, 1997) suggested that drawings are completely individualized. Her impression was that each construction is similar to a unique fingerprint, as well as personal, much like a dream. To her, drawings like a mother and child portrait offer personifications of the self, carrying both conscious, discernible images, and unconscious reflections not immediately accessible to everyday understanding. Although this method does not produce reliable indicators of pathology, it does assist clinicians in gaining a greater awareness of how their clients feel about and relate to their parents or other primary caretakers (Malchiodi, 1998).

The direction to this drawing method is simply to "Draw a mother and child." Although the task does not specifically request that clients draw their own mother, it is usually implied as an indicator of developmental issues, such as indices of separation and individuation. From this instruction, individuals can identify with either the mother (father) or child, since both illustrated figures may become the subject or object, depending on circumstances. Again, this modification to human figure drawings was designed to encourage projections of the inner life and to identify personality characteristics of the self that produce unusually strong components of unconscious perceptions and struggles.

In one of my prior books, *Clinical Uses of Drawings*, there was an illustration of mother-and-child symbols as separate trees with birds and nests on top to separate the emotional distance that characterized the 34-year-old client's estranged feelings from her mother (Oster & Montgomery, 1996). In that case example, the directive broke through many initial barriers in describing her childhood memories of perceived neglect and helped her to focus more on the reasons for re-entering therapy. This simple directive during the first session allowed her to experience these unresolved struggles with greater fortitude and focused the follow-up sessions on more specific goals to overcome these blockages.

Another demonstration of the benefits from a "Mother-and-Child" drawing occurred in the second edition of *Using Drawings in Assessment and Therapy* (Oster & Crone, 2004). An 18-year-old constructed a mother-and-child picture as part of a psychological evaluation after being admitted into an acute psychiatric unit due to out-of-control behaviors at home that included severe verbal and physical arguments with her older sister. After the instruction was given, this young woman graphically portrayed herself as a tiny child within a large hand that represented the mother.

She suggested that the image reflected her need for security and her mixed feelings regarding her impending independence in the form of leaving home for college. She also noted the large hand as representing an overbearing and dominant mother, with her own feelings of inadequacy stemming from the smallness of the child. In describing her reasons for acting out her distress, the young woman alluded to her fragile self-esteem and her inner anxiety and frustration that she could not express effectively. Through the illustration and other feedback, she realized the need for help and assistance during this important transition in her life.

In a case example of another person needing help, Alan W. also benefitted from this type of graphic intervention. The following description further demonstrated the enhancement to an evaluation that a simple drawing directive can produce.

CASE STUDY: **Alan W.**

Alan was 18 years old when admitted to the emergency room by his mother secondary to making suicidal threats. The mother was not able to control Alan's moods and subsequent behavioral reactions when he visited from his college disability program residential apartment. At the time he was seen in the ER, Alan was upset and tearful, and he suggested suicide plans (for example, cutting his wrists, electrocuting himself). Reportedly, the day before being admitted he had threatened to cut himself with a razor blade, but the father was able to intervene through a telephone conversation.

Alan had a long-standing history of ADHD, OCD, and Tourette's, in addition to bouts of depression. Symptoms expressed in the past had included: sadness, irritability, negative thoughts, fatigue, decreased sleep, reduced concentration, indecision, and feelings of helplessness, hopelessness, and worthlessness. Apparently, manic-like signs of distress had also been a concern, such as restless pacing, loud and rapid speech, scattered thoughts, disruptive sleep, and physical outbursts. He also displayed accounts of threatening and assaulting people, especially if he did not get his way. He had already been placed on a variety of medications for many years, and had also participated in outpatient therapy.

Alan had graduated high school (though apparently with poor grades despite educational support and numerous classroom accommodations). He had always participated in specialized academic programs since preschool. Although seemingly bright, he had difficulties in planning and organization, and in initiating work production. At the time of the interview with the intake counselor, he was beginning to take computer programming courses and wanted to develop video games.

Alan presented as a large, heavy-set young man of average height. He mentioned that he had only a few but close friends, and spent much of his time playing video games. He stated that he usually stayed up late and slept during the day. He said that he got upset quite a bit, but only on occasion did he become overly distraught. It was during these latter times when he felt needy for attention and expressed a wide range of moods, including self-harming thoughts. He also indicated that the summer months were more difficult for him (a time without structure).

While Alan was quite conversant and expressed a broad vocabulary, he seemed to lack insight into his behaviors. He also appeared quite limited in his interests and immature in his understanding of social relationships. Furthermore, he could not express his feelings at a depth expected from his seemingly high intelligence (previous reports had suggested superior functioning). His responses on questionnaires suggested that he tended to blame others for his problems and felt sorry for himself. His self-concept seemed quite fragile. He also seemed to be harboring considerable tension and anger that he was not able to express in an effective manner.

As part of the brief assessment, he completed a series of drawings that focused on his family and friendships. One of these directives requested a drawing of a "mother and child" ("See Figure

3.15

3.15). From this sketch, it became apparent how dependent and inadequate he still felt in her presence despite his seeming attempts at independence. He appeared embarrassed by the illustration after realizing how small and young the boy in the picture was compared to the mother. He acknowledged that he had many mixed feelings about getting older and was fearful of his future. With this understanding he was willing to talk more about the problems that he had experienced since leaving home. His fears were overtaking him and he truly needed someone to talk to about these unpleasant sensations. He agreed to be seen on a more regular basis in outpatient therapy and to participate in a social skills group with similar-aged peers.

REFERENCES

Appel, K. E. (1931). Drawings by children as aids in personality studies. *American Journal of Orthopsychiatry, 1,* 129–144.

Bolander, K. (1977). *Assessing personality through tree drawings.* New York: Basic Books.

Buck, J. N. (1948). The H–T–P technique: A qualitative and quantitative scoring manual. *Journal of Clinical Psychology, 4*(4), 317–317.

Buck, J. N. (1992). *House-Tree-Person projective drawing technique: Manual and interpretive guide.* Revised by W.W. Warran. Los Angeles, CA: Western Psychological Services.

Burns, R. C. (1987). *Kinetic–house–tree–person drawings (K–H–T–P): An interpretative manual.* New York: Brunner/Mazel.

Burns, R. C. (1990). *A guide to family-centered-circle-drawings (F-C-C-D) with symbol probes and visual free association.* New York: Brunner/Mazel.

Burns, R. C. & Kaufman, S. H. (1970). *Kinetic family drawings (K-F-D): An introduction to understanding children through kinetic drawings.* New York: Bruner/Mazel.

Corff, Y., Tivendell, J., & LeBlanc, C. (2013). A parsimonious projective drawing technique. In L. Handler & A. D. Thomas, *Drawings in assessment and psychotherapy: Research and application.* New York: Routledge.

DiLeo, J. H. (1983). *Interpreting children's drawings.* New York: Brunner/Mazel.

Gillespie, J. (1994). *The projective use of mother-and-child drawings: A manual for clinicians.* New York: Brunner/Mazel.

Gillespie, J. (1997). Projective mother-and-child drawings. In E. Hammer (Ed.), *Advances in projective drawings interpretation.* Springfield, IL: Charles C. Thomas, 137–151.

Goodenough, F. L. (1926). *Measurement of intelligence by drawings.* New York: Harcourt, Brace, & World.

Hammer, E. F. (Ed.). (1958). *Clinical applications of projective drawings.* Springfield, IL: Charles C. Thomas.

Hammer, E. F. (Ed.). (1967). *Clinical applications of projective drawings* (2nd ed.). Springfield, IL: Charles C. Thomas.

Hammer, E. F. (1997). *Advances in projective drawing interpretation.* Springfield, IL: Charles C. Thomas.

Handler, L. (1996). The clinical use of drawings. *Major Psychological Assessment Instruments,* 2, 206–293.

Handler, L., Campbell, A., & Martin, B. (2004). Use of graphic techniques in personality assessment: Reliability, validity, and clinical utility. *Comprehensive Handbook of Psychological Assessment,* 2, 387–404.

Handler, L. & Thomas, A. D. (2013). *Drawings in assessment and psychotherapy: Research and application.* New York: Routledge.

Harris, D. B. (1963). *Children's drawings as measures of intellectual* maturity. New York: Harcourt, Brace, & World.

Jolles, I. (1971). *A catalog for the qualitative interpretation of the House-Tree-Person (HTP).* Los Angeles, CA: Western Psychological Services.

Koch, K. (1952). *The tree test: The tree drawing test as an aid in psychodiagnosis.* Bern, Switzerland: Hans Huber.

Koppitz, E. M. (1968). *Psychological evaluation of children's human figure drawings.* New York: Grune and Stratton.

Koppitz, E. M. (1984). Psychological evaluation of human figure drawings by middle school pupils. Orlando, FL: Grune & Stratton.

Koppitz, E. M. & Casullo, M. M. (1983). Exploring cultural influences on human figure drawings of young adolescents. *Perceptual and Motor skills,* 57(2), 479–483.

Leibowitz, M. (1999). *Interpreting projective drawings: A self psychological approach.* New York: Brunner/Mazel.

Lichtenberg, E. F. (2013). Draw-a-person-in-the-rain test. In L. Handler & A. D. Thomas, *Drawings in assessment and psychotherapy: Research and application.* New York: Routledge.

Machover, K. (1949). *Personality projection in the drawing of the human figure.* Springfield, IL: Charles C. Thomas.

Machover, K. (1952). *Personality projection in the drawing of the human figure.* Springfield, IL: Charles C. Thomas.

Malchiodi, C. A. (1998). *Understanding children's drawings.* New York: Guilford Press.

Malchiodi, C. A., Kim, D. Y., & Choi, W. S. (2003). Developmental art therapy. In C. Malchiodi (Ed.). *Handbook of art therapy,* 93–105. New York: Guilford Press.

Milne, L. C., Greenway, P., & Best, F. (2005). Children's behaviour and their graphic representation of parents and self. *The Arts in psychotherapy,* 32(2), 107–119.

Mitchell, J., Trent, R., & McArthur, R. (1993). *Human figure drawing test: An illustrated handbook for interpretation and standardized assessment of cognitive impairment.* Los Angeles, CA: Western Psychological Services.

Naglieri, J. A., MacNeish, T. J., & Bardos, A. (1991). *Draw a Person: Screening procedure for emotional disturbance; DAP: SPED.* Pro-Ed.

Oster, G. D. & Crone, P. (2004). *Using drawings in assessment and therapy* (2nd ed.). New York: Taylor & Francis.

Oster, G. D. & Gould, P. (1987). *Using drawings in assessment and therapy.* New York: Brunner/Mazel.

Oster, G. D. & Montgomery, S. S. (1996). *Clinical uses of drawings.* Northvale, NJ: Jason Aronson.

Palmer, J. O. (1983). *Psychological assessment of children.* New York: Wiley.

Riethmiller, R. J. & Handler, L. (1997). The great figure drawing controversy: The integration of research and clinical practice. *Journal of Personality Assessment, 69,* 488–496.

Rorschach, H. (1942). *Psychodiagnostics.* Bern, Switzerland: Verlag Hans Huber.

Thomas, A. D. & Engram, D. (2013) Sexually and physically abused children. In L. Handler & A. D. Thomas. *Drawings in assessment and psychotherapy: Research and application.* New York: Routledge.

Thomas, A. D., Getz, J. W., Smith, J. D., & Rivas, E. (2013). Anorexic house–tree–person drawings: Profile and reliability. In L. Handler & A. D. Thomas. *Drawings in assessment and psychotherapy: Research and application.* New York: Routledge.

Torem, M. S., Gilbertson, A., & Light, V. (1990). Indications of physical, sexual, and verbal victimization in projective tree drawings. *Journal of clinical psychology, 46*(6), 900–906.

Verinis, J. S., Lictenberg, E. F., & Henrich. L. (1974). The Draw-A-Person-In-The-Rain technique: Its relationship to diagnostic category and other personality indicators. *Journal of Clinical Psychology, 30,* 407–414.

Wenck, L. S. (1986). *House–Tree–Person drawings: An illustrated diagnostic handbook.* Los Angeles, CA: Western Psychological Services.

Wolff, W. (1942). Projective methods for personality analysis of expressive behavior in preschool children. *Character & Personality, 10,* 309–330.

4 Alternative Drawing Directives

BROADENING THE INTERPERSONAL ENCOUNTER

Numerous nonverbal techniques (such as timelines, genograms, and projective drawings) have revealed their value as constructive supplements during clinical interviews and as crucial segments within standard psychological testing batteries.

Clinicians who work with children and adolescents, in particular, often use drawings during their assessment questions. As described and illustrated throughout this book, graphic images (or talking through them) can be equally effective when introducing various drawing directives to adults as well as families to expand their awareness and create different and unique interactive experiences.

Drawings and other nonverbal interventions are usually utilized during clinical interviews in one of two ways—as a projective tool, where certain aspects of a drawing are interpreted as an indication of personality traits (or relevant psychological distress), or as a communication tool, where the images enhance interpersonal exchanges and increase the amount of verbal dialogue between clients and clinicians. Although there remains controversy for the clinical uses of drawing as a projective tool, there is growing evidence to support their introduction as a tool to facilitate communication (Wesson & Salmon 2001; Haynes, 2012). In these studies, it was demonstrated that individuals in turmoil are more likely to reveal a wider range of their inner experiences and express their feelings in a broader range with the presentation of these types of nonverbal methods.

As conveyed in many previous books, graphic illustrations have the opportunity to provide rich and informative disclosures that are not usually obtained from standard psychological testing or from the customary verbal interview methods (Oster & Gould, 1987; Oster & Montgomery, 1996; Oster & Crone, 2004). When they are employed for diagnostic impressions within the context of other supporting clinical history, these visual (or articulated) images become an invaluable clinical tool and a productive source for gaining insightful information to the referral sources, as well as to the clients. These nonverbal techniques also enhance the overall client involvement and make the process of evaluation more enjoyable and easier to consume. Furthermore, with the assistance of a tangible platform to express one's thoughts and feelings, it becomes easier to disseminate the information to treatment team members so that meaningful interventions and planning can occur.

In everyday clinical practice, drawings and other nonverbal procedures have been shown to gain a special place of importance in this information-gathering process. They are easy to introduce, do not interfere in the flow of interpersonal exchanges, and add immensely to establishing rapport and increasing the exchanges of dialogue. They can also provide structure to introductory therapy sessions (when continued therapy sessions hit a roadblock), and significantly expand the client's revelations of intrapsychic conflicts and concerns.

By adding numerous graphic interventions to their repertoire, clinicians can truly gain comfort that various types of resistance can be overcome. Nonverbal directives provide a novelty within the interview or psychological testing session that stimulate enhanced narratives and reveal beneficial insights into long-standing struggles and current worries. Whether asking clients to "Construct a Timeline or Genogram," "Draw Your World," "Draw Your Mood," or "Draw a Problem and a Solution to the Problem," clinicians who are conducting interviews or evaluations have the opportunity to gain unique features within the sessions and propose a novel way of relating and increasing disclosure. Most clients readily accept this new path towards understanding their inner turmoil and appreciate this expanded, nonverbal view of themselves. The resulting visual illustrations become a salient and useful clinical device that allows for freedom, creativity, and insight. Additionally, they often focus the session towards core problem areas that can immediately be addressed and expanded upon.

This chapter elicits from those common drawing directives that have been discussed in the literature, as well as instructions from clinical practice that seem to add exponentially to an intake interview or testing session. These methods only take seconds to introduce, are instantly acknowledged by the client, and usually can be produced in a minute or two. With such brevity and the potential for such value, it is easy to see that having a variety of nonverbal directives at one's disposal can certainly augment any evaluative session. And the instructions used can be derived at any time during the interview or testing session—just have a paper and pencil easily accessible.

TIMELINES

A timeline is a method of displaying a list of events in chronological order. Most timelines use a *linear* scale, where a unit of distance is equal to a set amount of time that has passed (Grafton & Rosenberg, 2010). When collecting histories during initial assessment meetings or beginning therapy sessions, seldom do clinicians have a detailed and accurate timetable of events in the client's life. By taking a few moments to construct a graphical representation of events along a simple line on a piece of paper, much new and exciting data can be gleaned and incorporated into the remainder of the evaluation.

Timelines can be organized by dates or events, and this basic and direct method allows users to create a label of their life experiences with short or long descriptive texts. And by adding an image for each label makes a timeline more visually appealing! Even when clinicians have access to prior reports or medical records, much history may be inaccurate or remain a mystery, and through this straightforward method other important information can be easily obtained and documented.

What better way to gather this potentially new knowledge than by asking clients to write (or represent by symbols) their memories beginning at their earliest remembrances. In this format, a horizontal line is constructed across a sheet of paper and the direction becomes writing or drawing their earliest memories, (first holiday, first day in school or preschool, first friend) at the beginning of one edge. After this portion of the exercise is completed, then add a mark for each year (for example, first grade, second grade, and so forth), and just sit back and appreciate what the client does with the structure.

This brief visual intervention often elicits many recollections, especially for individuals who are reticent to disclose past events during initial sessions. This easy method is nonintrusive and enjoyable, and usually produces a plethora of material that can be elaborated upon throughout the evaluation. The horizontal line provides enough organization to begin a process of sequentially recalling past occurrences that may not have seemed relevant to share with a stranger. For instance, a past car accident may have been very traumatic at the time, but was not relayed to others when a background history was gathered at an earlier date. When introduced at the beginning of the session, many avenues can be explored from the historical knowledge that is disclosed. This process also sets forth the idea that the rest of the evaluation may not be as threatening (or boring) as first perceived!

CASE STUDY: **Lauren F.**

Lauren, aged 9, approached the examiner with much hesitation. Referred by her educational advocate, Lauren was uncertain about revealing too much of the reasons why she was being seen for this initial interview, or what to share about her family situation. From what little background information was available, Lauren's medical history was remarkable for prenatal exposure to narcotics, alcohol, and excessive cigarette smoke. There was also documentation from a much earlier evaluation documenting severe receptive and expressive language delays.

Lauren did not attend preschool and her entrance into kindergarten was marked by many adjustment difficulties. The skills she did obtain from first through third grades were rudimentary, and reports indicated a lack of progress in most areas of basic academic maturation. Due to many frustrations in learning, she began to "act out" her distress and experienced many altercations with teachers and peers. Subsequently, she was already beginning to view school in very negative terms and had begun to express somatic complaints to her parents so that she would not have to attend.

While Lauren presented as pleasant and engaging, she had difficulty staying focused and answering questions. She was distracted easily and could not attend to the activities presented to her. She was also reluctant to share personal information. Instead of a continuing in the usual interview style, she was offered the opportunity to explore her life through a timeline. This added structure was appealing to her and she readily agreed to this strategy. In this case, the examiner constructed the line and wrote for her (see Figure 4.1). This method seemed very approachable to Lauren and was successful in coaxing her to share her story narratives. It also stimulated other discussions about her difficulties at home and at school. With this appealing intervention, she was much more willing to sit longer for other questions and was more cooperative in completing inventories and other screening measures.

4.1

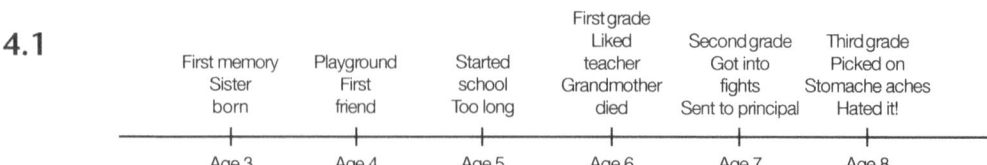

GENOGRAMS

Another informative nonverbal way of gathering valuable information during interviews or psychological testing is through the use of genograms. This graphic representation of a family tree provides clinicians a very observable detailed description of their clients' perceptions of important relationships and how these family members have shaped their lives. Genograms were initially popularized in clinical settings by Monica McGoldrick and Randy Gerson (1985). Through their books and workshops, genograms became commonly used by a variety of health and mental health professionals, as well as educators. And more recently, Eliana Gil (2014) has introduced the idea of using miniature play items as the family members. This expansion of genograms provides rich possibilities for helping family members explore their relationships and consider (in a creative, metaphorical way) to whom they belong (often including friends and pets), and to illustrate the best and the most difficult aspects of their relationships. There are now many books and websites on the topic and numerous designs for creating genograms (e.g., www.genograms.org/components.html).

The genogram's construction of interactive patterns goes beyond a traditional family tree by allowing the user to analyze physical configurations and emotional factors that impact known relations. Genograms allow the clinical interviewer or psychological examiner an opportunity to quickly identify and understand salient occurrences within the family's historical background that may have had significant impacts on their client's current functioning (for example, a suicide). The elaborate diagram provides a concrete and very observable map of past events that can then be discussed within a broader context for a more in-depth investigation of presenting problems.

By integrating genograms into a "toolbox" of commonly used techniques to overcome defensive clients and expand communication, clinicians will not only have obtained basic facts about interrelated individuals who have remained part of the client's history and memories, but will have perceptible details that can assist in the establishment of goals and treatment direction. Topics like education, occupation, major life events, chronic illnesses, and external social relationships can make for a very dynamic and informative interview, or add to the background history in a psychological evaluation. Also, salient aspects of the family history related to alcoholism and mental illness, or alternative living situations can be revealed through its construction. As with any added procedure introduced to gain extra information during evaluations, genograms emphasize a special significance to the interactions between clinicians and clients because there is no limitation as to what data can be included or questions asked.

Genograms also represent intergenerational family maps and are usually easy to construct (or can be requested before an interview or provided as homework between evaluative or beginning therapy sessions). Through symbols and notations, genograms allow clinicians to quickly grasp the key elements in the lives of family members, and to gain a better overview of relationship patterns. Most importantly, they also help clients gain a deeper understanding of the way they (and family members) respond to stressful situations, handle conflicts, or manage gender and cultural issues. And even as a nonverbal technique, it usually promotes (not limits) discussion and increases interchanges.

An important factor that influences multigenerational communication is culture. When people are asked to identify themselves ethnically, there is an attempt to focus on cultural continuity and cultural identity (McGoldrick, Giordano, & Garcia-Preto, 2005). Occasionally, individuals do not realize the impact of their cultural heritage on the ways in which they function in their current family system. Issues may focus on the extent to which clients have experienced discrimination due to their ethnic and racial background, the extent to which the family has lived in a separate community, or maintained religious or spiritual beliefs reflective of their cultural heritage. Furthermore, individuals may maintain strong beliefs about gender roles in families based on their cultural or religious heritage, as well as beliefs about the importance of individualism versus collectivism.

Although there is general agreement on the basic genogram structure and codes, there are some variations on how to depict certain family situations, such as cutoffs and adoptions (McGoldrick, Gerson, & Shellenberger, 1999). The male is usually noted by a square, the female by a circle. The male is placed to the left of the female in the father/mother dyad. Marriage is shown by a line connecting the two. Children are noted oldest to youngest left to right.

There are also many ways to interpret a genogram. A primary factor within the genogram could be the issue of losses. These factors could include: death, chronic illness, economic reversals, divorces, and other key areas that have influenced one's life or has plagued a family over the years. A key question, such as "To what degree was this event perceived as a loss?" could clarify the client's perception and provide the depth of the particular trauma.

Other themes within the family cycle or dynamic could address identity, core values and beliefs, and other important characteristics that define the qualities of the family's structure and uniqueness. Such statements that have continued throughout the lineage could be "only your best is good enough," "never accept your effort as the best," "only depend (and trust) your family members," or "only this family always watches your back." Furthermore, boundaries are a crucial area that defines a family system. These "interpersonal fences" distinguish the family from the rest of the world, whether physical or psychological. They may be totally open, or very rigid, and regulate the members' access to outside people, ideas, and values. With the construction of the genogram, clinicians have the opportunity to enter the world of the client and take a glimpse behind the generational context that has brought considerable influence upon the presenting problems.

CASE STUDY: Nosian H.

Nosian H. was a 32-year-old married woman when first evaluated during an initial interview. The oldest of three from a Middle Eastern heritage, her family had relocated to the United States after a cultural revolution. Nosian characterized herself as a "parentified" child who was given many responsibilities at a very young age. Although she had pursued acting earlier in life, her time was mainly spent caring for her sisters. She had participated in therapeutic activities several times in the past, but her current symptoms were intruding too much into her work and relationships. In the beginning of the session, she spoke readily about being very anxious, distractible, and having sleep problems. She also mentioned having low self-esteem despite her considerable school and work accomplishments (a master's degree and holding a job as director of a program).

Nosian's extended family was large, and the interconnections were important to her, as well as complicated. To intervene effectively with her, it was important to obtain a genogram that would detail these relationships and later use the diagram as a sounding board to verbally describe her present familial and personal conflicts (see Figure 4.2). A deeper understanding of her background was needed to accurately recognize her attempts at separation and individuation, and this method allowed this process to take place in a more comfortable manner.

When requested to complete this design, Nosian was pleased to take the time to remember her family members (both deceased and present) and review the varying relationships and how they

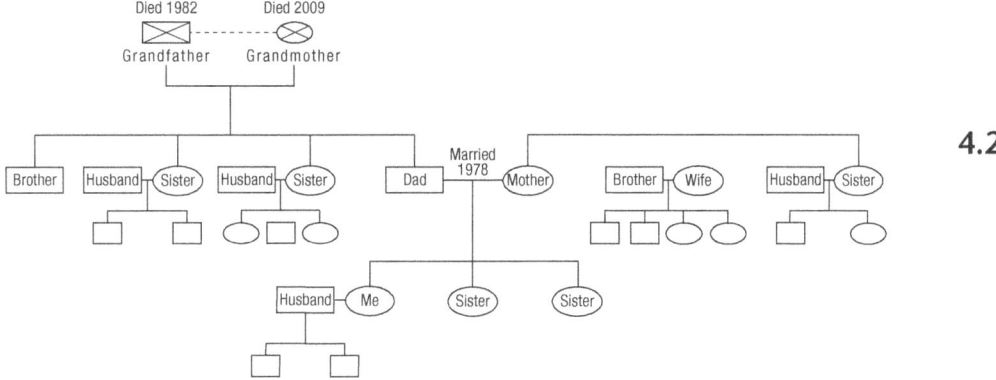

4.2

interacted and impacted on her life. For her, it became a very pleasurable experience. The product also allowed a fuller "picture" of her identity and the importance of the family interactions. This one creation started a long conversation that led to various resolutions once therapy was more established.

FAMILY SHIELD

A less complicated procedure to address the family's structure and values is to request the drawing of a "family shield." This visual technique makes history gathering at intake an enjoyable and highly informative exercise (Oster & Crone, 2004). The instruction for this task focuses the discussion and adds meaningful structure to the session. A directive to construct images of the family constellation at the beginning of an interview or assessment establishes an inventive form that communicates a distinctive experience is about to take place.

The creation of a "family shield" allows clients to portray their perceptions of a major part of their identity and provides the opportunity to amplify the shared views or values of what their families mean to them. Through the process of completing an image and sharing an impression of family beliefs, clients are readily attracted to this different aspect of sharing family history. The introduction of this directive also provides a brief and structured format to describe themes and concerns among individual family members.

A few examples may illuminate this interesting method towards sharing and self-discovery. An older man (a former pastor) described his "family shield" with a large heart (to define common values of love and caring) and tears (the hard work put forth by each member). Another client described her symbols of a hammer and nails, fishing pole, and American flag to reflect the family's standards of work, play, and patriotism. While a different, angrier male client reflected that his "shield" would include toilet bowls to signify the "bullsh . . ." he experienced as a youth within his household.

The easiest way to present this method is to construct a large outline of a shield onto the paper and request clients to complete the picture with illustrations of symbols that represent family values or beliefs. That is the central essence that defines their family and what makes them distinctive. In using this directive over the years, it seems like a useful springboard to contrast this picture with other drawings of fears, problems, and future dreams. The process allows for much spontaneity for interpersonal sharing, and documents current views of their families that might change over time in therapy.

CASE STUDY: **Albert J.**

Albert J., aged 14, presented for an intake session at an outpatient behavioral health clinic. Adopted at age 9 along with a twin sister, Albert had been experiencing adjustment problems while attending a new high school. According to his adoptive parents, he seemed distractible, was exhibiting poor concentration, and his ongoing struggles appeared to be blocking his confidence and self-esteem. Besides these difficulties, the adoptive parents complained about his excessive lying, as well as a lack of consistency in his grades. Despite his issues, Albert was a leader at camp, attended Bible school, and spent summers with his mother's family. In the neighborhood, he was considered friendly and outgoing.

At the time of the interview, Albert had not participated in prior individual therapy or psychological testing. He was reserved and tentative about disclosing personal information. With his reticence to engage in the session, the intake worker, a licensed social worker, thought that drawings would be a better method to access beginning information and enhance the verbal interchanges. After a few traditional drawing requests, Albert was asked to construct a "family shield." With this directive, he created the following image (see Figure 4.3).

Following the drawings, Albert seemed much more relaxed and was willing to talk through the images. He was proud of his "shield" and spoke openly about the family values and his spiritual beliefs. He and the family attended church regularly and their focus on love and caring came across in his discussions surrounding the family structure and the adjustments he had made since being fostered by the parents and eventually being adopted. This line of inquiry spurred many avenues of discovery for his treatment planning in individual and family therapy.

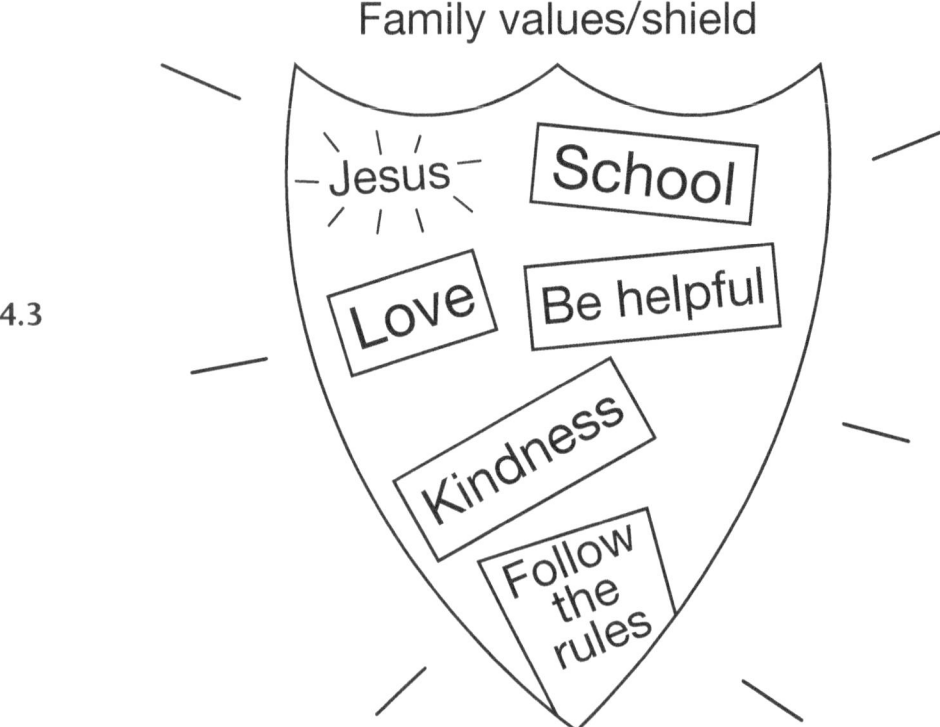

4.3

DRAW YOUR WORLD

Another easy way to establish rapport with new clients and to gain extra information about their lives stems from the directive, "Draw Your World." In this task, clients are requested to construct a large circle on a sheet of paper then place symbols within the circle to represent different aspects of their lives. Often, individuals will produce graphic images of their families, objects they own (e.g., bicycles, video game systems), or things they occupy or attend (e.g., home, school, church).

On occasion, however, clients will focus on their moods or concerns. A drawing with such instruction in one of our previous books portrayed a young woman's "world" as "being sliced apart and spinning out of control" (Oster & Crone, 2004). Another similar request produced a "world" illustrated with poignant words suggesting long-standing abuse and suicidal thoughts. And another was a construction of a heart that was broken and fractured down the middle, with one side suggesting love and happiness while the other segment expressed hurt feelings of "sad," "angry," and "upset."

When drawings such as these are completed, they can be reviewed to further clarify the thoughts and feelings behind such creations. At that point, alternative and hopefully more satisfying outcomes can be presented during the follow-up discussions that would enhance the client's problem-solving skills. This approach of adding a unique drawing directive can increase the client's cognitive and emotional repertoire, as well as assist in the pursuit of self-understanding. And with this new information, clients become more willing and forthright to accept intervention planning.

CASE STUDY: Amku L.

Amku L., now 17 years old, was born in Africa but moved to the US at age 10 upon adoption. Although native French-speaking, he also spoke English without problems. From all reports, Amku began displaying behavioral problems when he entered high school following relocation to a different neighborhood. Apparently, he began hanging out with a "wrong" crowd, and started smoking marijuana, became truant from school, and ran away from home. During this tumultuous period, he lived on the streets.

Although his medical chart noted normal birth and developmental milestones, at age 5 he was apparently injured in a grenade explosion while playing with friends (these two other children were killed). Afterwards, he was hospitalized for several months with scarring from burns on several areas of his body. He also had tested positive for tuberculosis.

Besides his past traumas, Amku had an extensive legal and psychiatric history. Past records mentioned several arrests for robbery, trespassing, and assault with subsequent juvenile detention. Later, he was hospitalized for bizarre displays of behavior (e.g., talking to himself, pouring milk over himself, and laughing and dancing for no apparent reason). He also eloped from the hospital on three separate occasions and was aggressive and threatening toward staff.

Other hospitalizations ensued with similar reports of unusual and regressive actions (urinating on the floor, smearing feces, spitting on the windows). Inpatient records documented reports of "amnesia" and "Multiple Personality Disorder." A treatment summary mentioned that Amku was inconsistent in his ability to think clearly and provide an accurate recall of events and experiences. It also stated that he exhibited poor impulse control, disregarded social norms, possessed impaired judgment and insight, and displayed aggressive behaviors.

When interviewed and evaluated prior to admission at a residential treatment center, Amku's mood and appearance were congruent with his chronological age. He was appropriately dressed

102 ALTERNATIVE DRAWING DIRECTIVES

and well groomed. He appeared oriented to time, place, and person, and his speech was normal in tone and volume. While he seemed focused and attentive to direction on self-report questionnaires, at times he responded hastily and without planning or forethought. Also, he seemed somewhat quiet and withdrawn, though he mentioned that he always had trust issues with adults.

Not wanting to pressure him at that point, the examiner, instead, requested a series of drawing directives. It was thought that these alternative pathways to communicate his history would seem more comfortable for Amku, and be more fruitful in elaborating about his past life. As a way to establish this type of rapport, Amku was asked to "Draw his World"; that is, to construct a large circle on a piece of paper and illustrate meaningful items that would portray his life and times. Amku seemed relieved at this opportunity to talk indirectly about his past and created the following picture to represent his life (see Figure 4.4).

Using this powerful tool to convey the depth of his struggles, Amku mostly wrote about previous struggles and fears. Through this image, Amku noted his past yearnings for remembering his real parents, his acknowledgement of past abuse, his feelings of loneliness and regret, and his basis of mistrust. Only then was he able to verbalize the key situations in his history. Subsequently, he was more willing describe his present issues (related to a negative self-esteem) and articulate his hopes for the future (e.g., having decreased conflicts with others and living a more normal life with appropriate aspirations for his age). The drawing seemed to lessen his anxiety, give him a structured way to express his concerns in a less directed manner, and gain a sense of trust that the examiner would truly listen to him using a variety of non-threatening methods.

4.4

DRAW YOURSELF WITH FRIENDS

For most people, especially teenagers, friendships are crucial and an extension of the developing self. Besides relatives, peers offer feedback from a same-aged perspective, provide a different set of eyes and ears to the world, and offer a safe sounding board to complaints and other salient pressing issues. Including the examiner in the world of friendships offers a glimpse into the world of another. This context is important in the information gathering stage of clinical interviews and evaluations. Like directives to construct images of families, having clients draw themselves with friends offers a chance to explore self-image, interpersonal dynamics, and gauges general interests. It is a quick, easy method and opens many doors to discover the person being assessed.

Simple to construct (just ask the client to draw themselves with friends), and non-threatening, this exercise can illuminate how social (or lonely) clients see their status among same-aged individuals. From this type of image, questions can explore various aspects of activities and gain a general sense of everyday life. The completed illustration enhances the framework of understanding the world of clients and engages them in a nonverbal activity that is enjoyable and productive. The introduction of drawing directives into the clinical assessment and psychological testing certainly usurps any preconceived tension that clients may produce through their resistance. In most situations, it makes the process much more enjoyable and active.

KINETIC SCHOOL DRAWINGS

Another avenue to pursue in overcoming guarded behaviour and defensiveness and to explore the client's perceptions of life is to request a drawing of school activity. An outgrowth of the kinetic family drawing series, the Kinetic School Drawing (K-S-D) is an adaptation for school-age youth. Originated by Prout and Phillips (1974) and later revised by Sarbaugh (1983), this directive generates numerous responses that students can represent such as teachers, friends, or themselves during daily activities. The following instructions were offered by the initial creator: "I'd like you to draw a school picture. Put yourself, your teacher, and a friend or two in the picture. Make everyone doing something." A post-drawing interrogation was later added to elicit associations. The clinician can ask the student to identify the people and actions within the drawings, along with any unidentifiable objects.

Sarbaugh (1983) was more interested in having students project personal attitudes and opinions onto their drawings and suggested a more open-ended directive with the instruction, "Draw a picture of people at school doing something." If students are uneasy about making this drawing or are perplexed over the direction, examiners can encourage the use of their ideas. The developer of this method also suggested a chromatic phase for the drawings where crayons could be added to enhance interpretive possibilities.

Impressions of the drawings paralleled the guidelines offered for the kinetic family drawing procedures (Prout & Phillips, 1974). The people within the drawings are analyzed according to Machover's (1952) guidelines. The images are then examined further in terms of action, style, and symbols.

By comparison, Sarbaugh (1983) used interpretations based on a symbolic perspective. Her view characterized students through their uniqueness placed onto the symbols. This method was in sharp contrast to using a formal psychological scoring system. In this manner, she believed, students already possessed existing inner symbols and their designs could be misunderstood. Sarbaugh's more subjective bias to this drawing directive was based on her numerous years of clinical experience.

Also, our previous books have reflected similar results (Oster & Gould, 1987; Oster & Montgomery, 1996; Oster & Crone, 2004). Mostly, people with negative attitudes toward school will represent themselves sitting at a desk in their classroom with their heads down in a sleeping, uncaring posture, or just looking overwhelmed and puzzled. All from a simpler directive, "Draw Yourself in School." Certainly, these constructions make a "loud" statement about their experiences in school (many times these are the reasons they are being evaluated).

Still later, Knoff and Prout (1985) integrated the K-F-D and K-S-D techniques into a system they called the Kinetic Drawing System. They emphasized the need to administer both directives to increase their clinical utility and interpretive depth. The integrated results could then a) determine a student's social–emotional difficulties across home and school settings; b) identify family issues that are related to school attitudes or behaviors; and c) isolate the setting where relationship problems are occurring that are contributing to other interpersonal complications (Cummings, 1986). Their manual thoroughly summarizes the research and literature from the K-F-D and K-S-D and introduces their own integrated system.

CASE STUDY: **Kesandra B.**

Kesandra B., aged 17, was being admitted into an intensive special education program due to an escalation of serious emotional disturbance. Previously, she had been hospitalized due to nightmares that she described as "being in hell." She also endorsed auditory and visual hallucinations during the day. At that time, Kesandra stated that she could see and hear the devil, and that demons were in her room. She also noted that in the past she had possessed "dark powers." With these symptoms overwhelming her, Kesandra presented as withdrawn, refused to participate in activities, and slept excessively.

Kesandra's history was noteworthy for emotional and physical abuse. She had also witnessed much turmoil between her parents. At one point, she was removed from her home and placed in supervised group situations. School placements had usually met with frustrations and failures. The system did not appear suitable to fit her considerable needs. Prior evaluations indicated very low functioning (IQ below 55) and achievement scores at a first to second grade level.

Before entering the new placement, Kesandra required a screening evaluation to assess her emotional functioning and attitude towards learning. She presented as cooperative and eager to perform, but her mood was quite labile over the two sessions; at times appearing sad and depressed, then immediately becoming loud and excited. Her rate of speech alternated between slow and rapid, depending on content of the session. And her thoughts were, at times, illogical and incoherent, and marked by loose associations.

When presented with the opportunity to construct a drawing of herself in school, Kesandra portrayed a very sad, overwhelmed, and helpless person (see Figure 4.5). It appeared that school had never been a positive experience for her, and through this poignant graphic image she elaborated on a history of failure and feeling different and not as competent as her peers. She used the platform of the drawing directives to talk about other school placements and why she never felt supported. The remarkable effect from the visual illustration suggested that she could certainly express herself through these types of artistic creations. A planning meeting was held with her future teachers and counsellor, and the drawings and interview were shared to form a basis for educational and treatment planning.

4.5

DRAW YOUR "IDEAL" SELF

Many times, clinicians are confronted by depressed and suicidal individuals who have lost all hope of living a worthwhile life and have been either hospitalized, or are struggling in their everyday lives. These individuals can no longer perceive a future that is pleasant or that has them emotionally connected to earlier ambitions or people. These feelings of helplessness and hopelessness are often overbearing and usurp their cognitive abilities to problem-solve successfully. When faced with these clients, it takes much effort to engage them and usually with only vague responses in return.

One brief intervention that offers a lifeline of hope for clients in such acute distress is to suggest the creation of their ideal selves (usually in 10 years' time). This drawing suggestion allows those in turmoil to look beyond their present condition to a time when things are more under their control. With the instructions to "Draw Your Ideal Self" (your fantasy of where you will be living in 10 years and with whom) offers many possibilities. For a younger child, this directive may represent the opportunity to channel their sports or singing fantasies (e.g., a center fielder for the Yankees or a rock and roll star). For a teenager, it permits a time of more freedom and control (i.e., living away from home, graduating from college, having their first job), and even for the graduate student it becomes a time of personal ambitions (status within their career choices, large homes and families).

For the adult, especially one who is presently in much turmoil, this drawing directive offers a concrete example of overcoming present negative self-biases and provides concrete examples for a future to be lived. One example was a 40-year-old school administrator who presented for an inpatient evaluation as anxious, apathetic, sad, irritable, and tired. She also suggested that she had lost interest in previously desired activities and that her self-esteem had been damaged. A depression scale provided many indicators of significant inner turmoil and a subsequent suicide questionnaire reflected a pattern of self-destructive and self-defeating actions. However, when requested to draw herself in 10 years her mood lifted as she constructed a picture of a more active and enjoyable life following a different career path. From this unique perspective, she was more willing to receive the assistance that she needed to overcome her then current condition of feeling frustrated and helpless.

Another case study, 15-year-old Carla S., faced similar feelings of hopelessness.

CASE STUDY: **Carla S.**

Carla S., 15 years old, was residing at a long-term inpatient facility due to a number of behavioral difficulties including outbursts of aggression, sadness, property destruction, and school problems related to many "incompletes" received in her classes. Previous intellectual testing had displayed numerous inconsistencies in her functioning with her overall scores well below average. Most notably, she experienced weaknesses in areas of information processing and verbal fluency. Her knowledge of social awareness and problem-solving also displayed lapses, resulting in interpersonal confusion and inappropriate responses. Furthermore, signs of attention weaknesses and distractibility were observed.

Despite her apparent cognitive liabilities, Carla was quick to respond to suggestions of drawing directives. She produced images easily, and her illustrations were very expressive. The suggestions of graphic responses lowered her guardedness to answering direct questions and overcame her resistance to prolonged testing. Through her series of drawings, she was able to share "a problem" ("her mouth") and her past conflicts with siblings. She also constructed a very attractive picture of her "ideal" self (see Figure 4.6).

By using this image, she was able to focus on many of her personal attributes and appeared to express much resilience despite a tumultuous childhood, and to communicate hope for her future. She realized that she required much support and encouragement and believed that she might be in the right setting to meet her varied needs. She was also willing to continue sitting for the remainder of the evaluation that offered suggestions for her treatment team to attempt more aspects of expressive therapies as a way to increase her self-esteem and everyday problem-solving strategies.

DRAW YOUR (CURRENT) MOOD

Oftentimes, clinicians are confronted with pure and intense emotions that make them uncomfortable. They are introduced to people in marked distress who are hesitant to reveal their shortcomings and fears, or cannot use "the right" words to describe their inner anguish. One simple method to offer these individuals to assist in describing their emotional hurt is to merely ask them to directly describe their depression, anxiety, anger, or feelings surrounding traumatic experiences.

person

4.6

left out face @ first
random person
happy

108 ALTERNATIVE DRAWING DIRECTIVES

An offer to represent their powerful moods on paper is frequently easier than attempting to verbally articulate their sadness or feelings of panic. Provided with this opportunity, clients have readily portrayed portraits of despair or pictures of anger (Oster & Montgomery, 1996; Oster & Crone, 2004). It is a method that speaks to alternative descriptions of themselves and can address multiple areas of torment. As in all methods of drawing techniques, it also becomes a different and novel approach to information gathering and often produces much relief in clients who view the process as a way to be "seen and heard" in many distinctive ways.

CASE STUDY: **Consuela L.**

Consuela L., a nearly 14-year-old young woman of South American descent, had been admitted into an inpatient unit of a community hospital due to increased symptoms of depression including suicidal thoughts, and an expressed plan towards self-harm. Other notable symptoms included: loss of appetite; decreased energy and motivation; social withdrawal; inability to concentrate; and stated feelings of loneliness, helplessness, and hopelessness. Although specific stressors were not identified, Consuela did mention general unhappiness, limited social relations, and family discord as major areas of concern.

When first approached for a psychological consultation (an interview and brief testing), she was distraught and unresponsive. While she acknowledged many instances of sadness and loneliness on self-report questionnaires, she was reluctant to expand her thoughts or express her feelings. As an adjunct to this evaluative process, Consuela was asked to draw a representation of her mood. At once, she lightened to this task and produced the following illustration (see Figure 4.7). As she explained, "I'm the flower with lots of petals that keep falling off—the rain is too much."

Through the use of this familiar metaphor to describe her inner pain, she related many negative self-perceptions, along with a home environment that was in constant discord. She spoke of not being able to trust her peers and her general reluctance to share her feelings with adults. She also perceived her environment as harsh and stressful with few emotional resources to defend herself ("the rain keeps falling, as do my petals").

By utilizing this unique approach to self-expression, Consuela was much more eager to discuss her situation without fear of becoming overwhelmed. The drawing exercise provided her a comfortable stage whereby she could talk through the graphic image and allowed her to view the remainder of the evaluation as a positive (rather than negative) experience. In this context, she was more willing to complete other tests and inventories. For instance, her intense sadness was also reflected on completion of sentence stems. She noted that—I hate "myself," my family "doesn't help me," there is nothing "that makes me happy," I just can't "handle the pressure," at school "I am unhappy." All of these written expressions concurred with the very revealing and expressive portrait of her depression, as well as other aspects of the assessment that included suicide questionnaires and projective techniques.

4.7

DEFINING AND RESOLVING PROBLEMS

The instructions to this directive include: "Everyone has problems. I want you to draw a problem you *may* have (on this one sheet of paper); then construct another illustration on the next sheet to show how you might resolve your problem." Many possibilities are in store for the clinician who utilizes this directive. Individuals may focus on "annoying" siblings and what they might want to do with them; while others often exemplify problems of social awkwardness, or an inability to make friends by illustrating how they might introduce themselves to other people they would like to meet. And some clients have focused on school problems with the revelation of studying harder as the solution.

In an example from a previous book (Oster & Crone, 2004), 12-year-old Meung of Asian descent was being evaluated for therapeutic inclusion due to failing grades and being argumentative with his single mother, a working professional who was overwhelmed by her personal responsibilities. She was frustrated by her inability to provide enough time for Meung, as well as his passive-aggressive actions towards her and his lack of communication. At the initial session, Meung was sullen and reluctant to delve into his problems. His self-defensive stance and excessive defensiveness were difficult to overcome.

As an alternative to this "difficult moment," the examiner requested Meung to construct a drawing of a problem on one sheet of paper and provide a solution on another. He immediately attacked this novel directive with vigor! In the first image, he sketched his mother yelling at him and portrayed himself as overwhelmed and shrinking in her presence. The other illustration (a solution) depicted Meung and his mother playing basketball together with a smile on both of their faces. When he shared this image with his mother, she hugged him and promised to find time and spend fun activities with him.

In a different setting and situation, Alysha G. was provided a similar directive:

CASE STUDY: Alysha G.

Alysha G., 19, had recently returned home from her first year at college after falling behind due to classroom absences and not completing required assignments. Prior to her freshman year, Alysha had displayed long-standing emotional and behavioral problems that culminated in hospital and medication interventions, as well as participation in alternative schools, such as a wilderness program and a therapeutic boarding school. During a clinical interview that occurred after a referral for psychological testing, Alysha, along with her mother, pointed to symptoms of apathy, defensiveness, irritability, and tiredness as target areas to overcome. She also alluded to areas of anhedonia (i.e., loss of interest in previously enjoyed activities), along with social withdrawal and loss of confidence.

While she was on medical leave from university, it was crucial to document her current cognitive and emotional functioning in addition to review her classroom accommodation needs when she returned to school. As part of the initial interview, Alysha was requested to construct a series of drawings to include everyday objects and situations (e.g., H-T-P, self in school) that would characterize her developmental maturation and provide indicators of possible emotional conflicts. When asked to draw a current problem and how she would resolve the issue, she immediately drew herself in bed, then constructed another image of her entering college (see Figures 4.8 and 4.9).

In constructing these figures, Alysha became more forthcoming in discussing her depression and overwhelming feelings of helplessness. Although she had been fairly quiet up to that point and was counting on her mother to do most of the talking, she jumped at the opportunity to portray

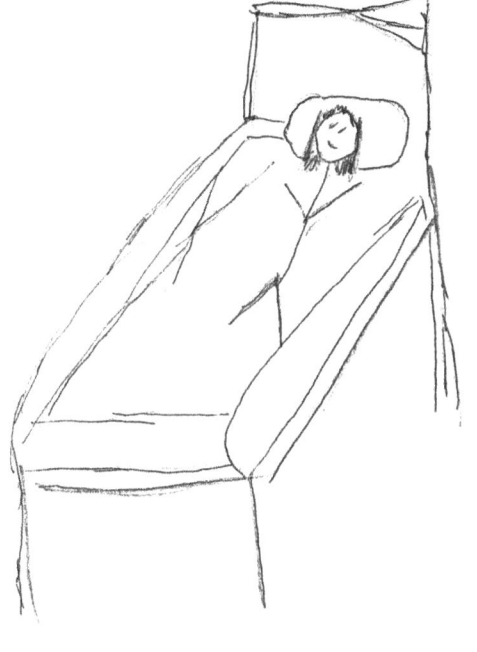

4.8

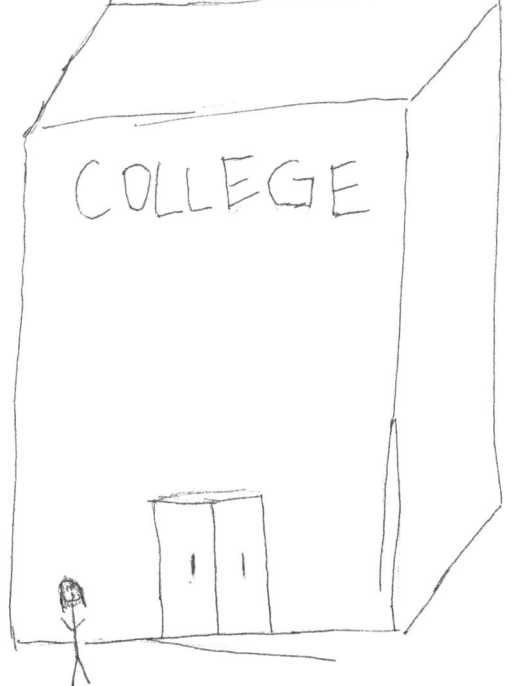

4.9

her feelings in this nonverbal format. By using these and other drawing directives, all initial resistance was overcome and she readily disclosed to the intake clinician and her mother the degree of her sadness. Her other drawings, as well, added to the overall impression of her crisis and the need for further assessment to clarify her intellectual, educational, and emotional strengths and weaknesses.

BEFORE, DURING, AND AFTER CRISES

During intakes in crisis centers, emergency rooms, or in hospital units, it has been a common experience that clients in distress can often more readily communicate their stressors onto paper rather than talking about their thoughts and feelings. In this manner, clinicians have the opportunity to concretely view the problems that culminated in this meeting, review current symptoms, and provide a glimpse of hope for the future. When utilizing this alternative method, drawings tend to reflect many aspects of the various difficulties the clients have had to face, and reveal their emotional resources and coping mechanisms.

For instance, in a poignant series of drawings constructed by one client, she depicted her life before her hospitalization as "raising hell." By contrast, an illustration portraying a figure that represented her feelings about her inpatient status spoke profoundly about the intensity of her struggles with the outside world. She viewed the efforts of the hospital as a large shoe crushing her with its "oppression and control" and her being squashed by the "big foot" (Oster & Montgomery, 1996). A final drawing, "Freedom," conveyed her wish to be independent. Through a successful stay on the unit, she was able to gain more effective ways of handling her emotions and gained additional insight. She finally constructed more hopeful future drawings that represented new-found skills.

Another example of using this drawing directive reflects its value:

CASE STUDY: Loren Y.

Loren Y. was 20 years old when assessed within a residential treatment program. With a long-standing history of neglect and abandonment, Loren had transitioned through a series of foster and group homes, as well as psychiatric hospitalizations due to impulsive, aggressive behaviors, and self-harming actions. A comprehensive evaluation was requested from her treatment team to access updated information regarding her emotional and cognitive status for therapeutic interventions and aftercare planning. Past diagnoses had included: Reactive Attachment Disorder, Intermittent Explosive Disorder, ADHD, and Intellectual Disability. Mood and substance abuse disorders were also shown to have impacted her growth and development.

During the course of the interview and testing procedures, Loren had displayed indices of anxiety and anger. Her cognitive vulnerabilities, lack of insight, and limited problem-solving abilities contributed to her being easily frustrated and overwhelmed during any stressful circumstances. These actions and their repercussions ultimately led to a poor self-concept, uncertainty, and confusion with few resources to respond appropriately. When confronted by ambiguous interview or testing situations, she would either withdraw or become very agitated and have to discontinue the sessions.

4.10

However, Loren approached requests of drawings in a more cooperative manner. She seemed to enjoy the process of expressing herself through this creative method (it wasn't like "school") and was certainly more engaged. Even though her illustrations were basic and unsophisticated, they allowed her the opportunity to discuss the events that occurred before she was transferred to the residential treatment center. Her images suggested much sadness in her life prior to admission and more hope for the future (see Figure 4.10). She seemed more stable than she demonstrated when initially entering the center and she noted that she had been working with her therapist on different avenues to express her needs more effectively. She appreciated the opportunity to have the time to communicate through novel techniques and was able to complete the entire assessment over the next several sessions.

ENDING REMARKS

Creative drawing procedures have been devised over many years and have offered clinicians brief, structured formats that enlarge the interpretive feedback derived during evaluative and beginning therapy sessions. These clinical tools have assisted the diagnostician in discovering different aspects of cognitive and emotional functioning, in addition to aiding the therapist in overcoming resistance and opening new avenues for increased dialogue. The graphic images yielded during these interchanges offer clinicians novel opportunities to pursue the inner and outer world of the clients in a unique and nonthreatening manner.

While numerous drawing directives have been reviewed in this chapter, many more exist and modifications of these procedures only take a bit of creativity to elicit varying responses. Additional directives may include: draw an unpleasant experience; draw your favorite animal; draw your worst memory; draw a dream, wish, or feeling; draw a group; or draw your earliest memory. All can produce much "food for thought" during intake and subsequent clinical interviews.

Diagnostic evaluations comprise a large segment of developing a workable treatment plan. During a relatively short time, clinicians must rely on various procedures and experiences to assess various aspects of client functioning. No single instrument can provide all this needed information. Thus, it becomes imperative for the clinician to gain knowledge about the strengths and weaknesses of many procedures before choosing a particular test battery.

REFERENCES

Cummings, J. A. (1986). Projective drawings. In H. M. Knoff (Ed.), *The assessment of child and adolescent personality*. New York: Guilford Press.

Gil, E. (2014). *Play in family therapy*. New York: Guilford Press.

Grafton, A. & Rosenberg, D. (2010*)*. *Cartographies of time: A history of the timeline*. New York: Princeton Architectural Press.

Haynes, R. B. (2012). *Clinical epidemiology: How to do clinical practice research*. Philadelphia, PA: Lippincott Williams & Wilkins.

Knoff, H. M. & Prout, H. T. (1985). *The Kinetic Drawing System: Family and school*. Los Angeles, CA: Western Psychological Services.

McGoldrick, M. & Gerson, R. (1985). Constructing genograms. In M. McGoldrick & R. Gerson, *Genograms in family assessment*. New York: W. W. Norton, 9–38.

McGoldrick, M., Gerson, R., & Shellenberger, S. (1999). *Genograms: Assessment and intervention*. New York: W. W. Norton.

McGoldrick, M., Giordano, J., & Garcia-Preto, N. (Eds.). (2005). *Ethnicity and family therapy*. New York: Guilford Press.

Machover, K. (1952). *Personality projection in the drawing of the human figure*. Springfield, IL: Charles C. Thomas.

Oster, G. D. & Crone, P. (2004). *Using drawings in assessment and therapy* (2nd ed.). New York: Taylor & Francis.

Oster, G. D. & Gould, P. (1987). *Using drawings in assessment and therapy*. New York: Brunner/Mazel.

Oster, G. D. & Montgomery, S. S. (1996). *Clinical uses of drawings*. Northvale, NJ: Jason Aronson.

Prout, H. T. & Phillips, P. D. (1974). A clinical note: The Kinetic School Drawing. *Psychology in the Schools*, *11*, 303–306.

Sarbaugh, M. E. (1983). Kinetic Drawing-School (KS-D) technique. *Illinois School Psychologist's Association Monograph Series*, *1*, 1–70.

Wesson, M. & Salmon, K. (2001). Drawing and showing: Helping children to report emotionally laden events. *Applied Cognitive Psychology*, *15*(3), 301–319.

5 Using Drawings During Clinical Interviews

INFORMATION GATHERING

Evaluations and therapies begin with the clinical interview, essentially a background exchange between clients and behavioral health workers. From the very first session, each client assessed will be vastly different in his or her presentation and expressed symptoms. As the information gatherer, clinicians need to: a) make this human contact comfortable; b) be able to establish rapport efficiently; c) build a working alliance; d) instill hope that problems being faced can be overcome; and e) provide clear goals and helpful interventions (Sommers-Flanagan & Sommers-Flanagan, 2013). Professional counselors, social workers, expressive therapists, psychiatric nurses, physicians, as well as psychologists can all be involved, yet they are not mind readers; they need to discover the background history, support system, presenting symptoms, and the resilience of the person sitting in front of them.

To assist in this elaborate process, both structured and unstructured clinical interview formats have been constructed and are used to gain valuable information that determines treatment direction. For example, a semi-structured interview was completed by one young woman who was entering a residential treatment center. As part of the history-gathering process, she was asked to write answers to a series of questions, such as basic background data ("Where were you born?" "List your parents and siblings," "Have you ever repeated a grade") in addition to more subjective questions (e.g., "How would you describe your childhood?" "How would you describe your life just before coming here?") and queries pertaining to mood state (e.g., "Have you experienced suicidal thoughts?").

Her answers to describing her childhood included, "chaotic, unorganized, traumatic, abusive, neglected, and scary." She indicated that she was physically and sexually assaulted on many occasions during her early years. Later in the interview, drawing directives were requested and underscored her underlying hurt and pain and how she "acted out" this anguish through cutting (see Figure 5.1). Certainly, these symbolic statements stimulated and enhanced many subsequent discussions. She stated that she finally felt "heard" by the intake counselor, who she indicated had asked all the "right" questions to help her adjust to this difficult transitional time in her life.

As exemplified in the above example, clinical interviews begin interactive dialogues between behavioral health professionals and clients that are designed to initiate a substantive evaluation of a person's problem areas and needs. The results of these interchanges will determine the necessity for additional testing, diagnostic impressions, and the direction of treatment intensions. Through this focused conversation that may include structured questions, checklists, and other clinical tools, extensive informational facts and impressions are collected to form a complete picture of the client's functioning and concerns. Of all the techniques utilized in hastening the goals of comprehensive

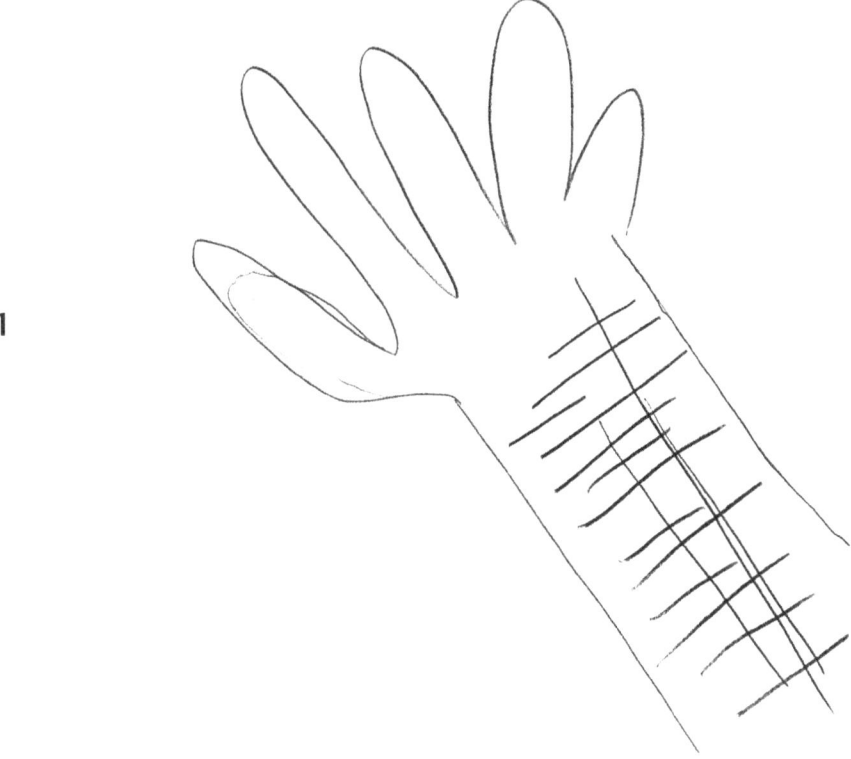

5.1

interviewing, drawing directives (such as genograms or symbolic drawings of family, school or work, mood, or future plans) appear to accomplish the objectives of developing individual expression and increasing interpersonal skills in the easiest and most profound manner (Oster & Gould, 1987; Oster & Montgomery, 1996; Oster & Crone, 2004).

Different from merely a conversation between two people, the clinical interview establishes distinct roles. And subsequently the questions pursued are directed toward understanding the client as thoroughly as possible. This progression of uncovering involves active listening, empathic responding, establishing feelings of validation, and skillfully learned attitudes that lead to positive rapport (Rogers, 1957). Additionally, there is typically a defined time frame, such as a single session in the case of the above intake interview for placement, an emergency room interview to assess need for inpatient status, or a beginning therapy session to determine need for ongoing treatment.

In the majority of interview situations, clinicians must begin by allowing clients to explore their own thoughts, feelings, and behaviors (Meier & Davis, 2010). While the natural urges are to help and intervene as soon as possible, effective clinicians need to consistently remind themselves to pause before giving advice or establishing diagnostic impressions too hastily. Mainly, though, they need to assist their clients to follow their own leads and make their own discoveries. Thus, their primary responsibility is to encourage clients to express themselves openly without too much resistance. By using drawings within this framework, this interactive process unfolds and enhances communication through multiple methods that consider aspects of both verbal and nonverbal language.

CASE STUDY: Jacob D.

Jacob D. was 16 years old when interviewed at the emergency room of a community hospital prior to being admitted to inpatient status due to symptoms of depression and expressed suicide ideation. Besides these unsettling thoughts and feelings, Jacob admitted to auditory and visual hallucinations as well as being preoccupied with death. Mainly he felt very alone. He denied alcohol and drug usage and never had legal complications. This was his first psychiatric hospitalization.

Through his developmental years, Jacob had spent an equal amount of time between parental households, since their divorce occurred when he was 4 years old. The parents were both working professionals and even after the separation lived fairly near one another. Jacob was a tenth grade student at the time of evaluation. His grades had always been inconsistent and he had few friends. During the interview, he mentioned that it was difficult for him to get motivated, especially for studying or completing homework. Socially, he appeared shy and awkward.

Jacob presented as a slender young man with longish hair and seemed his stated age. He was alert, oriented, and did not express unusual mannerisms. He was not in acute distress at the time of the interview and expressed an appropriate range of affect. While there was no overt evidence of thought interference, he admitted to hearing unfamiliar voices that made him feel "paranoid" and spoke of having visual hallucinations ("a person with a mischievous smirk").

Jacob spoke mostly about enjoying time alone. He mentioned having marked mood swings, and two out of five "bad" days a week. Although he denied current sadness, he noted that during the past year he had been cutting himself when feeling upset. He mentioned that these self-injurious behaviors were a result of being frustrated over school and friendships, in addition to being criticized for his lack of effort.

Jacob's responses to self-report inventories measuring signs of depression and suicide ideation were within a moderate range for clinical concern. While he mainly denied significant experiences of inner turmoil, he primarily focused on his preference for being by himself and on his expressions of frustration. Mostly, he stated that he felt angry about things most of the time and viewed his life as unfair. During the month prior to his admission, he had been preoccupied with thoughts surrounding death and dying, and not caring whether he lived or died.

Other salient information gathered during the interview pointed to increases in personal isolation and feelings of alienation. This hesitancy in reaching out to others seemed to undermine his confidence and motivation. He also suggested that he was very sensitive, which left him defensive and guarded in his interpersonal interactions.

Since Jacob appeared constricted in many areas of self-disclosure and he seemed to need a different way to reach him, a series of drawing directives were requested. One of these requests (constructing his life "before and after" the hospitalization) emerged as an effective way to discuss his problems and how to intervene. In these two drawings (see Figures 5.2 and 5.3), he portrayed himself first as lonely and confused. He then elaborated on the frustrations that his self-imposed isolation had caused. His next graphic image characterized his wish to begin talking to peers and obtain meaningful friendships. He was pleased with these visual illustrations and acknowledged that this alternative means of expressing himself might help him in the future.

It was apparent that Jacob needed much support to more accurately understand his thoughts and feelings and to enhance his problem-solving skills. Both group and individual therapies were offered to him in his brief inpatient stay and he began to accept this type of assistance. It was important that the interviewer communicate to the unit staff, and within his report Jacob's creative ways to communicate were emphasized in order to effectively intervene in his care. Family therapy was also established to better understand and express Jacob's needs to his parents and their expectations of him.

Before

5.2

After

5.3

CONDUCTING AN INITIAL INTERVIEW

During an intake screening, a mental status exam, a diagnostic evaluation, or one of many other types of clinical interviews (such as specific evaluations that focus on trauma or during family evaluations), there remain several elements that are crucial to the success of determining accurate diagnoses and therapeutic determination. First of all, clinicians conducting the interviews need to offer a protected space for questions and dialogue. For their part, the clients must perceive the situation as nonjudgmental and supportive in order to experience the freedom of sharing without negative consequences. Additionally, confidentiality is explored whereby clinicians need to reassure their clients that the information gathered will only be disseminated with their consent (Sommers-Flanagan & Sommers-Flanagan, 2013).

In the case of beginning treatment, this personal information will not be shared unless there is an immediate danger to the client or someone else. In other settings, such as an intake screening in an emergency room or crisis center, or to obtain residential assistance, the client will need to realize that the information will be distributed to other treating professionals. Taking the time to explore these issues of confidentiality will help to establish trust and allow all clients to be more relaxed and forthcoming.

When possible, the asking of open-ended questions may be more valuable than asking specific "yes" or "no" questions. Allowing clients time to process and answer open-ended questions will often provide personal reflections and possibly allow better insight into problem areas. For example, rather than simply asking "Do you feel depressed?" and expecting a direct affirmative or negative response, it is often better to explore thoughts and feelings behind the mood and oftentimes even better to "draw the mood" and elaborate on its construction (Oster & Crone, 2004). Taking the time to explore how clients feel, as opposed to direct questions related to depression, provides a myriad of possibilities that determine the uniqueness of the particular mood state. And verbal responses to illustrations of moods, such as "feeling stressed out," or like the "weight of the world" is on their shoulders, or completely "uninterested" in all the things they used to love, provide considerable richness to the interactions and a much broader picture of the depth of the client's experiences.

CASE STUDY: Lori S.

Lori S. was nearly 16 years old when placed on a psychiatric unit secondary to revealing suicidal thoughts to her high school nurse. She had never been hospitalized previously for her emotional or behavioral difficulties, but had participated in outpatient treatment for numerous years due to depression and social isolation. Prior to her admission, her feelings of sadnesshad increased along with suicidal thoughts. She had also cut her legs and thighs, and had begun experimenting with marijuana.

Even though her psychiatrist had changed her medication, the intervention was not effective. And the night before she disclosed her wish to die, Lori reportedly thought of cutting herself with a razor blade. And, in fact, she cut herself on the unit following a volatile family therapy session.

At the evaluation, Lori presented as a well-nourished young woman of average height. She had slashes on both forearms from cutting herself. She was alert and oriented, but her affect was somewhat constricted. Lori discussed feeling teased and ostracized from peers. She also described her frustrations with her parents who, according to her, did not understand the depth of her depression. She stated that she was "sad most of the time" and despite long-term treatment, she had rarely felt happy or content.

5.4

At that point, Lori was asked to portray her mood on paper. At first reluctant, she decided that this directive allowed her to reveal (through a different context) how she generally felt most days. This dramatic picture (see Figure 5.4) certainly reflected her remorse and feelings of isolation and helplessness. Through the drawing, she was able to elaborate on her hurt and anguish.

She spoke of her feelings more readily after constructing the image and was pleased that the examiner took the time to allow these alternative types of expressions. She acknowledged that most of the time she felt lonely, sad, and like crying. She rarely felt important and wanted mostly to hide from people. Additionally, she felt alienated from peers, viewed life as unfair, and harbored many self-degrading thoughts. She also indicated that she often felt hopeless as to whether things would improve in her life, and that she frequently wanted to run away or hurt herself. Overall, her responses reflected a "cry for help." The introduction of the drawing technique allowed her to visually demonstrate the intensity of her sad mood and feelings of hopelessness.

Finally, behavioral health professionals conducting a clinical interview need to be close observers of the client. They must listen not only to the words of the client, but also to nonverbal clues, like posture, affect, tone of voice, and bodily movements. For example, a client who responds "I'm fine" may be reacting defensively or angrily. Often there is much more going on behind these words.

BEHAVIORAL OBSERVATIONS

Careful observations during clinical interviews, diagnostic evaluations, and later psychological testing provide relevant avenues for obtaining vital clues about clients' current emotional and interpersonal conditions. During these assessments, the knowledge gathered through close scrutiny and the hypotheses generated during the interchanges are often as crucial to accurate diagnosis and treatment direction as any obtained test scores (Sattler, 1997; 2001). The behaviors gleaned through this careful surveillance also allow for meaningful directions toward thoughtful recommendations.

During the give-and-take of questions and answers as well as the administration of structured forms or drawing directives, clinicians have the opportunity to assess the client's attention span, frustration tolerance, anxiety level, motor coordination, problem-solving approach, degree of distractibility, and reflectivity (Kaufman & Lichtenberger, 2005). Through these astute observations, clinicians reach tentative conclusions about personal characteristics such as self-concept, work habits, or responses to encouragement. For instance, the degree of effort exerted during a drawing task may reflect a particular attitude toward new learning experiences, such as enjoyment or challenge versus those that may create anxiety and uncertainty.

Through careful observations, clinicians can decide whether their client's appearance is appropriate to the situation or too drab, unkempt, or disheveled; or too formal or casual. They can also deduce whether the client's activity level is within a normal range, and whether his or her gestures and affect are full-ranging or constricted. Furthermore, signs of interpersonal comfort become important as clinicians need to be alert and attentive towards signs of depression, worry, or unusual excitement. And interpersonally, clinicians need to be perceptive toward indicators of a guarded or aloof stance, a submissive or dramatic presentation, or a cooperative or oppositional attitude.

Questions of impulsivity, perfectionism, or compulsive traits can also be ascertained through diligent viewing of a client's verbal exchanges or approach to a questionnaire or drawing directive. Low frustration tolerance, for example, may be hypothesized when an individual becomes easily annoyed over minor mistakes and begins to erase or scribble over the details. Certain portions of the person's emotional expression, such as an angry voice, a sad face, or a nervous hand tremor, can also be regarded as possible indicators of acute inner turmoil or more permanent traits of personality.

An examiner's ability to make astute observations also enhances the value of the interactive process of clinical interviewing and assessments. Even the time spent establishing rapport with a client is a potential asset in the creation of working hypotheses that detail areas of strengths and weaknesses: for instance, assessing activity level, attention span, and logical thinking processes. While caution is prudent in attempting to make too many interpretations based on these observations, they still remain important bits of information that when integrated into other informational data and test results can help obtain a more accurate picture of the client. The following scenarios introduce the concept of behavioral observations as a main component of a thorough interview.

CASE STUDY: **Eduardo L.**

Eduardo L. was 18 years old when he was brought to an emergency room by his pastor secondary to substance abuse and declining functioning. Besides his substance usage (or because of it), he had withdrawn from activities and his grades had declined. Eduardo reportedly had been using IV heroin for the past eight months and overdosed on it just two weeks prior to the intake admission.

At that time, he was revived by emergency medical services (after his mother called 911) and taken to a different hospital where he was released after 12 hours of observation. While he had received brief outpatient treatment in the past, he never participated in extended therapies. However, he had been involved in past substance abuse education programs. On at least two occasions (eighth and tenth grades), he was suspended from school and arrested for marijuana possession. His probation entailed entering these programs.

At the time of the initial clinical interview, Eduardo presented as a well-nourished, muscular young man of average height without physical anomaly. He was right-handed and was not wearing glasses. He appeared alert and oriented, and did not offer unusual mannerisms. His speech was clear and goal-oriented.

There was no outward appearance of acute depressive symptoms; neither were there expressions of depressive or suicidal statements. However, his affect was constricted, as was his spontaneity. He denied most problems and did not view his drug usage as an addiction. He stated that he had used mostly in the fall (during football season) and had reduced his consumption considerably for his participation in wrestling. Reportedly, he was using 3–4 bags two to three times a week.

During his completion of questionnaires and screening measurements, Eduardo's problem-solving style was fairly consistent. He appeared challenged by the tasks and was focused when the activities were short and structured. He was able to sustain his attention over time and was not distracted by external noises. However, when demands became more complicated or novel in their presentation, his outward appearance seemed more strained, constricted, and anxious as he became uncertain of his responses and was visibly agitated.

CASE STUDY: **Randall M.**

Randall M., aged 15, was being interviewed for intake at an inner city behavioral health clinic. With a long-standing history of emotional and adjustment difficulties, Randall complained about physical abuse by adult family members. At a young age, he was seen in outpatient therapy due to conduct problems, including fire setting, lying, and stealing. During that time, he was evaluated with results indicating average intelligence, attentional deficits, and emotional conflicts stemming from mother–child disagreements. These latter disagreements led to this referral, as the mother complained about Randall's lack of respect towards her, disobeying household rules, curfew violations, and a lack of cleanliness.

Randall presented as a tall and slender young man without physical anomaly. He approached the session somewhat anxious, soft-spoken, and socially awkward. He was coherent, alert, and oriented to time, place, and person. He did not offer any signs of unusual communication or blockages in his expressed thoughts. He seemed at least average in his intellect and exhibited an excellent grasp of abstract reasoning. He denied intense feelings of sadness or suicidal ideation. He also refuted drug usage.

Randall was well-groomed in his appearance (except for dirty pants, which the mother noted was a major conflict between them (i.e., not caring about his dress)). In fact, the mother tended to speak for him, and then put pressure on him to speak up. This type of double message was typical of her interactions with him. Later, he admitted to hiding his emotions and being passive-aggressive with his mother.

From these early observations, it was apparent that much of the therapeutic work needed to be structured within a family perspective. Of course, Randall certainly needed his own time and space to vent personal frustrations and begin learning more effective problem-solving skills. Their relationship appeared enmeshed and suffocating, and both seemed very aggravated that they were not being heard and appreciated.

THE CRUX OF THE INTERVIEW

An interview resembles a test, whether psychological or educational (Kaplan & Saccuzzo, 2012). There are certain methods for gathering behavioral and emotional data such that the information is: a) applied to make informed predictions; b) evaluated in terms of reliability and validity; c) used with individuals or groups; and d) structured or unstructured. Interviews remain one of the most prevalent devices for employment (Posthuma, Morgeson, & Campion, 2002), as well as their benefits within the clinical arena (Groth-Marnat, 2009). Interviews also remain crucial in health-related professions, such as general medicine and nursing (Eggly, 2002). Even outside the professional realm, interviewing skills are important for everyone, even for parents when something has gone wrong in the family.

In general, the interview involves an interaction between or among individuals, whether it be a single person, a group, or for example, family members. But, similar to the controlled psychological testing environment, clinicians must remain in charge and resume responsibility for the direction and atmosphere. While there are many types and purposes for interviewing, all share certain commonalities. For instance, interviews involve mutual interactions wherein each party influences one another (Breggin, 2002).

A classic study detailing the transactional and reciprocal nature of the process found that participants increased or decreased their level of interactions based on the others' reactions. Therefore, interview participants significantly influence the behavior and verbal output of each other. Another even older study found that when professional actors performing as clients responded with anger to even highly trained and experienced clinicians, these interviewers became increasingly angry in return. This phenomenon of "social facilitation" demonstrated how anyone can be influenced by the other person in an interview situation. For example, uncomfortable feelings being displayed by interviewers are usually picked up easily by the interviewees and can make the situation and interactions very tense and uncomfortable. By contrast, interpersonal environments that remain warm and supportive usually elicit positive responses (cited in Kaplan & Saccuzzo, 2012).

Knowing that session participants have a major impact on one another, a proficient clinician knows how to create a relaxed and secure atmosphere through these principles of "social facilitation." However, it is crucial to remember that the effective interviewer remains on task and sets the tone for meaningful interactions. Clinicians must understand that their expressed feelings will be experienced by the client and reciprocation is likely; that is, a clinician's anxiety will almost always elicit stilted or agitated feedback. By remaining self-assured and relaxed, clinicians will have a calming impact on the environment of the room and instill trust from their clients. Even in difficult situations, such as prisons, or when working with seriously disturbed children or adults, the tone of the session truly matters.

TYPES OF CLINICAL INTERVIEWS

There are numerous types of clinical interviews that have been constructed and used for a variety of purposes. Clinicians may be seeing clients for the first time, or when an already established client is going through an acute crisis. Clinicians also interview distinct individuals in many different settings, such as a student in a college counseling center, a family in an inner city clinic, or someone who may be forced through the legal system or social services to make an appointment to establish criteria for disability support or intervention.

Practitioners who conduct these sessions need to be highly skilled in many methods of interpersonal counseling. They also must be knowledgeable in the usual structured formats for interviewing and the differential diagnostic criteria that will steer the conversation and the conclusions toward treatment. Many types of these encounters have been developed for use at different times and with varied people. Examining two of the most common clinical interviews (the intake interview and the mental status exam) are crucial formats to learn and to integrate into any clinician's "toolbox" of skills.

Intake Interviews

A beginning or intake interview occurs during first contact. While some of this information may be gathered on the phone or via email, the real substance happens in the office at first encounter. At that moment, behavioral health professionals have the opportunity to assess people's appearance, initial interactions, and forthrightness about problem areas. The clinician then begins the series of questions that defines the interactions—that is, a) asking about what has brought them to the office at this point in time; b) their history with other professionals; c) their general health and emotional difficulties; d) their current symptoms and how long they have persisted; e) what they hope to gain from this interview; and f) their expectations about future evaluations and treatment options (Burgess, 2013).

For example, by asking clients why they have come to see you may produce an initial reaction that might be quite vague ("Everyone thinks I'm fine, but I feel like a mess"). With further directed probing (either through structured questions or nonverbal techniques like drawings), clinicians begin to discover that the client is experiencing considerable underlying distress and for the first time is having panic attacks. Subsequent questions that may be more direct attempt to pinpoint: whether the stressors are acute or chronic; what methods the client has attempted to lessen the anxiety; and whether the symptoms are unique or an escalation of other feelings. During these interchanges, the discussion usually moves into discovering exactly when these unpleasant sensations began and how they may relate to life patterns or changes. By contrast, some clients will present as very confused or disorganized and it takes much skill to obtain the information needed. In these matters, it usually requires more systematic and structured questions to assess the core issues and provide more accurate diagnostic impressions.

Research-based principles of interviewing have suggested that accurate understanding leads to self-exploration (cited in Breggin, Breggin, & Bemak, 2002). These guidelines recommend beginning with open-ended questions, with the interviewer "listening, facilitating, and clarifying" during the beginning stages (Maloney & Ward, 1976). For instance, "Tell me about you," "What ails?" or "What brought you here today?" may be all a clinician needs to ask at the start of a session. It then becomes crucial that clients believe that they can best express their main complaints clearly and that the clinician is listening intently and actively to what they have to say.

More direct questioning, by contrast, is best utilized toward the end of the interview to complete missed details or gaps that have been unspoken to that point. However, these specific questions are beneficial when time is limited, the client is uncomfortable or uncooperative, or the individual is nonverbal or intellectually limited (Othmer & Othmer, 2001). A thorough history is required that entails: a) medical problems; b) past diagnoses and treatment; c) developmental milestones; d) past stressors; e) social relationships; f) school and work progress; and g) substance usage (Zimmerman, 2013).

Children in general may need more direct questioning and careful observation as opposed to openness or ambiguity. Typical questions that may be included in a beginning or intake interview with children and adolescents may include the following topics:

- What is your age and date of birth?
- What grade and what school are you attending?
- Tell me about yourself; your family . . . and school.
- How would your friends describe you?
- What kinds of drugs do you and your friends use?
- How many bad days during the week do you have?

These questions are both directed and open-ended. They involve the gathering of facts and also make assumptions (e.g., most teenagers are either exposed to or are using drugs; most have good and bad days). Listening acutely to the answers of these questions usually leads into long discussions about the reasons the client is at the site on this particular day, or elicits many other questions that clarify everyday functioning at home and school. The introduction of drawings can also facilitate these interactions through directives, such as "construct a timeline beginning with your earliest memory," "draw your world," or "sketch your ideal self in 10 years and include the setting and the people that you would like involved in your life." Even basic drawings, such as the H-T-P can reveal aspects of presenting problems or characteristics of home life or familiar dynamics. Through active questioning, participation in activities, and careful observations, a complete interview can produce not only a solid beginning, but can also lead to important elucidation of goals and treatment planning.

CASE STUDY: **Marilyn C.**

Nine-year-old Marilyn C. was referred by her parents to an outpatient expressive therapy clinic because she had been experiencing school-related and social problems. Admission notes gained from the telephone intake noted that Marilyn had few friends and exhibited signs of ADD and anxiety. When the mother was interviewed further, she described Marilyn as displaying poor concentration, taking an inordinate amount of time to complete homework, being easily overwhelmed, and seeming overly shy and nervous. Reports from school further described her as being passively uncooperative, isolating herself from other students, and appearing fearful and avoidant. These problems had persisted for several years, and more recently changes in her eating habits were observed.

When Marilyn was seen alone, she seemed nervous but alert and oriented. Her expressed thoughts were lucid and goal-directed. Her language, in fact, appeared sophisticated and she was fairly easy to engage in conversation. She concurred with her mother that she was easily distracted, daydreamed often, and preferred lone activities to group projects. When asked questions regarding her mood, she stated that she was overly sensitive and that her feelings got hurt easily, and that it was difficult keeping her mind on school work. She also suggested that she felt very nervous around peers and tended to avoid most social situations. However, she said that she felt happy, was well-accepted by her parents, and always hopeful.

In addition to questions, she was asked to construct a series of drawings. These illustrations were quite expressive and seemed a less threatening format to describe herself. Her picture of a tree was especially revealing of her temperament (see Figure 5.5). This figure seemed to reflect her vulnerability and need to hide and feel protected (the face inside the tree). Also, the bare and thorny branches appeared to signify her defensiveness and guardedness from interpersonal interactions. Interestingly, she added a lightning bolt to the picture, possibly as an expression of the perceived threats in her environment. This drawing and other images reinforced the indicators of her distress and the reasons why her mother had brought her for assistance. Through these creative activities and questions that clarified her everyday functioning, she was able to talk freely about her situation and was able to suggest ways that she would like to get help.

Mental Status Exam

The mental status exam (MSE) is considered more structured in pursuit of clinical answers (Strub & Black, 1993; Smith, 2011). It takes into account the client's behaviors, attitudes, and movements in addition to the responses to many questions regarding alertness, orientation, and general health and mental health status. This more comprehensive format of questions will often provide a broader view of the client's overall functioning. While a mental status exam can be used on any client, including those with lesser difficulties, it is more often used with clients who are presenting with more serious problems.

5.5

The mental status examination forms just one component of a comprehensive assessment. It augments other sections, such as history of the presenting complaint and provides cues regarding what more detailed testing needs to take place (e.g., cognitive assessment). The MSE also affords another way to structure data about certain aspects of a client's mental functioning. It typically follows a standard form with observations recorded under specific headings.

While the MSE might seem overwhelming and time consuming at first glance, in everyday practice this structured interview can be completed in a concise time framework. What is obtained through the MSE is specificity in certain areas of functioning, in addition to what information clinicians normally gather through their regular interviewing style and behavioral observations. Factors such as general appearance, interpersonal approach to the questions, alertness and orientation, mood and affect, motor coordination, articulation and fund of language, intellectual flexibility, and levels of consciousness are all key components to this quick, but comprehensive exam. The following elements are the primary features of the exam.

- *Appearance*: Factors such as gender, apparent age, height and weight, general grooming, appropriate attire for seasonal weather, posture, gross and fine motor coordination, and physical anomalies fall under this heading.
- *Interpersonal approach*: This section focuses on whether the client seems friendly or defensive; candid or cooperative; trusting or hostile; and relaxed or anxious. Other adjectives that may describe the client's readiness for the interview may entail seductive, negative, evasive, irritable, or unconcerned. This segment of the MSE also focuses on rate and production of speech, articulation, level of eye contact, attention span, as well as short- and long-term memory.
- *Alertness and orientation*: Primary assessment of time, place, and person, general alertness, coherence, ability to abstract, logical thinking, judgment and insight, and thought processes (including evidence of hallucinations and delusions) all fall under this category.
- *Affect and mood*: Answers to ascertain through this section of questioning include: how the client is feeling most days; what is his or her outlook (pessimistic or optimistic); whether rapport was easily established or not; indications of suicidal or homicidal ideation; maturity of defense mechanisms (e.g., overuse of denial is usually considered immature); and risk of violence.

Some questions that address the above sections of inquiry and explore the levels of distress may consist of the following.

- Do you have trouble falling asleep?
- How is your energy level throughout the day?
- Are there things that worry you a lot?
- Are there certain things that you feel compelled to do repeatedly?
- Have you felt your mind playing tricks on you?
- Are your dreams overly intense or unreal?
- Are your eating habits unusual, or have they changed?
- Do you find yourself doing many things without knowing why?
- Has your energy level changed, or do you feel you don't need to sleep?
- When you enter a new place, do you feel others are watching you?
- Do you feel others have harmed you or are out to harm you?

Answers to these questions form a strong basis for portraying the level of distress clients may be experiencing. Formulating diagnostic impressions at this point in an evaluation also provides clearer direction to other treating professionals and clarifies the client's need for therapeutic input. With the latest edition of the DSM (5th edition, American Psychiatric Association, 2013), clinicians have access to the most current diagnostic criteria at their disposal to better determine how emotional disorders are categorized. It becomes an essential educational resource for students and practitioners and provides a practical and functional guide for organizing information derived from interviews and responses from questionnaires.

CASE STUDY: Breanna P.

Breanna P. was a 17-year-old young woman referred for a diagnostic interview due to her deteriorating condition. She had recently run away from a residential treatment center and only returned after being apprehended by the local police. Breanna had a long-standing history of significant neglect and physical and sexual abuse. In the past, she had been diagnosed with Schizoaffective Disorder, Trichotillomania (pulling out her hair), and Generalized Anxiety Disorder. Previous reports from hospitalizations included presentations of auditory hallucinations, paranoia, and ideas of reference. When in school, she had displayed aggressive and assaultive behaviors. Past evaluations noted intellectual functioning within the "disabled" range (52–69).

A synopsis of the MSE included the following:

- *Appearance, attitude, and motor activity*: Breanna was casually dressed and appeared to be very cooperative, though mildly restless during the interview.
- *Mood and affect*: She described her mood as "okay," and her affect was appropriate.
- *Speech*: Output was slow, low tone, problems in articulation.
- Thought processes: Generally relevant and pertinent, no evidence of circumstantial or tangential thinking.
- *Perception*: She denied current auditory or visual hallucinations while taking medications.
- *Alertness*: She was alert and oriented to time, place, and person.
- Concentration: She had no difficulty with concentration.
- *Recent and remote memory*: She was able to recall three out of three objects at one and five minutes. She had no difficulty with remote memory.
- *Language*: She displayed adequate vocabulary and was able to express her needs and future plans. She had limited capacity for abstraction.
- *Interpretation of proverbs*: She had difficulty with explanations.
- *Insight and judgment*: Both areas were limited.

The findings from this MSE allowed the examiner to integrate these impressions into a more comprehensive report. She ordered extended psychological testing to document Breanna's overall cognitive functioning and to detail her specialized needs after she would leave the treatment center at a more appropriate time. The MSE guided the staff and unit psychiatrist in more immediate interventions. It appeared that her running away was part of impulsive, disinhibited, and unregulated behaviors that she was displaying after refusing medication. Once returned, she was more cooperative in accepting the treatment regimen and her improved condition was noted by all staff.

TRAUMA INTERVIEWS

Posttraumatic stress disorder (PTSD) is a chronic and debilitating condition that develops in response to catastrophic life events, such as military combat, sexual and physical assault, and repercussions of natural disasters (van der Kolk, 2014). It can also develop from long-standing neglect and abandonment from childhood (Walker, 2013). Symptoms of traumatic stress can additionally result from the lasting consequence of traumatic ordeals that cause intense feelings of fear and helplessness, such as the unexpected death of a loved one or an accident.

PTSD can happen to anyone who has experienced a harrowing and upsetting event. Individuals who have been abused as children, or who have been repeatedly exposed to life-threatening situations, are at greater risk for developing PTSD. Most people who experience a traumatic event will have reactions that may include intense shock, anger, nervousness, fear, and even excessive guilt. These reactions are common; and for most people, they go away over time. For a person with PTSD, however, these feelings continue and even increase; becoming so strong that they keep the person from living a normal life (Williams & Poijula, 2013).

People with PTSD have symptoms for longer than one month and cannot function as well as before the event occurred. Symptoms associated with PTSD usually express themselves through three clusters—re-experiencing, avoidance, and hyperarousal. Furthermore, survivors of trauma can sometimes experience dissociative states and alterations in personality. They also have difficulty regulating their emotions and appear to have marked impairments in intimate relationships and attachment. Additionally, comorbid symptoms are oftentimes expressed; including depression and substance abuse.

Symptoms of PTSD often are grouped into three main categories, including:

- *Reliving*: Individuals suffering with PTSD repeatedly relive the ordeal through thoughts, feelings, and memories of the trauma. These often include flashbacks, hallucinations, and nightmares. They may also experience considerable distress when certain situations or events remind them of the trauma, such as an important anniversary date.
- *Avoiding*: The symptoms of PTSD may contribute to the need to avoid people, places, thoughts, or situations that trigger reminders of the original trauma. These associations can lead to detached feelings or wanting to isolate from family and friends, in addition to losing interest in previously enjoyed activities.
- *Increased arousal*: This cluster of symptoms may include the expression of excessive emotions; problems in relating to others; having difficulty falling or staying asleep; outbursts of anger; difficulty concentrating; and being easily startled. Individuals experiencing these sensations may also suffer physical symptoms, such as increased blood pressure, muscle tension, or stomach problems.

There are a number of reasons why behavioral health care providers should assess clients for a history of trauma exposure (Foa & Yadin, 2011). Some of the most important factors are: a) trauma-related problems are common; b) symptoms of PTSD contribute to other health effects; and c) PTSD remains under-recognized among various practitioners when conducting regular screening interviews. During the past several decades, researchers have developed a variety of structured and unstructured interviews and assessment instruments that address trauma exposure and related symptoms. A wide variety of measures and protocols that can provide psychometrically sound and practicable measurement of PTSD for almost any application across settings is available, including art therapy-based assessments. The growing focus on the use of evidence-based assessment procedures will foster the continued dissemination of such measures until they become part of routine clinical practice.

Clinicians can begin with questions that relate to trauma-related symptoms. Alternatively, a practitioner can distribute a self-report screening instrument prior to an initial appointment. Completed screens are collected and reviewed to identify clients who are likely to be experiencing symptoms of severe distress. Such areas to be questioned might include: a) frequency of nightmares about a frightening event; b) avoidance of situations that remind clients of stressful situation; c) being constantly hypervigilant and easily startled; and d) feeling detached from relationships and surroundings.

An example of an individual who completed these screening instruments is a 49-year-old man who presented for an initial evaluation at an outpatient clinic. During the interview that focused on possible PTSD symptoms, he revealed instances of persistent nightmares, fears, and intrusive thoughts, as well as efforts to avoid the disturbing thoughts that were producing unpleasant physiological reactions. He also experienced several indications of past trauma (including gaps in awareness, paranoid thoughts, and depersonalization) that all translated in severe personal, social, and occupational impairment. Moreover, his background was replete with alcoholism and abuse within his family of origin. Past court-ordered outpatient substance abuse treatment programs had met with little success. Although he was reluctant to receive intensive treatment, he was willing to participate in an extended evaluation after time was taken to inform him of the repercussions of PTSD.

After obtaining preliminary information from clients, the following suggestions may facilitate subsequent discussions about their responses to screening measures (Wilson, 2004). Clinicians need to: a) respond empathically to the need for privacy in talking about these matters without making assumptions that may be inconsistent with the person's feelings; b) provide information about the bodily effects that traumatic events can create; c) acknowledge their distress in reporting their experiences; and d) demonstrate interest and concern when they have revealed these "secrets." After reviewing the screening results and discussing these responses with clients, it becomes important for providers to decide whether there is a need for more specialized mental health evaluations.

Two of these measures, CAPS-5 that is associated with the newest version of the DSM (DSM-5; Weathers et al., 2013) and the Trauma Symptom Inventory (for adults) and Checklist (for children), will be discussed in the following sections. A comprehensive assessment of PTSD attempts to evaluate the current definition that includes exposure to a traumatic exposure with the development of the characteristic syndrome that has persisted for at least one month and continues to undermine social and occupational functioning. While the structured questions and checklists offer a starting point for a differential diagnosis, follow-up clinical interviews and psychological testing provide even more opportunities to clarify responses and to use clinical judgment and observations in the cumulative ratings. During these more extended evaluations, such nonverbal techniques as timelines or genograms, drawing unpleasant memories, or constructing a problem and how to resolve it, can all lead to pertinent discussions about past trauma and how to overcome its impact.

CLINICIAN-ADMINISTERED PTSD SCALE

The Clinician-Administered PTSD Scale (CAPS), which was originally developed in 1989 at the National Center for PTSD, is a comprehensive structured interview for PTSD (Blake et al., 1995). CAPS was designed to be administered by clinicians and clinical researchers who have a working knowledge of PTSD, but can also be administered by appropriately trained paraprofessionals. The full interview takes 45–60 minutes to administer. Over the years, it has been revised to meet with the newest definitions of PTSD.

The CAPS has been considered the "gold standard" in PTSD assessment. The latest edition, CAPS-5 is a 30-item structured interview that can be used to:

- make a current (past month) diagnosis of PTSD;
- make a lifetime diagnosis of PTSD;
- assess PTSD symptoms over the past week.

In addition to assessing the 20 DSM-5 PTSD symptoms, questions target the onset and duration of symptoms, subjective distress, negative influence on social and occupational functioning, improvement in symptoms since a previous CAPS administration, overall response validity, overall PTSD severity, and specifications for the dissociative subtype (depersonalization and de-realization). For each symptom, standardized questions and probes are provided. Administration requires identification of an index traumatic event to serve as the basis for symptom inquiry. The Life Events Checklist for DSM-5 (LEC-5) is recommended in addition to the Criterion A inquiry included in CAPS-5.

The CAPS-CA (for children and adolescents) has also been developed as a 33-item clinician-administered PTSD modified scale for youths aged 8 to 18 years. Items were revised to make them age appropriate and picture response options were added. The Life Events Checklist is used to identify traumatic events. Like CAPS, CAPS-CA measures the frequency and intensity of symptoms associated with PTSD symptoms, as well as the impact of those symptoms on such aspects of functioning as overall distress, coping skills, and impairment, in addition to current and lifetime diagnoses, and coping strategies (Nader, 2004, 2015).

CASE STUDY: Kienna T.

Kienna T., a 17-year-old young woman, was being assessed for inclusion into a specialized educational program. With a documented history of abuse and removal from her parents' home at age 4, she had exhibited long-standing behavioral and emotional problems that resulted in multiple hospitalizations and placements in various group homes. In fact, her earliest psychiatric intervention occurred at age 7, when she presented as responding to internal stimuli, displayed looseness of associations, and made statements about hurting herself and being hurt by others. Her lengthy mental health history also included later attempts at self-injury, as well as violence and aggression toward others.

As part of her clinical interview, she was administered CAPS to assess her past experiences of trauma-related events. On the CAPS, Kienna reported experiencing several noteworthy and hurtful events; including witnessing a neighbor's house burn down, being the victim of a physical assault, being the object of an assault with a weapon, and causing injury to someone else. Upon further inquiry, she stated that she also caused harm to her mother during a physical altercation, attempted to kill her middle sister, and pushed her aunt down several stairs.

Kienna also identified an instance of being the victim of sexual assault at age 12 as being the most disturbing and difficult. She acknowledged that the event increased her distress and upset during that period of her life (a time when her behavioral altercations had escalated). However, she was unable to stay focused on the discussion, and appeared to be avoiding the thoughts and feelings that reminded her of this past trauma.

5.6

Throughout the remainder of the interview, Kienna expressed feelings of excessive fear and helplessness, seemed to be re-experiencing intrusive recollections of past events and unwanted memories, and mentioned that these reflections were constant in her life and often caused her thoughts of self-harm. She also reported dreams about specific incidents in her past and acknowledged frequent nightmares, typically involving her being harmed or beaten. With these areas mentioned during the CAPS, in addition to other expressed themes of violence that caused her to be hyperaroused and overly reactive in her actions (in addition her difficulties in attention combined with a low frustration tolerance), her responses signified enough criteria for a diagnosis of PTSD.

Along with these emotional indicators, drawings were also included in the interview to assess her motivation towards learning. As portrayed in a drawing of herself in school (see Figure 5.6), she obviously had strong reactions about traditional classrooms. Her struggles were evident by past assessments indicating very low functioning. Despite these vulnerabilities, it was believed that she could best be served by placement in this particular academic program.

TRAUMA SYMPTOM INVENTORY

The Trauma Symptom Inventory (TSI) is a 100-item self-report measure of posttraumatic stress and other psychological sequelae of traumatic events (Briere, 1995). Because it is a fairly brief inventory, it is usually used to screen for trauma before a decision is used to include a lengthier interview, such as CAPS, during an initial assessment. It can also be included in a psychological testing battery.

Respondents are asked to rate how often each symptom has happened to them in the past six months. Items are rated on a four-point frequency scale ranging from 0 ("never") to 3 ("often"). The TSI has 10 clinical scales that assess a variety of symptom domains related to trauma: Anxious Arousal, Depression, Anger/Irritability, Intrusive Experiences, Defensive Avoidance, Dissociation, Sexual Concerns, Dysfunctional Sexual Behavior,

134 USING DRAWINGS DURING CLINICAL INTERVIEWS

Impaired Self-reference, and Tension Reduction Behavior. The TSI also includes three validity scales that may be useful in identifying response tendencies that would invalidate the test results. These scales assess Atypical Responses, Response Level (very low reporting), and Inconsistent Responses.

The TSI contains items that correspond to DSM-4 symptom criteria (B, C, and D) for PTSD, but does not specifically assess these criteria. Raw scale scores are converted to T scores for the 10 clinical scales and the three validity scales based on a normative sample (with separate norms based on gender and age). A computer scoring program is available from the test publisher. The TSI is recommended for measuring a variety of trauma-related symptoms in clinical or research settings.

CASE STUDY: **Nina F.**

Eighteen-year-old Nina F. was being interviewed for admission into a therapeutic group home. In her past, she had resided in multiple foster care and residential placements due to aggressive and self-injurious behaviors. She was also hospitalized on numerous occasions, especially after transitioning to a less restrictive environment.

Developmentally, Nina was born with a very low birth rate (one pound, ten ounces), subsequent to drug exposure in utero. Because of her mother's neglect, she was subsequently raised by another family member. Over the years, she became a victim of sexual abuse, as well as the perpetrator of sexual actions against a minor, which caused frequent mood and social instability.

Prior reports noted intellectual abilities within a range from Extremely Low to Borderline functioning (IQ 62–75). However, given her extraordinary emotional difficulties and missed classroom opportunities, it was believed that her true potential was somewhat higher. She also demonstrated a specific learning disability in her capacity to write and copy efficiently that reduced her academic output and motivation to complete tasks.

5.7
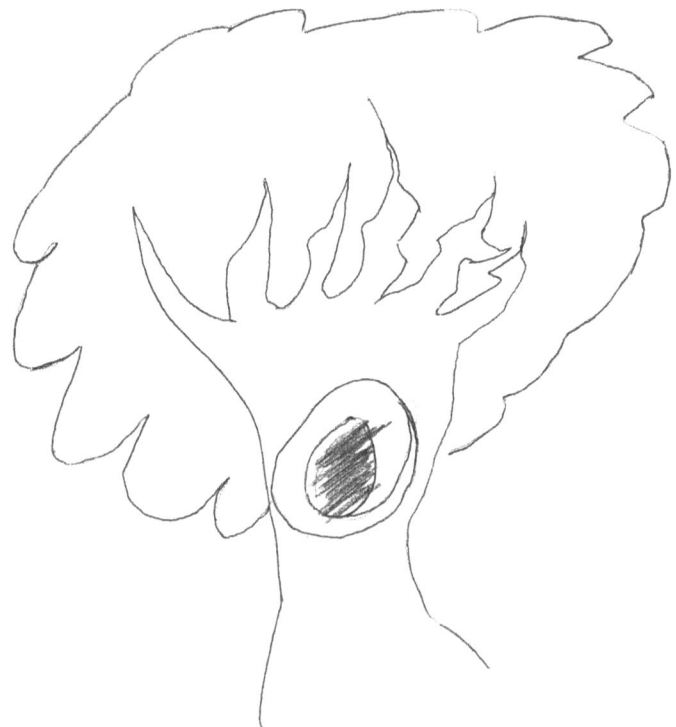

Emotionally, Nina was perceived as displaying significant depressive symptoms, as well as harboring excessive anxiety. It appeared that her anger and irritability, combined with her underlying mood disturbance, led to her unpredictable presentation. Her present feelings of hopelessness and pervasive low self-esteem seemed to suggest a long-standing consequence of her past traumatic experiences. Therefore, she was administered the TSI as part of her intake interview.

The TSI was selected as a measure to identify potential traumatic events in Nina's past and their current effects. Her completed profile indicated that she experienced significant anxiety symptoms, as well as "classic" troubling signs associated with PTSD (e.g., intrusive thoughts). In particular, her responses suggested substantial fears related to previous victimization. She reported that she could not stop thinking about past negative events, could not put these events out of her mind, and wished things had not happened to her. She also specified that she often felt sad and unhappy, and that scary ideas and pictures "popped" into her head. Significant distress and preoccupation related to sexual experiences additionally created much discomfort. As a result, she attempted to avoid many social interactions and withdrew constantly from interpersonal situations. Same-aged peers who respond in a similar manner usually view themselves as "bad" and "unworthy" and are at an elevated risk for suicidality and self-harming behaviors.

Besides the TSI, Nina completed a series of drawings to glean a better sense of her personality functioning. One of the drawings, in particular, seemed to emphasize her past trauma (See Figure 5.7). Her construction of a tree was noteworthy for the highlighted knothole in the trunk (usually an indicator of past trauma and emotional vulnerability). It also displayed a ring around the shaded area, suggesting the time she had devoted towards healing. The other drawings appeared to reflect her impulsivity and poor coping mechanisms when confronted by stress. With this combined information, she was allowed acceptance in the group home with specialized assistance that was determined by the evaluation required for her to succeed.

TRAUMA SYMPTOM CHECKLIST FOR CHILDREN

The Trauma Symptom Checklist for Children (TSCC) is a 54-item self-report scale used for youth between the ages of 8 and 16 that was originally designed for trauma symptoms related to sexual abuse and other traumatic events (Briere, 1996). It is composed of two validity scales (indicating over- and underreporting of symptoms) and six clinical scales (Anxiety, Depression, Posttraumatic Stress, Sexual Concerns, Dissociation, and Anger). The boy or girl is presented with a list of thoughts, feelings, and behaviors and he or she is asked to mark how often each thing has occurred to him or her. Items are rated on a four-point scale (from 0 = "never" to 3 = "almost all the time").

The scale is written at an 8-year-old reading level for easier delivery and to gain more accurate information. It is useful in the evaluation of children who have experienced traumatic events, including physical and sexual assault, victimization by peers, major losses, the witnessing of violence done to others, and natural disasters. The instrument is suitable for individual or group administration. Again, it is mainly used as a screening measure to assess the need for a more focused and lengthier interview directed at previous trauma. It is often included in many of the questionnaires provided during a more comprehensive psychological evaluation.

CASE STUDY: **Leyana G.**

Leyana G. was 14 years old at the time of her clinical interview for admission into a treatment program for emotionally disturbed and conduct disordered youth. She was initially referred by juvenile services due to a history of anger management difficulties, as well as auditory hallucinations telling her to kill herself or other people. These latter problems could not be managed through her temporary detention facility.

Leyana was born suffering from withdrawal symptoms, as her mother apparently smoked crack cocaine throughout the pregnancy. After birth, Leyana was placed through social services with a close family member, where she remained until she was 5 years old. She was then returned to her biological mother, who had successfully overcome her drug usage through rehabilitation services, and was married. However, over the years there were reports of family violence and physical abuse that necessitated in-home family preservation services.

Leyana's academic history was replete with an extensive record of school difficulties, including refusal to attend school regularly and numerous suspensions. At one point she attended an alternative behavioral school due to fighting in her regular middle school. Her actions became even more troubling during the second quarter of her enrollment, as she exhibited behaviors such as: anger, excessive silliness, pressured speech, lying, and severe arguments with teachers and peers where she cursed and threatened them.

Leyana was also an adjudicated delinquent in matters involving violation of probation, theft misdemeanor, second degree assault, and disturbing school activities. Leyana's probation was violated for three reasons: non-compliance with medication, failure to appear in court, and not attending school regularly. As a result, she was placed in detention. Apparently, her aunt was an instigator of her theft and drove Leyana and other children around to stores in order to steal.

Additionally, Leyana had an extensive history of emotional disturbance and psychiatric hospitalizations as well as potentially traumatic events. Reportedly, she began taking psychotropic medications in the first grade. She began hearing voices that told her to do "crazy stuff" at about the age of 6. Reports had indicated that Leyana also seemed to be paranoid and appeared to be responding to internal stimuli, for example, jumping up and yelling, "stop messing with me!" or talking out loud when she was alone in her room. During her intake interview, she reported that the voices she heard were "sometimes mean and sometimes nice;" they instructed her to hurt herself and others, but they also complimented her. Her past psychiatric hospitalizations were primarily due to suicidal and homicidal ideation and gesturing, and medication noncompliance.

She had also been described as having problems with inattentiveness, hyperactivity, and impulsivity and had previously been diagnosed with ADHD. Her records further mentioned that she had frequent mood swings, and often displayed signs of irritability, as well as paranoia and a general distrust of others. Additionally, Leyana had a history of sexual promiscuity. She reported that she "loves" sex, and she had at least five sexual partners since the age of 12, with no pregnancies.

As part of the intake process, the administrator (a clinical social worker) utilized the TSCC to assess current and past trauma symptoms. Based on Leyana's responses, she certainly endorsed a variety of experiences related to PTSD. She had experienced significant trauma and abuse in her past. Consequently, she harbored extreme anxiety and fears that something bad would happen to her. She also stated that she often had nightmares and memories associated with trauma. And these occurrences frequently caused her to have problems concentrating during the day, which made it difficult to remain focused on daily responsibilities and school work.

She also viewed many of her life experiences as "strange" or "unusual" and thought she was different from other adolescents. As a result, her self-concept appeared damaged. Furthermore, she was mistrustful of men, viewed the world as threatening, and often believed that she was being plotted against. She additionally acknowledged being preoccupied with intrusive thoughts about her previous abuse, as well as struggling with sexual conflicts. There were also admissions to instances of apparent dissociation when becoming fearful or overwhelmed by her intrusive thoughts and persecutory ideas.

With this extra information provided by the trauma checklist, Leyana was admitted into a specialized unit with individuals of similar backgrounds. A psychiatric re-evaluation was ordered, as well as individual and group therapies. These latter interventions would focus on helping Leyana learn alternative ways to cope with her past trauma and anxiety, such as psycho-education and stress-reduction methods (e.g., yoga). They would also provide role-playing opportunities to increase her ability to relate and interact with her peers.

SEXUAL ABUSE INDICATORS IN DRAWINGS

At this juncture, a mention of using drawings during evaluations of sexually abused clients needs to be discussed. While the topic is too extensive to cover in this section, it would be helpful for clinicians to gain some awareness of several possible indicators within constructions of graphic images. For instance, many clients may present for interviews with an entirely different presenting problem (e.g., depression or anxiety) and may never have disclosed sexual abuse previously. In this case, if an astute clinician observes possible signs of abuse in several drawings, he or she might further explore possible occurrences in the client's life and highlight this area of concern in treatment recommendations. It is certainly possible that the core of the client's presenting problems may be that sexual abuse history that was never investigated or discussed in more depth. Without the introduction of drawing directives into the evaluative process, the clinician may have overlooked this important focus. The addition of graphic images allows for a nonthreatening way to facilitate and enhance this communication.

Therefore, it becomes salient to emphasize a list of possible indicators that have been observed within drawings that might assist clinicians in their quest for discovery of potential abuse. The following indicators within drawings of sexually abused victims are a compilation of some of the commonalities that have been discovered (cited in Malchiodi, 1997):

- overt sexual connotation in the content, such as images of genitalia, graphic emphasis on the pelvic area of figures, seductiveness in subject of content (Faller, 1996);
- heads without bodies or bodies without their lower half (Hagood, 2000);
- encapsulation (Malchiodi, 1997);
- phallic shapes, often trees (Hagood, 2000);
- shapes (hearts, circles, and wedges) (Hagood, 2000);
- self-deprecation (Malchiodi, 1997);
- repetitive marks, blending (Hagood, 2000).

As always, caution should be utilized in any interpretation, especially in judging the developmental aspects of children's drawings. Also, signs of sexual abuse should be detected repeatedly as part of a pattern across several drawings rather than assumed by a sole indicator. Clear evidence of sexual abuse should not be based on drawings alone; rather ongoing discussions, suggestions from other psychological instruments, and clear disclosure by the client should be established before recommendations are put into place (Hagood, 2000).

CASE STUDY: **Louis R.**

Louis R. was a third grade, 9-year-old public school student who was referred for an evaluation by his mother due to his inattention, disruptive behaviors, and impulsivity. According to his mother, Louis had regressed in his behavior and work habits during the academic year after the removal of some classroom accommodations, especially 1:1 support assistance. While seemingly on grade level, his latest IEP review suggested ongoing concerns in organization, needing to add details to his writing, and comprehension. Behaviorally, he appeared to be viewed as immature and impulsive.

Louis was deemed a child at risk at a young age. He was originally diagnosed with sensory integration problems, along with attention deficits. Additionally, there were questions related to pervasive developmental issues and autism spectrum symptoms. Although he was perceived as being capable of learning, he required 1:1 support during kindergarten and first grade. In the past, he had received occupational therapy, as well as speech and language interventions. He had also participated in special needs camps and social skills training. He was then taking medication for anxiety (liquid Prozac), but he continued to express inappropriate behaviors, both aggressive and sexual in nature, in various settings.

For this evaluation, Louis presented as a well-groomed, polite, and well-nourished youngster who separated easily from his mother, and accepted all direction. There were no indications of severe distress. His speech was clear and his expressed thoughts relevant and goal-directed. However, at times, he required extra prompting and redirection to complete tasks, but did respond positively to encouragement when stuck on problem-solving. In general, though, he was restless, fidgety, and made noises if he was not immediately engaged in an activity.

On IQ and academic tests, Louis obtained average functioning. However, there was a broad disparity within his scores ranging from Below Average to Superior that reflected specific strengths and lesser skills among his unique abilities and academic progress. Although Louis would be expected to achieve at an average to somewhat higher average level in a regular academic environment, the unevenness in his skill development was believed to produce many frustrations during his school performance, and led to inconsistencies and carelessness in his work efforts.

On a test of fine motor coordination and copying effectiveness, Louis' reproductions were difficult and uneven. He exerted considerable effort in drawing the figures, and although primarily accurate, it took him much time to finish. Problems in perceptual-motor control probably constricted his efficiency during written assignments, produced much frustration, and lowered his work output. Also, planning and organization were difficult for him, and these liabilities would suggest a high need for structure to perform maximally.

Object and figure drawings additionally disclosed many weaknesses in his fine-motor coordination and expression. There were numerous indicators of perceptual immaturity and his constructions tended to be in a developmental range several years behind his chronological age. This immaturity was also seen on projective techniques related to his emotionality. His responses suggested a high degree of underlying anxiety that might make him appear overreactive when confronted by stressful situations. These vulnerabilities were especially visible in his "tree" drawing that not only reflected his immaturity but also suggested sexual inferences (see Figure 5.8). When this avenue was explored, he admitted to having "discovered" pornography on the internet.

5.8

BENEFITS AND LIMITATIONS

The clinical interview, whether informal at intake or through a more formal MSE or CAPS, is an opportunity for behavioral health professionals to gather valuable background and family histories about the entire person. It becomes a critical time for information gathering and gaining insight for the client, as well as the clinician. A skilled clinician can review an abundance of personal and interpersonal assets and liabilities in a relative short amount of time. Also having memorized parts of structured interviews and mental status exams can provide a strong foundation to being an efficient examiner.

Asking relevant questions can guide an interview and allow the client to realize that the clinician is truly interested in his or her welfare. Clients will have to recall or review an enormous amount of life and personal histories with the clinician, who will often ask many of the above questions that are related to various life stages. While some components of beginning interviews have even been computerized (especially in gathering demographic information), it becomes crucial for clinicians to understand the points of the questions and where they fit into the overall diagnostic picture. It is also important to approach interviews with an abundance of clinical tools at their disposal to overcome difficult clients, including the introduction of drawings. Thus, reviewing the previous chapters to access appropriate moments for providing structured formats such as timelines, genograms, family shields, school and work diagrams, or images of an "ideal" self may all be fruitful in the discovery process.

CASE STUDY: Cheryl N.

Cheryl N. was a 16-year-old, eleventh grade public school student who was referred for a psychological evaluation by her mother and step-father due to faltering grades, school absences, and ongoing adjustment problems related to the parent's divorce of 5 years. She wavered between needing attention from her biological father (who lived nearby with her brother), as well as her step-father. She had participated in previous counseling with mixed results.

Presenting symptoms described by her mother included: defensive, irritable, sad, and lacking in self-esteem. She also mentioned that Cheryl was easily angered, exhibited poor concentration, seemed distractible, barely ate, and often had sleep problems. Referral questions for testing included: "Does she truly have ADD/ADHD (history of distractibility and inattention)?" "How severe was her apparent depression (she had family members with diagnosis of bipolar)?" and "Was there any evidence of learning disabilities?" A school meeting had been established and the parents needed input and documentation for potential accommodations and interventions.

Cheryl was initially upset to be "wasting her time" talking to yet another therapist. She grudgingly answered questions about her life and current situation and was quite provocative. She described a previous boyfriend as a "loser," and indicated that her current friends were older, had cars, and enjoyed partying. She did relate, though, that she was quite resourceful; having had a summer job hosting in a restaurant and seemed passionate about her interests in sports, dance, and social media.

On self-report measures, Cheryl portrayed herself as indecisive, easily influenced, nervous and worried, and lonely with indicators of low self-esteem. In school, she appeared anxious about test-taking and her concerns often interfered with her work. She also suggested that she experienced "panic" during important exams. Furthermore, she indicated that she daydreamed often during school and was excessively disorganized in her efforts. In fact, there were many indices of executive function difficulties on the various psychological tests; including procrastination, inattention, poor planning abilities, and feeling overwhelmed easily when confronted by complexity. She also acknowledged much intrapsychic distress pertaining to her extreme moodiness, inability to sleep fitfully, underlying sadness, and viewing life as unfair.

Despite her despair, when asked to construct her "ideal" self in perhaps 10 years, Cheryl constructed a very stylish woman who she described as successful and in control (see Figure 5.9). Although the drawing seemed to still suggest some problems in her stability and impulse control, the main focus was its hopefulness about her future. She spoke through the drawing of her need of independence and the hope that she would be prosperous and assertive one day. She enjoyed this process and indirect approach to history taking. The format allowed her to relax and become more responsive and cooperative to the examiner's requests. The remainder of the testing was completed and results disseminated to her parents and school officials who offered accommodations. Without the benefit of another "clinical tool" to establish rapport and gain trust, the results would probably have taken a different and unproductive path.

5.9

FAMILY EVALUATIONS

Introducing drawings into beginning family therapy sessions has two main purposes—they provide a tangible assessment and evaluative technique, and they become a therapeutic process tool (Rubin, 1978). These functions usually overlap. By using drawings at the outset, clinicians can establish rapport with the family members by connecting with them through structured activities. At the same time, the therapist begins the process of assessing complicated interpersonal dynamics and roles. The process of drawing and the completed images assist clinicians by: a) gaining a clearer indication of the hierarchies and boundaries within the family structures; (b) viewing how members perceive themselves and the entire family organization; and (c) understanding how the family members communicate, support, and understand one other. All these elements are vitally important to discover the core beliefs and issues in order to establish treatment goals.

In regards to exploring the evaluative process, the activity of drawing usually produces a common and enjoyable experience to an initial family session. And the sharing of symbols within the graphic images increases familial interactions and establishes an overall positive and memorable tone! The unique aspect of constructing graphic images creates shared fun, provides a sense of intimacy, and assists the family to reestablish its sense of a unique identity. The procedures also enhance verbal communication across generations (Kerr et al., 2007).

Additionally, drawing directives are introduced during evaluative sessions to assist in strengthening or destabilizing familial coalitions so that productive change can occur. Also, drawing techniques can make hidden problems visible to the family members through their tangible illustrations, which then can be used to identify, understand, and resolve problem issues. Through their use as a creative agent of change, clinicians who use drawings during their beginning sessions can promote numerous interventions regardless of family therapy model (Oster & Gould, 1987).

In the second edition of Using Drawings in Assessment and Therapy (Oster & Crone, 2004), an example of a 40-year-old mother of four, "Carla," was feeling overwhelmed, suffocated, and could no longer remember her true identity. She felt exhausted, had little time for herself, and no time to reflect on her own abilities and personal dreams. In essence, she was a mystery to herself and was beginning to feel lost within her family role as primary caretaker. When Carla attempted to describe her concerns to her family members during an initial evaluative session, they were bewildered and did not know how to react to her expressed feelings of ineptitude.

This open confession was confusing and fearful to all family members. This description was especially lost on the husband. He could not fathom that his wonderfully active and multitalented wife and mother who was always so involved in all of their activities was expressing these feelings, especially to a new person. He was truly astonished and clueless. This reaction pained him since he thought that he had successfully secured everything that she had originally wanted—children, a nice house (all the good things in life). The children were equally perplexed for they loved their mother and could not imagine that she was not happy. From their perspective, all their needs were being met and they were certainly happy. What happened to the mother they thought they knew?

What the clinician requested next astounded the family! He asked Carla to create an image that might represent her primary problem. This directive was attempting to convey to her family her inner experience and the resulting visual projection could be used to discuss and express her underlying feelings in a less threatening manner. To Carla, the drawing said it all! What she produced (a mirror without a reflection) seemed to symbolize her feelings of anonymity. She was then able to use this "portrait" as an ingenious platform to express her feelings of alienation and lost identity to her husband and children in a way that could be understood by all participants. Through this graphic illustration, Carla was able to identify her primary issues and the family realized that they could rearrange their activities to provide her the opportunity to plan time for herself, which made her feel appreciated and less overwhelmed.

It is not uncommon for both the non-art-therapist clinician and family members to feel somewhat awkward when drawing directives are first introduced during a beginning family session. This uncomfortable feeling is typical, since the use of drawings is stepping outside the anticipation of the usual verbal interactions. However, this alternative path towards relating can be quite beneficial when families find themselves rigidly stuck in their own patterns of ineffective communication. The clinical uses of drawings can provide a playful environment within a tense session and can lighten the mood of usual criticism that often begins a session when parents attempt to relay what is going wrong in their family (Oster & Montgomery, 1996). Drawings can often alter these negative interactions and stop a downward cycle of harsh remarks that inhibits effective communication among family members. And the resulting products create novel avenues of self-expression and add deeper understanding to the expression of problem areas. By overtly recognizing the shared nervousness of expressing oneself through graphic images, clinicians can establish common ground with the family (regardless of background or culture) and model healthier ways of relating complex feelings (Kerr, 2015).

SHARING OF CONFLICTS

With the introduction of drawing directives to family evaluative sessions, clinicians assist the entire family by providing specific themes for reviewing areas of conflict that may be too threatening to share openly. These visual talking points also lend themselves to the process of generating hypotheses regarding salient family concerns and worries. They also can provide clinicians with introductory premises that can begin to answer many of the referral questions and initiate a more direct channel toward the various aspects of treatment intervention.

When using drawings within the context of family assessments, each member has the opportunity to portray his or her problems in a safe arena without talking. They can then share these struggles during subsequent discussions and discover new solutions to gain control over them. The images serve as a focal point for this dialogue and provide a permanent record of the process for future sessions. The drawings can even become visual records of family transactions that can be preserved and reviewed throughout treatment.

CASE STUDY: Jason A.

Jason A. was a 9-year-old youngster who lived with his parents and older sister who he annoyed constantly. When he was seen for a psychological evaluation it was decided that a family session would be included to assess the expressed concerns and current dynamics. While the parents were mainly worried about Jason's inattention, anxiety, emotional variability, and lack of self-esteem, there were also complaints by the parents about the sibling rivalry and constant squabbling.

As a way to visually describe the situation, each member was asked to draw a problem within the family and how to resolve it. While the other family members were hesitant to produce their own images, the older sister, Jordan, was quick to illustrate the conflict between her and Jason and her unique solution. As can be seen in Figure 5.10, Jordan seemed to be expressing much frustration

5.10

5.11

but was also able to control her temper. In the next picture (see Figure 5.11), Jason can be seen receiving a reward for his "good" behavior. Jordan thought that maybe these types of encouragements could redirect her younger brother's actions.

It was obvious to all the family members that Jason wanted their attention and that it might take an incentive to get what they and he wanted. Although the parents viewed this as manipulation, they were in agreement that they would try a different approach (praise and rewards) to shape Jason's behavior towards more pleasing actions. By the next session that was scheduled to assess Jason's overall functioning, it was disclosed that Jason indeed was flexible enough to reduce his usual antics and to express his need for closeness in more accepting ways. At that point, it was evident that simple interventions with cooperative members could make profound effects on the family dynamics.

Art tasks offer the couple, or the entire family, the opportunity of working together and underscore the important message that mutual problem-solving is a primary goal of their therapy. The communal activities also emphasize the important theme that the difficulties being discussed are everyone's concerns and that a family working together can be a forceful agent of change (Riley, 1993; Kerr, 2015). The drawing methods often reveal therapeutic issues and creative solutions that are not always available through traditional approaches to information gathering.

The use of nonverbal techniques, such as drawings, is especially useful for exploring emotionally laden issues with families of depressed teenagers, who discover that it is often easier to express uncomfortable feelings through joint products or experiences (Oster & Caro, 1990; Oster & Montgomery, 1996). Drawings offer a safer outlet for the destructive or angry impulses of troubled adolescents, who may otherwise feel overwhelmed by what is being expressed during the interview and who may be afraid of losing emotional and behavioral control. Additionally, the adolescent and family, who may already be creative in their self-expression, have another basis for further enlightening explorations through these nonverbal procedures.

AN ENHANCEMENT TO PRACTITIONERS

Clinical tools, such as drawings, offer considerable advantages to the practitioner during initial evaluations or beginning individual or family therapy sessions. In these first visits, behavior and expression of feelings may be excessively rigid, fragmented, or unfocused. It becomes incumbent on the interviewer, examiner, or therapist to make this first contact as comfortable as possible. Because drawing directives have their own unique structure and facilitate selective information, they offer special opportunities for establishing rapport and for building a bridge that provides direction for change. The activities initiated by drawing directives and the resulting products constructed send a compelling message to individuals and family members that they are an active party to the information-gathering process. And more specifically, the uses of alternative methods, such as drawing or expressing internal images, allow the participants to increase their awareness to their presenting problems.

To assist in this elaborate "dance," both structured and unstructured clinical interview formats have been constructed to gain valuable information that determines treatment direction. For their part, drawing directives have been devised to promote the enhancement of communication and to explore the complexity of personal and interpersonal dynamics that need to be revealed during evaluative sessions. The opportunity to add nonverbal expressions of emotions and conflicts increases access to experiences that are usually beyond the give-and-take of questions and answers or completions of brief checklists. These one-step-removed experiences can become a focal point to enhance interactions, explore difficult areas of distress, and initiate different, yet meaningful pursuits of gathering the salient information required for answering referral questions. For this to occur, clinicians need to become astute observers of the human condition and to gather the myriad of interviewing tools necessary to uncover the client's secrets.

REFERENCES

American Psychiatric Association. (2013). *Diagnostic and statistical manual of mental disorders* (5th ed.). Arlington, VA: American Psychiatric Association.

Blake, D. D., Weathers, F. W., Nagy, L. M., Kaloupek, D. G., Gusman, F. D., Charney, D. S., & Keane, T. M. (1995). The development of a clinician-administered PTSD scale. *Journal of Traumatic Stress*, 8, 75–90.

Breggin, P. R. (2002). *The Ritalin fact book*. Cambridge, MA: Perseus.

Breggin, P. R., Breggin, G. R., & Bemak, F. (2002). *Dimensions of empathic therapy*. New York: Springer.

Briere, J. (1995). *Trauma symptom inventory: Professional manual*. Odessa, FL: Psychological Assessment Resources.

Briere, J. (1996) *Trauma symptom checklist for children: Professional manual*. Odessa, FL: Psychological Assessment Resources.

Burgess, W. (2013). *Mental status examination: 52 challenging cases, DSM and ICD-10 interviews, questionnaires and cognitive tests for diagnosis and treatment* (2nd ed.). Amazon: Create Space Independent Publishing Platform.

Eggly, S. (2002). Physician-patient co-construction of illness narratives in the medical interview. *Health Communication*, 14(3), 339–360.

Faller, K. C. (1996). A clinical sample of women who have sexually abused children. *Journal of Child Sexual Abuse*, 4(3), 13–30.

Foa, E. B. & Yadin, E. (2011). Assessment and diagnosis of posttraumatic stress disorder: An overview of measures. *Psychiatric Times*, 28, 63–71.

Groth-Marnat, G. (2009). *Handbook of psychological assessment* (5th ed.). New York: Wiley.

Hagood, M. (2000). *The use of art in counseling child and adult survivors of sexual abuse*. London: Jessica Kingsley.

Kaplan, R. M. & Saccuzzo, D. P. (2012). *Psychological testing: Principles, applications, and issues* (8th ed.). Independence, KY: Cengage Learning.

Kaufman, A. S. & Lichtenberger, E. O. (2005). *Assessing adolescent and adult intelligence* (3rd ed.). New York: Wiley.

Kerr, C. (Ed.). (2015). *Multicultural family art therapy*. New York: Routledge.

Kerr, C., Hoshino, J., Sutherland, J., Parashak, S. T., & McCarley, L. L. (2007). *Family art therapy: Foundations of theory and practice*. New York: Routledge.

Malchiodi, C. A. (1997). *Breaking the silence: Art therapy with children from violent homes* (2nd ed.). New York: Brunner/Mazel.

Maloney, M. P. & Ward, M. P. (1976). *Psychological assessment: A conceptual approach*. New York: Oxford University Press.

Meier, S. T. & Davis, S. R. (2010). *The elements of counseling* (7th ed). Independence, KY: Cengage Learning.

Nader, K. O. (2004). Assessing traumatic experiences in children and adolescents: Self-reports of DSM PTSD Criteria B-D symptoms. In J. Wilson & T. Keane (Eds.), *Assessing psychological trauma and PTSD*, (2nd ed.) New York: Guilford Press, 513–537.

Nader, K. O. (2015). *Understanding and assessing trauma in children and adolescents: measures, methods, and youth in context*. New York: Routledge.

Oster, G. D. & Caro, J. (1990). *Understanding and treating depressed adolescents and their families*. New York: Wiley.

Oster, G. D. & Crone, P. (2004). *Using drawings in assessment and therapy* (2nd ed.). New York: Taylor & Francis.

Oster, G. D. & Gould, P. (1987). *Using drawings in assessment and therapy*. New York: Brunner/Mazel.

Oster, G. D. & Montgomery, S. S. (1996). *Clinical uses of drawings*. Northvale, NJ: Jason Aronson.

Othmer, E. & Othmer, S. C. (2001). *The clinical interview using DSM-IV-TR*. Arlington, VA: American Psychiatric Press.

Posthuma, R. A., Morgeson, F. P., & Campion, M. A. (2002). Beyond employment interview validity: A comprehensive narrative review of recent research and trends over time. *Personnel Psychology, 55*(1), 1–81.

Riley, S. (1993). Illustrating the family story: Art therapy, a lens for viewing the family's reality. *The Arts in Psychotherapy, 2*, 253–264.

Rogers, C. R. (1957). The necessary and sufficient conditions of therapeutic personality change. *Journal of consulting psychology, 21*(2), 95.

Rubin, J. A. (1978). *Child art therapy*. New York: Van Nostrand Reinhold.

Sattler, J. (1997). *Clinical and forensic interviewing of children and families*. San Diego, CA: Jerome M. Sattler.

Sattler, J. (2001). *Assessment of children: Behavioral and clinical applications* (4th ed.). San Diego, CA: Jerome M. Sattler.

Sattler, J. (2006). *Assessment of Children: Behavioral and clinical applications* (5th ed.). San Diego, CA: Jerome M. Sattler.

Sattler, J. (2014). *Foundations of behavioral, social, and clinical assessment of children* (6th ed.). Jerome M. Sattler: Publisher, Inc.

Smith, H. G. (2011). *Mental status exam and brief social history in clinical psychology*. Lulu.com.

Sommers-Flanagan, J. S. & Sommers-Flanagan, R. (2013). *Clinical interviewing* (5th ed.). New York: Wiley.

Strub, R. L. & Black, F. W. (1993). *The mental status examination in neurology*. Phiadelphia, PA: FA Davis Company.

van der Kolk, B. (2014). *The body keeps the score: Brain, mind, and body in the healing of trauma*. New York: Viking.

Walker, P. (2013). *Complex ptsd: From surviving to thriving: A guide and map from recovering from childhood trauma*. New York: New Harbinger.

Weathers, F. W., Blake, D. D., Schnurr, P. P., Kaloupek, D. G., Marx, B. P., & Keane, T. M. (2013). *The clinician-administered PTSD scale for DSM–5 (CAPS-5)*. Washington, DC: US Department of Veteran Affairs.

Williams, M. B. & Poijula, S. (2013). *The ptsd workbook: Simple, effective techniques for overcoming ptsd symptoms*. New York: Harbinger.

Wilson, J. P. (2004). PTSD and complex ptsd: Symptoms, syndromes, and diagnoses. In Wilson, J. P. & Keane T. M. (Eds.). *Assessing psychological trauma and PTSD* (2nd ed.). New York: Guilford Press.

Zimmerman, S. (2013). *Interview guide for evaluation of DSM5 disorders* (2nd ed.). New York: Psychology Products Press.

6 Comprehensive Psychological Evaluations

CASE STUDY: **Max T.**

Max T. was a 12-year-old, seventh-grade student who had been achieving inconsistent grades for many years, despite an established Individual Educational Plan (IEP). Though his teachers had introduced modifications to boost his academic success (such as providing him with a small learning lab for taking exams), few improvements were seen. His teachers were increasingly baffled with his inability to express his ideas in writing, and with his progressively negative attitude towards school.

While Max did not display behavioral outbursts, he seemed constantly frustrated. During his elementary years, a pediatrician suggested that Max was on the borderline of an ADHD diagnosis, but he was never evaluated more extensively or treated. While he had received extra tutoring, he remained below grade level. Also his achievement motivation was decreasing, as his disappointments were being reflected by his constant misbehavior.

Max's teachers, case manager, and counselor determined that a thorough psycho-educational evaluation was warranted to more clearly delineate his intellectual and academic strengths and weaknesses, and to plan for more extensive services, if necessary, through an expansion of his IEP. Personality characteristics were also of interest to assess how his moodiness, impulsiveness, and low frustration tolerance might be undermining his learning progress. At the beginning of the assessment session, Max's father completed a checklist to describe Max's continued symptoms. He noted anger, anxiety, defensiveness, distractibility, irritability, and a lack of self-esteem as the primary concerns.

During the testing session, Max constructed one very poignant drawing of himself in school. In this image, he portrayed himself as sitting at his desk appearing overwhelmed (crying with his head in his hands) and wondering what to do next and how he was going to obtain help. The remainder of the evaluation provided a complete picture of Max's needs that were delineated through the report's recommendations. With this thorough documentation in hand, the treatment team and his parents were provided clear directions on how to best assist in Max's academic and social growth.

CASE STUDY: **Janette B.**

Janette B. was 15 years old when she was admitted to the psychiatric unit of a community hospital. She was first brought to the emergency department via ambulance after telling her mother that she had overdosed on assorted medications found in her jewelry box (for instance, Vicodin and Benadryl). According to the ER reports, Janette was experiencing a "bad day," for which she apparently had many. During an initial clinical interview, she expressed feelings of estrangement and thinking that no one understood her. At that time, it seemed obvious that she was exhibiting significant signs of depression and anxiety; including social awkwardness and hopeless feelings with suicidal thoughts.

Janette mentioned at intake that she always attempted to hide her true self and was mistrustful of her peers. A drawing constructed of "her world" displayed many barriers between herself and others at school, as well as in her neighborhood. She stated that she was uncomfortable in school and did not like to work in the classrooms. She admitted to many instances of suicide ideation during the past month and thought that she would be "better off dead." The most recent attempt that brought her to the hospital seemed more intentional and purposeful compared to past behaviors, where she was seen walking carelessly on a busy road.

When placed on the unit, Janette was referred for a psychological evaluation to gain a clearer understanding of her cognitive and emotional assets and vulnerabilities. Assessment questions pertained to what degree her mood experiences were interfering with her daily functioning and to assist in treatment direction and aftercare planning. She had been previously assessed at a younger age, diagnosed with ADHD, and stated that she "had always been hyperactive, inattentive, and forgetful." Apparently, these characteristics that were basically left untreated contributed to her decreased functioning and lowered self-esteem.

PSYCHOLOGICAL TESTING WITHIN THE ASSESSMENT PROCESS

Behavioral health professionals who perform clinical interviews, diagnostic evaluations, and psychological testing attempt to explain their clients' range of presenting problems. Through various techniques, they assess current cognitive and emotional functioning in order to integrate a deeper understanding into applicable conclusions and appropriate interventions (Oster & Crone, 2004). Once referral questions have been clarified, interviews conducted, and diagnostic impressions considered, questions might still remain regarding the need for specific information and documentation that will determine a particular classroom accommodation, degree of deterioration in functioning, or the need for specialized residential, rehabilitative, or aftercare programs. Through self-report questionnaires, behavioral observations, and the administration of intellectual and neuropsychological tests, educational batteries, personality inventories, and projective techniques (like drawing directives), a comprehensive depiction of performance based on normative data and the examiner's judgment and experience is created from client responses. This global picture can then detail specific strength and weaknesses and more accurately summarize and clarify diagnostic conjectures (Gregory, 2013; Urbina, 2014).

In many instances, especially regarding school-aged children, psychologists receive messages from parents and guardians whose children have been referred by a school professional for psychological and educational evaluations (Brenner & Oster, 2013). These caretakers are usually surprised, and almost always uncertain, about the reasons for the referral. "How can these test results be helpful?" "What do you mean it will provide objective data—don't we already have enough?" "How can this benefit my child's IEP when modifications have recently been made?" Apprehensions about cost, necessity, and introducing extra family information also come into question.

As described in the first case study (Max T.), referrals for psychological and further educational evaluations are made when, despite preliminary investigation and classroom modifications, it remains unclear why the student continues to fall behind academically, or acts out his or her distress in an avoidant or disruptive manner. By requesting this comprehensive assessment, parents and teachers can remove any degree of guesswork that might still be present regarding the child's true struggles. Test results can more effectively clarify what is behind the expressions of learning or emotional difficulties, and what can be done to rectify the issues and bring the child to his or her full potential.

Additionally, broad-based testing can delineate a more accurate portrait of important challenges and concerns about a student's attention span, visual-motor integration abilities, and copying efficiency, as deficits in these functional areas of cognitive development are often at the root of learning struggles and disabilities (Brenner & Oster, 2013; Oster, 2013). A clearer understanding of the child's struggles with these vulnerabilities based on a thorough evaluation becomes invaluable to the parents, as well as school officials. The resulting data and interpretations help to explain behavioral acting out during class, for example, or why "Johnny" is not completing assignments on time.

If the referrals stem from a parent or guardian, someone in the child's school (such as a recent teacher or counselor), or an outside practitioner (for example, a tutor, pediatrician, or therapist) who is puzzled regarding proper diagnosis or treatment direction might want to review the need for further testing. Common questions might include:

- How can testing properly diagnose ADHD symptoms?
- Could my child have a specific learning disability?
- We know our child has great learning potential, so why is she not doing better with classroom assignments?
- Is my child depressed?
- Is my child too anxious while taking tests to perform well?
- Why is my student having so much trouble socializing with his peers?
- How can an evaluation help us discover the best plan of action?

A wide-ranging battery of psychological tests can provide insight into a child's (or adult's) emotional functioning—this includes details about an individual's personality structure and how it impacts his or her academic or work demands, as well as current symptoms that may need to be addressed through counseling or, if necessary, medication. One very important benefit of further examining is that, once psychologists have obtained the results and begin to understand the client's underlying performance issues, they can construct individually tailored recommendations for interventions and treatment directions. Suggestions can be provided for new classroom accommodations (such as having a volunteer assigned to a child or gaining access to teacher notes), or adaptations at work to overcome sensory or attention problems. In fact, psychological testing is often required to provide these or other specialized services, such as speech or occupational therapy.

REQUESTS FROM TREATING PROFESSIONALS

Many requests for psychological testing also stem from psychiatrists, pediatricians, fellow clinicians, and adult clients who are seeking added information to clarify diagnoses, or perhaps changes in medication. Documentation of the degree of moodiness, impulsivity, attention span, and suicide risk are all relevant requests for this type of specialized information. Referrals may also come from lawyers and the court system to rule out mental illness, assess deterioration in functioning following automobile accidents, evaluate for disability services, and conduct investigations of parental suitability during custody disagreements, as well as to assess willingness for treatment interventions. They can additionally stem from Employee Assistance Program personnel to conduct "Fitness for Duty Evaluations" on such individuals as law enforcement officers or pilots. These latter assessments often attempt to document such aspects of functioning as declining performance, decision making, or malingering.

In the other example at the beginning of this chapter, Janette B. was evaluated within an inpatient setting at the request of the unit psychiatrist. In that situation, documentation was needed to clarify her diagnosis, as well as to provide evidence to the insurance company of her need to remain within a restricted setting. As most admissions to this particular adolescent unit were for only two days, it appeared that her intent toward self-harm was very serious and more than just an impulsive action. However, more objective testing was requested from the prescribing physician and required by the insurance company to justify a lengthier stay. After a thorough assessment, it was determined that detaining her for extra days was pertinent and valuable for her protection, in addition to planning for her aftercare.

CASE STUDY: **Carlos B.**

Another example, Carlos B., aged 39, was a self-referral for psychological testing. His main complaints surrounded issues of low frustration tolerance, increased irritability around seasonal changes, anxiousness within crowded settings, and mood changes ranging from energetic to "down periods." He had recently seen his oldest child placed on medication for ADHD with positive results and wondered about his own symptoms and possible interventions. Before soliciting evaluations from psychiatrists and not really wanting to be placed on medication, he wanted to obtain a clear view of his concerns and whether psychological testing could clarify possible ADHD symptoms, or something else related to his mood such as Bipolar issues or Seasonal Affective Disorder. A thorough history was conducted and plans for cognitive and personality tests were initiated.

RESPONDING TO REFERRAL QUESTIONS

As mentioned earlier, referrals for psychological testing derive from a variety of sources: including physicians (usually pediatricians or psychiatrists, though also from primary care doctors); the legal system (judges, lawyers, probation officers); or directly from other mental health professionals (social workers, psychiatric nurses, professional counselors, expressive therapists). Referrals are also made by educational officials and often directly by families, usually due to the presence of disruptive behaviors within the family, at school or at work (Oster et al., 1988). Underlying the referral questions are the need for supplemental knowledge that would clarify diagnostic decisions, detail strengths and weaknesses, clarify deficits in functioning, recommend a specific type of treatment service or educational placement, and/or measure treatment or academic progress.

The first step in assessing any individual is to clearly delineate these initial questions from the referring source and elucidate the probable expectations. When working within a multidisciplinary setting or a broader health or legal system, there is usually a high degree of variability in sophistication regarding knowledge of child development, experience with severe psychopathology in adults, and a general awareness of capabilities and limitations of psychological testing. Referral questions often come in vague terms (for instance, "I need a psychological"), and underscore the confusion surrounding both the presenting behaviors and concerns of the identified client as well as the benefits that could be secured from the assessment process.

Those individuals making referrals often have many unanswered questions in mind (for example, "Is this teenager reacting to past trauma?" "Can this person maintain their current work duties?" or "Why is my child lazy") that may not lend themselves to being directly addressed through a brief interview. The primary requirement from the psychological examiner is to further clarify these initial questions and to amplify the interactive process and what might result from these queries. To gain maximum benefit, it becomes incumbent upon the examiner to communicate effectively with the referring professionals or parents in order to pinpoint objectives from their requests. It also becomes salient to direct their questions, and the subsequent testing and report, toward providing appropriate conclusions to better meet the needs of the client.

Psychologists and other clinicians engaged in the assessment process are aided by referral sources who supply clear, concise, and direct statements, verbally or in writing. These statements could include why a particular youth or adult is being referred, what is known about the person (and family), and of special importance—what expectations does the referral source have concerning the examiner and the results of the assessment (Gabel, Oster, & Butnik, 1986). Most importantly, it needs to be emphasized that the responsibility for gathering this information clearly lies with the individual conducting the evaluation. And it becomes especially pertinent for the clinician to assist the referral sources in organizing their questions in such a manner as to specify what issues can readily be answered by psychological testing and what questions are beyond the scope of the assessment process. Also, the examiner needs to become aware of the choices confronted by the referral source (for instance, will the results be used to determine delinquent or school placement, disability decisions, or direction in clarifying diagnosis for medication?).

Specific information to be solicited from the referral sources needs to include the following requests:

- *What is the nature of the presenting problem as understood by the referral source?* For instance, if a family is requesting a psychological evaluation, what is the major complaint and how will the evaluation be used? If a physician is requesting diagnostic information, will the data be used to determine therapeutic direction or medication effectiveness?
- *At what point in the contact with the referral source is this request for diagnostic assistance being made?* For example, a residential treatment program requests an assessment for intake requirements or towards the end of treatment to help in placement decisions.
- *What prior assessments have been completed?* Often referrals are received without the knowledge of previous evaluations having been provided in the recent past. It is essential to request from the referral source all known past testing, or if the opportunity arises review the medical records before making an appointment. Not only do tests become invalid when given frequently, but they become a waste of valuable time and money when the information already known is valid to answer any questions that have arisen.
- *What is going to be the role of the examiner after the evaluation and report have been completed?* Will the psychologist be expected to review the results directly with the client or family, and will the referral source brief the client, family, or other professionals on the results?

CASE STUDY: **Malcolm S.**

Malcolm S. was a 6-year-old, first grade public school student referred for a psychological evaluation at an outpatient clinic by his parents to clarify whether attention weaknesses, learning delays, or emotional factors might be hindering his academic potential and interpersonal maturation. There had been expressed concerns by his teachers regarding Malcolm's inattention, anxiety, and moodiness. He apparently struggled in his beginning efforts at reading and writing, and was starting to show aversions toward expressing his knowledge in the classroom. He was also very tentative in new situations and displayed much nervousness in social situations.

According to his mother, Malcolm appeared to be a perfectionist, was overly sensitive, and did not like to be judged. Additionally, he demonstrated much displeasure around loud noises. She viewed him as distractible and anxious, and he was especially worried about revealing his weaknesses despite appearing quite capable in math, loving science, and displaying a good memory. He also reportedly had a difficult time focusing for any length of time and would become restless and off task when attempting to complete in-class assignments or homework.

Malcolm's vulnerabilities seemed to undermine his confidence and he sometimes felt like a failure, causing him to withdraw into himself. Before the testing was initiated, the psychologist contacted the parents to clarify their expectations of the results and to discover whether the findings would be needed for placement decisions during individualized educational planning meetings. The psychologist also needed to clarify whether the family was expecting her to attend these school meetings or contact the school professionals. Additionally, informed consents were gathered to communicate with the child's teachers and school counselor.

IDENTIFYING PRESENTING PROBLEMS

In everyday practice, referral sources may have many unanswered questions about the behavior of their troubled and struggling clients. Generally, they must seek extra data in the form of standardized testing from those professionals who conduct such evaluations (Gabel et al., 1986; Oster et al., 1988). Health and mental health clinicians who initiate referrals, whether they be pediatricians, primary care physicians, social service workers, school counselors, or other behavioral health personnel, have specific concerns that necessitate further inquiry. At the point of referral, they need to determine whether additional interventions are necessary and viable. And in the case of family referrals, it also becomes a matter of cost and its worth: whether they realize what is involved and the likely end product.

This judgment in determining whether comprehensive testing is required is most salient within a managed care environment that oftentimes limits the number of tests or days in treatment. This process of decision making relies on many considerations and sources, but mainly on clinicians who routinely conduct intake interviews (e.g., social workers, professional counselors) and initial diagnostic evaluations (e.g., psychiatrists and psychologists). Other clinicians, such as expressive therapists and substance abuse counselors, are often included in this process when they are part of a multidisciplinary team to add their perspectives to this information-gathering phase of diagnostic clarification.

In order for effective treatment to occur, a client's presenting problems must be clearly identified and interventions delineated that offer deeper understanding, clarity of symptoms, and practical solutions. For example, it becomes imperative for the referring agents to plainly state the reasons why someone in emotional turmoil may require emergency services or hospitalization, or why a physician or another health or mental health professional may be referring a client to an outpatient clinic or a private practitioner for psychological evaluation. In many cases, a "drawing" requested from the referral source characterizing emotional hurt, examples of being bullied, or suicidal thoughts might begin the recommendation for further testing. And with this clearer view of presenting problem areas, various paths toward treatment recommendations based on more comprehensive testing could be undertaken.

Even within a brief treatment setting, it sometimes becomes imperative to take a sufficient amount of time for an accurate and thorough evaluation. Referring practitioners need relevant client portraits that can be succinctly communicated to all clinicians who are involved in case management or treatment. To access this knowledge and document it accordingly, information needs to be gathered by a) clarifying questions from the referral source; b) conducting a thorough review of background history; c) observing behaviour; d) providing self-report questionnaires; and e) determining intellectual capabilities and personality traits by administering objective and projective tests.

THE ROLE OF PSYCHOLOGISTS

Psychologists as behavioral health providers play a major role in understanding how biological, behavioral, and social factors influence health, and illness (Gregory, 2013; Urbina, 2014). They are equipped with training, skills, and knowledge to understand how basic behavioral and cognitive processes (e.g., cognition. emotion, motivation, development, personality, social and cultural interaction) prepare the body to develop normally or begin to exhibit dysfunctions. They are also instructed to perceive how these behavioral and cognitive functions are altered, the factors that contribute to their alteration, and how these symptoms are diagnosed and treated. In dealing with such problems, they are skilled to use psycho-diagnostic and psychotherapeutic techniques that help and affect the abilities of individuals to function more effectively in diverse settings and roles.

Psychologists bring this unique expertise into the assessment decision-making process after attempts have already been made to determine an individual's degree of intrapsychic distress, but remaining questions persist and more certainty is needed for diagnostic clarity or treatment direction. With added documentation that characterizes psychological evaluations, the referral source can make much more informed and relevant recommendations toward treatment options. Through this comprehensive testing process, specific strengths and liabilities are noted so that effective planning can evolve into suitable action, whether through medication evaluations or changes, school or work accommodations, or therapeutic interventions. The methods and procedures chosen during this process become more important than mere diagnostic tools—they guide practitioners and their clients on a path toward healthy problem solutions. And when drawings are included in the test battery, opportunities arise for enhanced communication and sharing through nonverbal images (Oster & Crone, 2004).

The two following case examples provide even more clarity to this process and illustrate how referrals can be initiated and shaped into testable questions.

CASE STUDY: Deborah M.

Deborah M was a 14-year-old youngster who was entering ninth grade at a public school. She was referred for psychological testing to determine her current intellectual and educational status, as well as specify any emotional issues that might be obstructing her progress. There were also expressed concerns regarding Deborah's overwhelming anxiety when approaching new situations. She apparently struggled excessively when faced with novel transitions and was becoming quite tentative in even minor risk taking. For Deborah, the transition into high school seemed overwhelming.

According to Deborah's mother (who called about the evaluation), Deborah was experiencing panic attacks during her initial adjustment to high school. After attending a few weeks in September, she began to display school refusal. Although she had been selected for an honors program in biotechnology, she felt ill-prepared for the amount of work that was required, resisted any attempts at participation, and fell considerably behind in the expected work demands. Furthermore, she appeared easily angered, irritable, and oppositional to the point of threatening her family and exhibiting self-destructive actions. Ultimately, social services and the police intervened.

Before a testing appointment was established, the psychologist obtained permission to contact the school where it was discovered that a brief diagnostic interview had already occurred. Even though they had gathered considerable initial information (including a family drawing characterizing the household in turmoil), they required further intellectual and personality testing to establish clear direction and conclusions. Through the phone call, it was also discovered that several school interventions had been attempted but failed. The school officials were able to articulate the specific information that they needed to offer alternative services and individualized accommodations for Deborah. At that point, the psychologist was more effectively able to tailor a testing battery that would answer their questions and provide a baseline for future treatment alternatives if needed.

CASE STUDY: Charles L.

Charles L. was a 24-year-old male who was brought to the emergency room of a local hospital by his parents after it was discovered that he emailed "goodbye" notes to family members. He had planned to stay at his own apartment after work on the day of admission to shoot himself with a gun he had purchased online. When initially evaluated on the unit, Charles had stated that he loaded two bullets into his handgun just in case the first bullet did not kill him. He did not follow through with his threat, though, because he wanted to see his family one more time. When the family read the email notes, they immediately came to Charles's house and subsequently called the suicide hotline.

Although Charles acknowledged a two- to three-year history of depression, he had not received recent outpatient treatment and had never been hospitalized previously for behavioral or emotional difficulties. He mentioned that he had been conflicted over having little direction in his future and reported feeling overwhelmed by work expectations and everyday life stressors. He also stated that he had a difficult time fitting in socially. In the past several months he had felt extremely lonely and isolated. A drawing revealing his depressed condition before his admission reflected these feelings of estrangement from his world. The pencil sketch portrayed him appearing puzzled and sad in a corner of a dark room looking out the window with a gun by a bed table.

Charles had apparently ordered his gun in the springtime when he started experiencing thoughts of suicide. Due to the lengthy background check, he did not receive the gun until the fall months.

After receiving it, he felt "relieved" because he stated that he could kill himself whenever he chose the time. When first entering the hospital, he explained that he regretted that he did not follow through on his plans. During his initial interview, he disclosed that he had been diagnosed with ADHD by his primary care physician and provided stimulant medication. However, this intervention reportedly increased his moodiness, especially the experiences of depressed feelings.

The psychologist on call for testing first met with the psychiatrist to review the symptoms and gain his view of the situation, as well as the need for all-inclusive testing. It was discovered that the psychiatrist had talked to the patient's primary care physician regarding past medication side effects. With this in mind, he was uncomfortable starting Charles on different medications without further data determining his mood disturbance and whether there were any signs of psychosis. The psychiatrist was also concerned about the degree of suicidal risk. This conversation between the psychologist and psychiatrist clarified the need for further assessment.

PUZZLES THAT NEED SOLUTIONS

In the above examples, the primary referral sources (that is, a mother, a school counselor, and a psychiatrist) had many questions regarding diagnostic indicators and alternative directions for treatment and interventions. To accurately gauge the degree of disturbance, pertinent information was needed to assist the examiner determine the extent of the presenting problems. First and foremost, the need for communication became necessary to explore the background history, access previous evaluations, and assess current status in order to determine the direction of assessment.

The answers to referral questions always lie within an elaborate puzzle. As these case studies pointed out, numerous bits of data were required and collected to clarify an overall picture of a person's cognitive and emotional functioning. A carefully designed evaluation provides the framework for the pieces to fit accurately into this overall portrait. The process of interviewing and testing, including multiple avenues of assessment (that should include drawing directives for nonverbal expression) establishes a broad baseline of verbal and nonverbal information that allows direction for decision making, treatment planning, and desired changes.

The gathering and documentation of background history, clarification with referral sources, behavioral observations, diagnostic interviewing, and test results supply everyone involved with the client an active treatment direction where change can then be effectively measured. Even these diagnostic and assessment sessions with the client are themselves a form of therapeutic intervention, and the decision to interview or administer a particular battery of tests must consider the possible influence it will have on the client. The beginning interviews and initial techniques that are used have the potential to initiate an individual's self-examination and self-reflection, producing alternative views of his or her life and possible resolutions of problems.

The final objective in this comprehensive evaluation consists of integrating all responses into an organized and clearly written report. This document profiles the client's strengths and weaknesses, indicates how these characteristics interact in everyday functioning, and culminates with short- and long-term goals and objectives. With this working knowledge, direction for gathering accurate diagnosis and treatment planning can then be communicated to all treating professionals. The resulting written portrait of the client or patient allows the primary therapist or referral source to pinpoint the problems, explain the findings, and target specific symptoms for intervention relief.

PRINCIPLES OF PSYCHOLOGICAL TESTING

Psychological testing refers to all possible uses, applications, and underlying concepts of psychological and educational measures (Kaplan & Saccuzzo, 2012). Such techniques assess individual differences in ability and emotional resources and assume that the variance described from these measures reflects actual distinctions among individuals. The fundamental ideas that determine these differences are based on statistical concepts such as *reliability* of the measurements (that is, its accuracy and consistency over time) and *validity* (or usefulness). Other principles consist of how a particular test is constructed and administered. As with any test (including the use of drawing techniques) there is controversy, especially surrounding its reliability, bias against certain cultural or minority groups, and the ethics of its usage.

Since each client is unique and the types of referral questions and problem behaviors differ, many types of measures have been developed. Psychological tests have been constructed for individuals, as well as groups. These techniques can also be categorized according to what is being assessed. For instance, some ability measures are scored in terms of speed, accuracy, or both. By contrast, achievement tests mostly reflect previous school learning. Other measures have also been developed to assess aptitude; referring to the potential to learn and not necessarily the individual's current progress. Intellectual tests usually combine these goals by incorporating verbal dexterity, general knowledge, and nonverbal problem-solving items, in addition to assessing auditory and visual memory, attention span, abstract reasoning, mental flexibility, fine-motor integration, and copying speed.

Personality tests, on the other hand, attempt to describe an individual's tendency to display a particular behavior or reveal how he or she responds during a given situation. These measures are more likely to demonstrate a person's emotional capacities when confronted by stressful circumstances, or describe his or her inner feelings when faced with a new or challenging event. Personality techniques are usually divided between structured ones (self-report inventories or questionnaires) and projectives (where the stimulus is novel or ambiguous). Thus, when clients are requested to respond to an inkblot or construct a drawing, their answers are not forced by a "yes/no" decision or a rating continuum, rather they respond in a spontaneous and very unique way based on their personal perceptions and personal histories.

COMPONENTS OF PSYCHOLOGICAL EVALUATIONS

The introduction of psychological testing after initial interviews have been completed and relevant background history gathered often provides a broader and more objective determination of the skills and performance of clients based on age norms, as well as a more complete portrait of their emotional resources and inner experiences. The primary value of psychological tests lies within their objectivity, whether they attempt to reduce the possible distortions that frequently occur in clinical judgments through omissions and subjective biases (Berger, 1976). Additionally, comprehensive testing with numerous procedures allows for greater interpersonal engagement between examiner and client to adequately assess an individual's behavioral and expressed symptoms, personality style, intelligence, and perceptions of his or her world (Anastasi & Urbina, 1997). Because answers to referral questions can be complicated, they often cannot be adequately addressed during one interview session or by simply introducing and interpreting one technique. They need to consider other relevant information that is gathered through extensive testing of intelligence, achievement, behavior, and personality that more accurately portrays the entire person. Only through a consensus-building perspective derived from a comprehensive, multi-method evaluation can clinicians be more certain of their impressions to accurately provide diagnostic impressions, plan for classroom or work accommodations, or initiate therapeutic interventions.

To assist in the process of psychological testing, extensive techniques have been created to a) measure intelligence (e.g., the Wechsler Intelligence Scale for Children, 5th version, Wechsler, 2014; Kaufman Adolescent and Adult Intelligence Test, Kaufman & Kaufman, 1993); b) screen for brain impairment (e.g., the Bender Visual–Motor Gestalt Test; Bender, 1962); c) gauge educational attainment (e.g., the Wide Range Achievement Test 3rd edition, Jastak & Jastak, 1993); d) describe behavioral characteristics; e) assess trauma experiences; f) evaluate severe emotional disturbance (e.g., the Rorschach Test, Rorschach, 1942); and g) address personality styles (e.g., the revised Minnesota Multiphasic Personality Inventory, MMP-2, Butcher, Dahlstrom, & Graham et al., 1989; and the Personality Assessment Inventory, PAI, Morey, 1991). With the abundance of information derived from these tests, a more complete portrait of the person's intrapsychic and interpersonal dynamics that have contributed to his or her distress and the issues leading to the original referral questions can be identified and provided.

SELECTING A TEST BATTERY

The decision as to which tests to administer varies according to referral questions, the referral source and agency involved, time constraints, and other situational factors. A battery of tests is usually selected in order to permit the examiner the opportunity to observe performances in a vast array of problem-solving situations and allow clients to express their abilities, learning preferences, emotional resources, and personality style. Responses from an individual technique cannot be expected to answer all the relevant questions that have been posed by the clinicians attempting to formulate a diagnosis and treatment strategy. Additionally, no single instrument can measure all abilities of an individual, some of which are hidden or undermined by the presenting symptoms.

Most psychologists tend to reuse the same set of tests by which they have been trained and gained comfort with a reference of typical answers. Through repeated usage, these measures provide the psychologist with a baseline for comparing normal versus abnormal responding and functioning. Although a particular set of tests may be useful in delineating problems areas in most clinical cases, there are many instances in which a variety of other specialized tests are needed for handicapping conditions. For instance, the use of nonverbal tests for language-disabled people is one such example. The examiner needs to be aware of these alternative tests, in addition to being kept informed of new tests being developed and revised normative data being collected on existing measures. By keeping abreast of developments in the field of psychometrics, examiners can enhance their usefulness to their clients and referral sources.

Besides the usual tests of intelligence, achievement, and personality, the realization of the complexity between brain and behavior has initiated a movement in psychology toward the uses of extended neuropsychological batteries. These groups of individual tests attempt to assess specific deficits in abilities relating to motor coordination, memory, attention, flexibility in thinking, and other problems in information processing. Since most individuals present with multifaceted difficulties, neuropsychological testing can often be more sensitive to brain damage or specific learning disabilities, and can be more objective in its results.

In general, the development and use of psychological tests entails a series of interrelated steps ranging from theoretical assumptions, item development and choice, and statistical methodology, to normative investigations (Oster et al., 1988). This process evolves beyond the initial scale construction to continual refinements in order to enhance the general usability of the device. This constant upgrading is required since no one test is ideal, and each setting, individual need, and group is different (Gregory, 2013; Urbina, 2014). The ideal in test development includes research that guarantees that a particular test is appropriate to a specific sample, a particular cohort, and a variety of clinical issues, in addition to empirical feedback that helps ensure maximum clinical utility.

Intellectual Assessment

Referrals for psychological evaluations frequently include questions that can only be answered by assessment of both intellectual and academic functioning. Given the central place of school performance in a child or adolescent's life, questions concerning behavioral and emotional problems, as well as academic achievement, require information surrounding cognitive abilities and actual levels of school achievement. The examiner, therefore, needs to be familiar with the technical aspects of both types of assessment and with the broader issues surrounding their use.

Part of the continuing controversy over the use of intelligence tests stems from the lack of an agreed-upon definitions of the concept of intelligence. And in fact IQ scores are not direct measures of innate intelligence. Rather, they are imperfect measures of a limited sample of maturational abilities at a particular point in time compared to same-aged peers. The varied tests are subject to change over time and sensitive to what people have been exposed to through interactions with their cultures (Gregory, 2013; Urbina, 2014). Therefore, IQ scores are estimates of an individual's current level of functioning on the types of tasks included in the assessment. Most commonly used intelligence tests measure verbal abilities, fluid reasoning, perceptual organizational skills, mental focus and flexibility, and fine motor coordination and speed as well as sustained concentration. And revised measures, such as the Wechsler Intelligence Scale for Children (5th ed) (WISC-V), even have a computer tablet-form version that may tap other skills. These tests, however, do not adequately measure other abilities that might be considered "intelligent"—for example, musical talent, mechanical aptitude, and artistic abilities. In today's culture, rarely are decisions made on merely IQ scores; yet they are an important component of broader-based evaluations that determine inclusion or exclusion to certain settings or programs.

Academic Achievement

The assessment of academic functioning is often an integral part of the comprehensive psychological assessment. When combined with measures of cognitive functioning, the information from an academic assessment can answer questions concerning school progress or underachievement, learning disabilities, or readiness for post-secondary education. A seemingly sudden deterioration in a youngster's school performance, for instance, will frequently occasion a referral for psychological testing. In such cases, the insertion of an academic assessment can assist substantially in determining the nature of the difficulty. And while most severe learning disorders will have been identified before adolescence, some students will have been overlooked and their struggles will only gradually be noticed during middle school. Even in cases where learning disabilities are identified at an early age, reassessment during the teenage years can explicate current patterns of skill development and suggest new educational goals.

Psychologists often include in their test batteries a brief measure of academic functioning, such as the Wide Range Achievement Test (Wilkinson & Robertson, 2006), or the Peabody Individual Achievement Test (Markwardt, 1989). These tests serve a screening function by providing rough estimates of the individual's progress in a number of important subject areas. When a more extensive assessment of functioning is needed, a lengthier battery of tests is usually provided. These more extensive measures usually include the Woodcock–Johnson Psycho-education batteries or the Wechsler Individual Achievement Tests (cited Gregory, 2013; Urbina, 2014) and are composed of a cognitive cluster of tests, and specific subtests of achievement in such areas as language skills, science, math, and humanities.

Neuropsychological Testing

At times, the standard battery of intellectual and achievement testing may not be sufficient to confront subtle deficits of a frontal lobe syndrome: for example, where signs of lacking initiative or blunted social sensibility may be viewed as behavior weaknesses, as opposed to any specific patterns of test scores alluding to brain impairment. In these circumstances, psychologists administer ancillary tests beyond their core battery to test hypotheses that were developed and still remain unanswered during the evaluation. An example of this approach is to use a test of mental flexibility (e.g., the Wisconsin Card Sorting Test (Berg, 1948) to more clearly define the problem. A simple test of concept formation and the ability to shift sets, this test will demonstrate the struggles of utilizing feedback that someone may exhibit who has minor (or major) deficits in their executive functioning. The Auditory-Verbal Learning Test (Taylor, 1959) is another example of adding select tests to a core battery when questions about behavior and performance are still unanswered. This neuropsychological measure is a useful test of auditory-verbal memory that attempts to assess immediate recall, learning after rehearsal, and the ability to remember over time following intervening activities.

Trained neuropsychologists might also provide more complete batteries of tests. These tests, like the Halstead–Reitan Neuropsychological Battery (Reitan, 1985), attempt to detect deficits in such areas as speech sounds and motor flexibility. An overall impairment index is calculated, along with specific cutoff scores that might reveal specific deficit areas in need of specialized intervention. Another popular battery of tests is the Luria–Nebraska Neuropsychological Battery (Golden, Hammeke, & Pruisch, 1980). These techniques examine motor, tactile, and visual functioning, rhythm and pitch, receptive and expressive language, basic achievement tasks, as well as aspects of attention, memory, and learning. Because of their expense and the time needed to undertake such an evaluation, neuropsychological batteries are best suited for clients who have experienced physical trauma to assess baselines before and after treatment interventions.

Personality Inventories

The goal of administering personality inventories is to assess client traits that are descriptive of possible emotional disorders and to determine how these traits relate to the presenting problems. Psychologists have developed paper-and-pencil and computerized self-report questionnaires that attempt to measure interpersonal, motivation, and attitudinal characteristics. These structured tests attempt to be objective by taking an individual's pattern of responses and comparing these answers to specific reference groups (for instance, other depressed or hospitalized individuals within the same age group).

The most widely used and most researched of these personality inventories is the Minnesota Multiphasic Personality Inventory (MMPI). The MMPI was revised in 1989, and MMPI-2, which incorporated a number of culturally relevant features, has continued the tradition of the original method as a preeminent multiscale personality inventory (Butcher, Dahlstrom, & Graham, 1989). It was constructed to assist in the identification of severe psychopathology. Besides clinical scales like Depression or Schizophrenia, recent additions have focused on substance abuse and ego strength. The MMPI-2 also assesses the wide range of problems typically seen in the clinical presentation of PTSD and provides sophisticated methods for detecting malingering and other types of response bias.

Another popular personality inventory is the Personality Assessment Inventory (PAI; Morey, 2007). Developed in 1991, the PAI has grown rapidly in popularity in clinical, research, and forensic settings. Studies that have emerged indicate that the PAI has considerable promise and is very useful as a research and clinical tool with trauma survivors. As with MMPI-2, the PAI rigorously evaluates various forms of response bias, assesses a wide range of comorbid syndromes, and contains a specialized PTSD scale. The PAI provides a straightforward assessment of contemporary constructs related to diagnosis and clinical management.

Behavior Rating Scales

Another useful objective method for obtaining preliminary information is the use of behavior problem checklists and rating scales. These forms are usually completed by parents, teachers, or other direct caretakers. The collected information screens for the incidence and severity of presenting problems, as well as serving as a platform for further discussion with the client or family. Besides these screening functions, these descriptive rating forms can be used to pinpoint target behaviors (such as ADHD) for intervention purposes, provide a way to monitor progress, and conduct evaluations for treatment effectiveness. Through the uses of such forms, clinicians can survey a vast number of activities in a timely fashion, then concentrate on specific behaviors through the successive stages of the assessment process.

The Achenbach Child Behavior Checklist (Achenbach & Rescorla, 2001) is a prime example of this method. The scale assesses social competence as well as behavioral difficulties. Areas of interpersonal relations, extracurricular activities, and academic performance are just a few of the areas that it reviews. Another popular rating form, especially in the school system, is the Behavior Assessment System for Children 2nd Edition (BASC-2) (Reynolds & Kamphaus, 2015). It is a norm-referenced diagnostic tool designed to assess the behavior and self-perceptions of children and young adults aged 2 to 25 years. It is completed by clients as well as caretakers. The scale is a multidimensional and multi-method tool that measures numerous behavioral and personality characteristics. Such aspects of functioning as activities of daily living, effective communication, adaptability, and hyperactivity are just a few of the areas assessed.

Projective Techniques

Projective measures are designed to allow clients to respond to ambiguous designs or situations in such a way to reveal hidden emotions and internal conflicts. In essence, individuals are "projecting" their own thoughts and feelings onto the presented material. This situation is vastly different than merely responding to a questionnaire or objective test seeking certain answers. While the responses may be analyzed subjectively based onthe clinician's experiences, there have also been many attempts at standardizing the scoring systems of these measures. These techniques have a long history with their origins existing in psychoanalysis theory that emphasizes unconscious attitudes and motivations.

Advocates of projective tests emphasize the ambiguity of the situation and argue that clients can express themselves on a deeper level through this method as compared with straightforward questions related to specific symptoms. These indirect techniques allow spontaneity that is beyond immediate awareness, such that they reduce the temptation to fake, do not depend entirely on verbal abilities, and underscore both conscious and unconscious personality traits.

The most popular of these methods is the Rorschach Test (Rorschach, 1942). Clients respond to 10 inkblots and their answers are then interpreted through either their sequences (process interpretation) or by complex scoring systems (typically Exner,1995). The Rorschach is used to address referral questions related to personality traits and emotional resources. The method remains one of the most widely used among psychologists. The main difficulty in utilizing this test in today's world is its proliferation of the images, which have be seen and discussed in movies or on the internet.

Another popular projective technique is the Thematic Apperception Test (TAT, or story telling test). The TAT was developed during the 1930s by the American psychologist Henry A. Murray and lay psychoanalyst Christiana D. Morgan at the Harvard University Clinic (Aronow, Weiss, & Rezinkoff, 2001). Like the Rorschach, its main purpose is to explore the underlying dynamics of personality. This method asks clients to relate a complete story based on a series of cards that picture people or objects in various situations. In this regard, the clients tend to interpret ambiguous situations in accordance with their own past experiences and current motivations. Murray reasoned that by asking people to tell a story about a picture, their emotional defenses to the examiner would be lowered and they would not realize the personal information that was being divulged in their created stories.

The TAT is popularly known as the *picture interpretation technique.* Clients are asked to tell a complete story with a beginning, middle, and end for each picture presented. They are often queried about what is happening in the story, what the characters are thinking and feeling, and how will the story end. Many of the picture cards pull for certain themes, such as academic motivation, frustration tolerance, competition, jealousy, aggression, depression, and suicide.

A similar version for children and young adolescents, the Roberts Apperception Test (Roberts, 1994) was developed later. Most themes are similar in content, but address some situations related specifically to childhood, such as parental response to misbehavior, or peer relationships.

DRAWINGS IN THE TEST BATTERY

As part of the psychological testing process, drawing directives have become key elements in generating working hypotheses during the assessment sessions concerning organic dysfunction, learning difficulties, and emotional distress (Hammer, 1997; Handler & Thomas, 2013). Drawings provide the examiner with extraordinarily valuable information when used as supplements to traditional psychological batteries and historical information. Observing the actions during drawing and interpreting the important cognitive and emotional indicators within the constructions also offers an abundant and rich source of documentation about the individual's strengths and weaknesses and style of relating to the world. Graphic images reveal a realm of pertinent information that is beyond most observations, objective measurements, or personality questionnaires; that is, the dimension of inner fantasy and imagination (Klepsch & Logie, 1982), as well as a pathway to explore the client's inner struggles (Oster & Gould, 1987; Oster & Montgomery, 1996; Oster & Crone, 2004). Even when talking through the images, these drawings offer salient opportunities to gauge hidden worries, interpersonal conflicts, and hopes about the future.

As highlighted throughout much of this book, the visual symbols derived from various drawing directives offer an entry point into the subjective world of clients that may differ substantially from what was read from their background history, observed through their behavior, or presented by their verbal presentation. After initial evaluations and later in the assessment process, these graphic renderings can be used as a baseline to judge progress or deterioration. Their special value remains, though, as clinical tools and as adjunctive interviewing devices that stimulate diagnostic impressions, gain different avenues for discussions, and provide assessment direction surrounding cognitive functioning and personality traits. With the use of drawings providing this supplemental knowledge, examiners acquire greater insights into the conceptual and emotional responses of the client and can provide more effective feedback to the referral source (Leibowitz, 1999).

Drawings for assessment purposes may include "free drawings," where the task is left completely to the individual being assessed, or more structured directives ("draw a house-tree-person"), where specific instructions are provided and scoring systems have been discussed in the literature. And as emphasized throughout the preceding chapters in this book, these graphic illustrations can also be helpful to elicit the examinee's interpretations of the drawings and to view them within the context of his or her developmental stage of life (Malchiodi, 1998; Oster & Crone, 2004). With this organized way of gathering salient information, clinicians can form more invaluable insights into the examinee's conceptual, intellectual, and emotional functioning as well as provide a tangible platform for further discussion of current problem areas.

The significant impact of using drawings in the assessment of personality has also made tremendous strides (Malchiodi, 2012; Handler & Thomas, 2013). This popularity in the use of drawings among clinicians has prompted the development of numerous variations in what is to be drawn. As seen in Chapters 3 and 4, the instructions provided to the client about what to draw or visualize can emphasize specific areas of potential conflict ("Draw You and Your Family Doing Something Together;" "Draw Yourself in School"), various emotions ("Draw Your Mood"), or novel experiences ("Draw-A-Person-in-the-Rain") to name a few. Each directive can offer clients a unique situation, as it places them in different circumstances that access distinctive aspects of their perceptions.

CASE STUDY: Janice L.

Janice L. was a 13-year-old, eighth grade student when referred by her parents for a comprehensive psychological battery of tests. Her parents noted problems in concentration, self-esteem, and moodiness as her primary difficulties. She also apparently was "freaking out" about germs. Already being treated for ADHD with a variety of medications and participating in therapeutic group activities, she still had trouble with being distractible, was lacking in motivation, and talked excessively. The evaluation was primarily due for high school placement, as the parents were considering private schools, in addition to what the public schools had to offer.

6.1

According to the parents, Janice had been struggling in her parochial middle school. They mentioned that Janice did not participate in many activities and regular classes were difficult despite accommodations being implemented (such as a separate room for testing and no time requirements). Janice concurred with her parents' description of her lack of efforts and expressed little interest in her coursework. To emphasize her negative outlook, she constructed the following drawing during the session (see Figure 6.1). Through this expressive avenue, Janice seemed relieved that everyone "got the picture" of her failings and frustrations.

Through my many years of testing and clinical experiences, I have found the utilization of drawing directives to be fruitful in establishing rapport, enhancing communication, and enriching the projective section of the assessments. Drawings are usually a brief and non-threatening ice breaker and they are efficient in producing areas of worry and conflict that are visible and straightforward and that can be discussed and corroborated within the test battery. In different settings (both in psychiatric hospitals as well as outpatient clinics and independent practices), I have used drawings at the beginning of an interview or testing session, in the middle of a conversation to amplify what is being discussed, or later as part of the structured evaluation.

CASE STUDY: John R.

John R. was a nearly 15-year-old young man referred for a psychological assessment by his therapist to gain a better understanding of his intellectual and emotional functioning and to identify specific areas of concern. John's history was replete with ongoing difficulties with peers. Also, his high degree of distractibility created many problems in completing his school work. Over the years, he had received numerous disciplinary actions due to impulsive and reactive behaviors. His low frustration tolerance and anger also was directed toward school staff and authority figures.

Additionally, past records noted arrests for theft and assault. One event occurred after he "stole an old lady's lawn chair off her porch." During the interview, he also indicated alcohol usage since 8 years of age, and later had smoked marijuana and experimented with prescription medications. While he bragged about his exploits, he was resistant to completing many of the standardized tests. The ones he did finish portrayed him as someone who externalizes behavior in an aggressive manner. Other data suggesting immaturity and few coping defenses were gleaned from projective measures.

When requested to construct an image that represented his mood, John immediately sketched a figure that was directly related to his many problems (see Figure 6.2). He had no qualms about discussing his anger and stated that it was his main feeling. With this information, he agreed to accept a suggestion to participate in an anger management group and this recommendation was placed within his report.

In one outpatient setting for children and adolescents, I (as the principle psychological examiner) provided a standard series of drawing instructions for each client that was constructed in a different room setting (along with completing self-report questionnaires), while I interviewed the parents in a separate location. This efficient use of my time allowed me to gather considerable information about the history of the youth, in addition to the family's view of the problem areas before I finished the remainder of the testing session. The drawings completed were then reviewed and the responses captured within the integrative report. The typical drawing requests included a series of 10 drawings on separate sheets of paper. By using the following same set of instructions over many years, I gathered an important baseline of key indicators for further interpretation and discussion in that particular setting and population:

- Construct a House–Tree–Person
- Draw a Person-in-the-Rain
- Draw Your Family
- Draw Yourself in School
- Draw Yourself with Friends
- Draw Your "Ideal" Self (fantasy of self in 10 years' time, to include setting and other people who may be involved)
- Draw "A Problem You May Have" (preceded this request by noting that everyone has problems and I just wanted to know one that they might have)
- Draw "How to Solve that Problem."

These requests provided a plethora of exciting images that directed discussions toward the core of a variety of conflicting issues related to: self-esteem, views within the home and family relationships, academic motivation, peer support or difficulties, abilities to

6.2

see beyond the present crisis, and resourcefulness in overcoming problem areas. Each drawing yielded substantial information that was elaborated upon during the remainder of the testing session to generate impressions concerning the person's cognitive and emotional levels that ultimately led to diagnoses and recommendations.

In other settings where I am faced directly with clients from the beginning of a testing session (usually in a hospital) or in beginning therapy, I have used other nonverbal strategies to "break the ice" or estimate their functioning. These directives have included:

- Construct a timeline, genogram, or family shield (to better "see" the historical patterns of problems and their support system).
- Portray your "World" (a picture request of the important people and objects in the everyday life).
- Draw a picture that symbolically represents experiences before admission into the hospital, demonstartes thier current condition, and illustrates their perspectives upon leaving the inpatient setting.
- Draw a picture that symbolically represents your most pronounced feeling (such as "anxiety" or "depression").
- Draw "an unusual experience."

These suggestions at graphically expressing clients' conflicts and feelings in a totally different manner than they may have anticipated, usually establishes a framework for exciting interchanges that can break down any preconceived resistance. Using drawings during interviews and psychological evaluations has broadened my clinical world exponentially. The examples constructed have also assisted clients in overcoming their initial anxiety and created an enjoyable experience within a potentially uncomfortable situation. The addition of drawings directives within a test battery also points out the importance of assessing the whole person and seeing other dimensions of expressing their worries and concerns. Furthermore, the drawings expose an alternative medium for new students of assessment of the various ways that inner pain, suffering, and conflicts can be described, rather than rely only on the use of verbal language.

THE PSYCHOLOGICAL REPORT

The psychological report is the culmination of the assessment process (Groth-Marnat, 2009). It represents the clinician's efforts to integrate the gathered information into a comprehensive picture of background history, current symptoms, emotional resources, and strengths and weaknesses in cognitive functioning. This end product provides that meaningful knowledge required by the referral source and guides the client in better understanding him- or herself at a deeper level. This collected evidence culminates in diagnostic impressions and goals that assist in directing a comprehensive treatment plan. The mixture of intellectual, educational, and personality tests, including drawing samples, allows for a consistent and complete portrait that must be explained in a manner that is clear and relevant to any number of readers.

Evaluations are constructed in different ways depending on the clinician's training, writing style, and experience. During previous years, psychological reports were considered "classified for professional use only" and written for other practitioners. In today's world of consumer rights, the client has primary discretion of reviewing the report and providing it to others in their network. Depending on the referral source, the report is likely open to many people including judges, teachers, physicians, lawyers, therapists, social service practitioners, and other family members. The report needs to make sense to anyone with a moderate degree of sophistication; thus, the language needs to be written in a thoughtful but straightforward manner.

Usually, the format has fairly standard guidelines. It includes methods for elaborating on essential areas such as referral questions, relevant history, previous assessments, tests to be administered, behavioral observations, sections of test data and interpretation that typically include cognitive measures, self-report questionnaires, personality inventories, and projective techniques. A summary of results that integrates the data into a meaningful whole is then constructed. Finally, diagnostic impressions and recommendations that cover interventions for therapists, school officials, allied professionals and individuals charged with placement decisions are included at the end. These latter sections are the ones that are mostly read and thus must be fairly specific and practical.

In certain types of referral, especially clients who are referred for psychotherapy, an important goal may be to help them increase their level of personal insight. In these cases, drawings can provide a wider description of the client that includes a number of different topics that describes what is unique to this individual (for instance, the depth of depression, school motivation, or how family relationships are perceived).

Another point in writing reports that make sense in quality and usefulness is the emphasis on elucidating the issues that the client is experiencing. The knowledge gained through the assessment process and that drawings expand upon increases the depth of the results and interpretations, enhances a portrait of the problem conditions, and provides a clear view of the areas that require intervention. Drawings can add substantially to these goals in diagnosis and treatment direction due to their visibility and clarity. Oftentimes, a picture with sensitive interpretations and elaboration can enhance the feedback session with the client, family members, unit staff, and referral source.

SUMMARIES OF PSYCHOLOGICAL EVALUATIONS

CASE STUDY: Marvin S.

Marvin S. was a 12-year-old, seventh grade public school student who was referred for psychological testing by his mother to clarify whether attention weaknesses, learning delays, or emotional factors might be hindering his academic potential and interpersonal maturation. Marvin had never had therapeutic treatment previously, neither had he been placed on medication for his activity level or behavioral adjustment. According to the mother, Marvin had become increasingly oppositional over the past couple of years. He was especially more provocative this past summer and displayed many tantrums and poor interpersonal boundaries. Also, he had begun to resist homework and as a result his grades had been inconsistent. She described his current condition as being apathetic, distractible, irritable, overactive, and exhibiting poor concentration.

Reports from earlier school years suggested that Marvin was shy, lacked self-control, and needed reassurance. Problems also included remembering directions, failing to finish classroom assignments, being easily led, excitable, and impulsive. More recent progress notes stated that Marvin had been highly inconsistent in his approach to problem-solving.

Marvin was the older of two boys who were both adopted from Russia at 18 months old. Developmentally, Marvin was malnourished when he was adopted and too weak to walk (he did not begin walking until 22 months). However, over time he had thrived nutritionally and physically.

Marvin attended preschool and day care since 2 years of age. He entered kindergarten on time and remained there through fifth grade. During these years, the mother described many struggles over homework, and described Marvin as not wanting to put forth sustained effort. Instead, he apparently was sloppy and careless in his work and wanted to rush through things without thinking about the consequences. He also exhibited poor boundaries with peers, never took responsibility over conflicts, and viewed the world as unfair.

Despite his behavioral problems, Marvin had attempted a variety of organized activities and camps. He had also tried violin lessons and more recently was taking piano. He especially enjoyed music and dance, and other adults mentioned that he appeared gifted in these areas.

For this evaluation, Marvin presented as a well-groomed and well-nourished youngster of average height without physical anomaly. He separated easily from his mother, and was able to work fairly independently. There were no indications of severe distress, or other signs of significant anxiety or sadness. Overall, he was pleasant and cooperative.

During the testing portion of the evaluation, Marvin was attentive and put forth a maximum of effort. He did not appear fatigued or restless. He was challenged by the various tasks and persevered to the end of testing. In general, he demonstrated a broad array of reasoning skills, though with some variability in his copying speed and concentration.

On the WISC-V, Marvin obtained an overall IQ score of 103. His functioning fell within the Average range of intelligence (Average = 90–109) and at the 58th percentile for his age group. However, there was a broad disparity within his subtest scores, ranging from Low Average to High Average that reflected specific strengths and lesser skills among his unique abilities.

Marvin demonstrated solid functioning in areas pertaining to higher academic potential. His subtest scores related to both verbal and nonverbal reasoning, language development, practical judgment, short-term rote memory, and hands-on learning were solidly developed. However, when sustained concentration and mental flexibility were required, as well as handwriting efficiency, he exhibited lower scores and these vulnerabilities contributed to carelessness in his work and lessened output. The effort he expended on written work seemed to undermine his academic confidence and motivation.

On basic academic tests, he demonstrated grade level to above grade level functioning. His abilities seemed commensurate with his overall potential (as demonstrated on the WISC-V). His scores did not suggest specific learning disabilities. Of the measured tests, he seemed most competent in his reading and most challenged by math problems. Spelling appeared somewhat lower, as he was less confident and more careless in his approach.

Marvin's reproductions of the Bender Gestalt Figures, a test of fine motor coordination and copying effectiveness, were completed with some difficulty and unevenness (approximately six months behind in his perceptual maturation). Also, his approach to the task indicated problems in planning. His object and figure drawings additionally disclosed weaknesses in his fine motor coordination and expression. These problems in perceptual-motor control and organization probably constricted his efficiency during written assignments.

More significantly, emotional indices derived from the drawings suggested many internal conflicts that would probably interfere in his growth and development. These constructions reflected identity concerns and exhibited signs that he harbored much inner tension that he was having difficulty expressing in an appropriate manner. They also seemed to indicate that he is struggling with his self-esteem and feelings of mastery and confidence. These exertions were observed in several drawings, but one in particular ("a person in the rain") revealed few emotional resources when confronted by even minor stressors (see Figure 6.3). In this illustration, there were signs of helplessness and underlying sadness that alluded to blockages in his interpersonal maturation.

6.3

A checklist of descriptive phrases pertaining to ADHD symptoms at home indicated that Marvin lost a lot of things, and was easily distracted, restless and fidgety, impatient, impulsive, and overly talkative. In school, Marvin was perceived as needing extra direction, as not attending to classroom instruction, as displaying a short attention span, and as openly defying authority.

In previous years, Marvin's behavior was more characterized by ADHD symptoms that included a low frustration tolerance, poor concentration, and volatile moods. It was also suggested that Marvin was destructive of property and was poorly organized. This latter quality made homework efficiency especially problematic.

Similarly, Marvin portrayed himself as highly sensitive, quick tempered, and impulsive in what he said to adults and peers. He also mentioned that his mind wandered frequently and found it very hard to read written material unless it was particularly interesting or very easy. He also indicated that he was restless and fidgety, and struggled to stay focused on tasks or conversations.

On items focused on self-confidence, tension, and anxiety, Marvin acknowledged many areas of distress. He described himself as indecisive, nervous, and highly sensitive. He noted that he worried a lot of the time, was concerned about how others viewed him, often felt sick to his stomach, and saw others as more capable and happier.

Additionally, he suggested that he perceived himself as being very frightened in many situations (e.g., at night and during medical exams), and often experienced panic-like sensations. He also indicated that he got mad easily.

In areas of affective discomfort, Marvin reported that he felt loved by his family, but struggled with peer interactions. He suggested that other students did not like him and that he never felt like talking to them. There were no indications, however, of severe distress where he would want to avoid everything in his life.

His reactions to more ambiguous items (Rorschach, TAT) seemed to suggest a moderate degree of underlying anxiety and sadness that would make him appear moody and overreactive when confronted by stressful situations. He appeared to become easily overwhelmed by ambiguity and constricted in his abilities to problem-solve effectively. During these times, he overlooked important details of interactions and situations, and as a result reacted impulsively and in an excessive manner without thinking through the consequences.

Further, during novel problem-solving experiences or new social situations, Marvin could withdraw from the challenges and likely become more resistant to put forth much effort. This emotionally immature approach to stressful situations indicated that Marvin probably harbored much inner tension and anxiety that he apparently could not express in an appropriate manner. During these times, he seemed bored and withdrawn, while missing salient details that would be important for appropriate responses and interactions. These inconsistencies in his interactions and behaviors would likely meet with negative consequences and interfere with his developing achievement motivation and self-confidence.

As a result of his emotional vulnerabilities, Marvin felt ineffective rather than attempting active problem solutions. While he seemed to have the potential to overcome the problems that he confronted, his lowered capacities to cope with stress significantly interfered with his initiative and learning process. This realization only added to his daily frustrations and most likely created more tension and expressed irritability.

Consequently, he appeared to depend on others to resolve these conflicts. Marvin also harbored some angry and oppositional feelings that he was not able to communicate adaptively. He often felt bored and restless, and acted out his feelings in a somewhat provocative manner. And if someone was not there to assist him, faulty reasoning led to simplified logic, ineffective responses, and continued negativity.

CASE STUDY: Allison T.

Allison T. was also a 12-year-old public school student who was entering seventh grade. She was referred for this evaluation to assess her cognitive and emotional functioning. According to her parents, Allison had experienced severe adjustment problems over the past year. She contracted health issues, including headaches and fatigue, which caused her to miss many school days. During the year, her grades declined and she appeared highly sensitive and excessively irritable. Other symptoms included signs of anxiety, sadness, apathy, defensiveness, and social inhibition.

Allison's birth and developmental history were fairly unremarkable. Until this past year, she had not suffered from physical health issues or experienced trauma. Also, no learning disabilities had been apparent. Her elementary years were considered excellent regarding grades and attendance. It was not until this past year that she became sick with a virus and difficulties persisted.

Despite her recent academic problems, Allison had attempted many activities (including horseback riding and gymnastics) and participated at camps. She was mostly interested in dance and music, and had been a competitive dancer for many years. She was also considered an excellent artist.

Allison presented as a fairly tall (5'6"), well-nourished, and well-groomed youngster without physical anomaly and appeared somewhat older than her stated age. Although she was alert and oriented, she seemed affectively constricted and did not offer much interpersonal spontaneity. However, she was compliant to direction and put forth adequate effort.

During the testing portion of the evaluation, Allison displayed inconsistent decoding skills and problem-solving strategies. She seemed very creative and detailed in her drawings, expressed a broad vocabulary and general knowledge, and was adept during nonverbal, hands-on problem-solving tasks. Her only hesitancy and relative weaknesses appeared in areas of complex problem-solving that required sustained concentration, and on a test of working memory.

On the WISC-V, Allison obtained an overall IQ score of 114. Her functioning fell within the High Average range of intelligence (High Average = 110–120) and at the 82nd percentile for her age group. However, there was a wide disparity among her specific abilities, ranging from Low Average (88) to Very Superior (130).

Allison's expressive language skills were her main attribute. Her strong command of verbal dexterity and abstract reasoning, in addition to her general knowledge, provided a strong basis for high academic potential. Also, she displayed solid abilities in hands-on learning, word knowledge, and nonverbal reasoning when objects were familiar. However, relative delays in areas that emphasized novel learning and auditory concentration probably reduced her classroom and interpersonal effectiveness, and possibly created inner confusion and uncertainty.

On basic academic tests, her overall scores were similar to what would be expected from her intellectual functioning. Once again, she demonstrated her highest functioning in language areas (95th percentile). She scored outstanding on subtests of word recognition and spelling. She displayed some hesitancy, though, and made careless errors during mathematical calculations. This relative area of weakness in sustained mental effort likely undermined her classroom confidence and lowered her academic initiative.

Tests of fine motor coordination and copying efficiency were completed without errors. There were no indications of perceptual-motor difficulties that would make written work problematic. However, her approach to the tasks suggested some degree of organization problems, alluding to the need for structure to work optimally. Drawing directives were produced in a very creative manner and very detailed, indicating much inner expression. However, the amount of detail that she provided made her less efficient in completing all the assignments given her to work independently.

Also, emotional indicators from her drawings suggested that she tended to be guarded and overly defended in her interpersonal interactions, which would reduce her spontaneity and effectiveness. These signs were visible in several of her drawings that attempted to portray herself in a positive light and overlook her current problems. One drawing specifically signified her general use of denial. From the directive, "Draw Your Ideal Self" she sketched a woman who was "happy, smart, successful, funny, and healthy" (see Figure 6.4). Her attention to presenting herself in a positive light was noteworthy for her unwillingness to reveal the extent of her current problems. These manifestations of disavowing her vulnerabilities were a consistent theme throughout the evaluation.

While Allison's parents did not mention significant difficulties in her attention capacities on behavioral checklists, they did allude to Allison's sensitivity, sadness, low frustration tolerance, and tendency not to complete classroom work. As usual, Allison mainly denied all problem areas of concern related to attention and concentration. She only implied that she found her mind wandering from tasks that were uninteresting or boring. While Allison and her parents denied many of the usual indicators of ADHD that would interfere with her social and academic maturity, the parents were most concerned about Allison's emotional immaturity. Of course, Allison would not admit to these types of issues.

Responses from a self-report scale related to depressive symptoms also did not suggest inner distress. Allison mainly pictured herself as happy, loved, and content (both on checklists and through her drawings). Only at times did she feel bored, angry, or upset. In general, she appeared to have a positive self-regard, but seemed to use denial as a main defense mechanism, which often points to naïvety and a lack of emotional spontaneity.

Only on ambiguous items (Rorschach, TAT) did Allison's responses suggest underlying anxiety that might make her appear guarded and avoidant when confronted by stressful situations. On these measures, her answers suggested estrangement from her emotions that probably limits interpersonal interactions and distanced her from events she viewed as threatening. Because of her avoidant style, she probably overlooked important details of interactions and situations, and reacted impulsively and in an excessive manner.

Allison also appeared to harbor angry and oppositional feelings that she was not able to communicate in an effective manner. She often felt frustrated when demands were placed on her, but felt that she could eventually get her way. However, if blocked from her wants, her faulty reasoning seemed to lead to simplified logic, ineffective responses, and somewhat naïve behavior. Because of these limitations in her emotional repertoire, Allison appeared to avoid challenges that created the slightest apprehension as a way to reduce uncomfortable feelings. As a result, these actions may have detracted from her opportunities for new learning. Rather than express her irritability or frustration, she would rather not face these obstacles and passively resisted demands placed on her. Consequently, she tended to deny problems and not work on important issues that could otherwise enhance her self-confidence and motivation, leaving her potential to enhance her self-esteem underdeveloped.

6.4

Happy
Smart
Successful
Funny
Healthy

CLOSING WORDS

From birth on, tests have a major influence on our lives. They form initial impressions of our adaptive growth and development. During the school years, they are used to measure academic progress, gauge learning delays, and determine needs for specialized accommodations and assistance. And still later, tests are used to evaluate work place efficiency, quantify deterioration when diseases occur, or determine necessary interventions for disability services.

Because of their unique educational background in statistics and understanding test development, psychologists remain at the forefront for assessment administration. However, other disciplines are now emphasizing the importance of creating tests that can demonstrate accuracy in determining various types of cognitive and emotional functioning. The main uses of testing, though, are to appraise individual differences in abilities and personality. Throughout this book, the emphasis has been on demonstrating the value that drawings possess to estimate cognitive functioning and view emotional traits. Of all the tests that have been developed, drawings seem to be the most expedient and the most poignant in providing these clues to uncovering the whole person.

REFERENCES

Achenbach, T. M. & Rescorla, L. A. (2001). *Manual for the ASEBA school-age forms and profiles.* Burlington, VT: University of Vermont, Research Center for Children, Youth, and Families.

Anastasi, A. & Urbina, S. (1997). *Psychological testing* (7th ed.). Bloomington, MN: Pearson.

Aronow, E., Weiss, K. A., & Rezinkoff, M. (2001). *A practical guide to the thematic apperception test.* Philadelphia, PA: Brunner Routledge.

Bender, L. (1963). *Bender-Gestalt test.* Los Angeles, CA: Western Psychological Services.

Berg, E. A. (1948). A simple objective technique for measuring flexibility in thinking. *The Journal of General Psychology, 39*(1), 15–22.

Berger, M. (1976). Psychological testing. In M. Rutter and L. Herson (Eds.), *Child and adolescent psychiatry: Modern approaches.* London: Blackwell Scientific.

Brenner, R. A. & Oster, G. D. (2013). *From abcs to ieps: Empowering parents to communicate with their children's teachers and schools.* Seattle, WA: Amazon Digital Services.

Butcher, J. N., Dahlstrom, W. G., & Graham, J. R. (1989). *Manual for the restandardized Minnesota Multiphasic Personality Inventory (MMPI-2).* Minneapolis, MN: University of Minnesota Press.

Exner, J. E. (1995). *The Rorschach: A Comprehensive System. Vol 1: Basic foundations.* New York: Wiley.

Gabel, S., Oster, G. D., & Butnik, S. M. (1986). *Understanding psychological testing in children: A guide for health professionals.* New York: Plenum Medical.

Golden, C. J., Hammeke, T. A., & Purisch, A. D. (1980). *The Luria-Nebraska Battery manual.* Palo Alto, CA: Western Psychological Services.

Gregory, R. J. (2013). *Psychological testing: History, principles and applications* (7th ed.). Bloomington, MN: Pearson.

Groth-Marnat, G. (2009). *Handbook of psychological assessment.* (5th ed.). New York: Wiley.

Hammer, E. F. (1997). *Advances in projective drawing interpretation.* Springfield, IL: Charles C. Thomas.

Handler, L. & Thomas, A. D. (2013). *Drawings in assessment and psychotherapy: Research and application.* New York: Routledge.

Jastak, J. F. & Jastak, S. (1993). *WRAT-3: Wide Range Achievement Te*st (3rd ed.). Wilmington, DE: Jastak Associates.

Kaplan, R. M. & Saccuzzo, D. P. (2012). *Psychological testing: Principles, applications, and issues* (8th ed.). Independence, KY: Cengage Learning.

Kaufman, A. S. & Kaufman, N. L. (1993). *The Kaufman adolescent and adult intelligence test.* Circle Pines, MN: American Guidance Service.

Klepsch, M. & Logie, L. (1982). *Children draw and tell: An introduction to the projective uses of children's human figure drawings.* New York: Brunner/Mazel.

Leibowitz, M. (1999). *Interpreting projective drawings: A self psychological approach.* New York: Brunner/Mazel.

Malchiodi, C. A. (1998). *Understanding children's drawings.* New York: Guilford Press.

Malchiodi, C. A. (Ed.). (2012). *Art therapy and health care.* New York: Guilford Press.

Markwardt, F. C. (1989). *Peabody individual achievement test-revised (PIAT-R).* Circle Pines: MN: American Guidance Service.

Morey, L. C. (2007). *Personality assessment inventory professional manual.* Lutz, FL: Psychological Assessment Resources.

Oster, G. D. (2013). *Unmasking childhood depression.* Seattle, WA: Amazon Digital Services.

Oster, G. D., Caro, J. E., Eagen, D. R., & Lillo, M. A. (1988). *Assessing adolescents.* New York: Pergamon.

Oster, G. D. & Crone, P. (2004). *Using drawings in assessment and therapy* (2nd ed.). New York: Taylor & Francis.

Oster, G. D. & Gould, P. (1987). *Using drawings in assessment and therapy.* New York: Brunner/Mazel.

Oster, G. D. & Montgomery, S. S. (1996). *Clinical uses of drawings.* Northvale, NJ: Jason Aronson.

Reitan, R. (1985). *Halstead-Reitan neuropsychological test battery: Theory and clinical interpretation.* Tucson, AZ: Reitan Neuropsychology.

Reynolds, C. R. & Kamphaus, R. W. (2015). *BASC-3: Behavior assessment system for children* (3rd edition). Bloomington, MN: Pearson.

Roberts, G. E. (1994). *Interpretive handbook for the Roberts Appercetion Test for Children.* Los Angeles, CA: Western Psychological Services.

Rorschach, H. (1942). *Psychodiagnostics.* Bern, Switzerland: Verlag Han Huber.

Taylor, E. M. (1959). *The appraisal of children with cerebral deficits.* Cambridge, MA: Harvard University Press.

Urbina, S. (2014). *Essentials of psychological testing* (2nd ed.). New York: Wiley.

Wechsler, D. (2014). *WISC-V: Administration and scoring manual for the Wechsler intelligence scale for children* (5th ed.). Bloomington, MN: Pearson.

Wilkinson, G. S. & Robertson, G. J. (2006). *Wide Range Achievement Test* (4th ed.; WRAT4). Lutz, FL: Psychological Assessment Resources.

Index

abuse 137–139
academic achievement 159–160
Achenbach Child Behavior Checklist 161
ADD *see* Attention Deficit Disorder
ADHD *see* Attention Deficit Hyperactivity Disorder
affect 128
AIDS 18
alertness 128
alternative drawing directives 94–114
amnesia 101–102
anger 69–70, 165–166
anxiety 129, 134–135
appearance (mental status exams) 128
arms (D-A-P tests) 72
arousal (trauma interviews) 130
Artful scribbles: The significance of children's drawings 26–27
Artistry of the Mentally Ill 37
art therapy 41–50
Attention Deficit Disorder (ADD) 74–75
Attention Deficit Hyperactivity Disorder (ADHD): in Family-Centered-Circle-Drawing 87–88; Mother-and-Child drawings 90–91; psychological evaluations 155–156, 163–164, 171
Auditory-Verbal Learning Test 160
avoidance (trauma interviews) 130

Bardos, A. 71
bared teeth 69–70
before, during and after crises 112–113
behavioral observations 121–123
behavior rating scales 161
Bender, L. 42
brain injury and dysfunction 43
Brooke, S. L. 47
Buck, J. N. 63, 65
Burns, R. C. 86–87
Burt, C. 27, 30

CAPs *see* Clinician-Administered PTSD Scale

cautionary tales 50–51
Chapman, L. 42
chimneys (of houses) 60
The Clinical Applications of Projective Drawings 43, 47
Clinician-Administered PTSD Scale (CAPS) 131–133
closed fist 39
cognitive maturation 32–34
Cohen, B. 47
comprehensive psychological evaluations 148–176; components 157–158; identification of presenting problems 153–154; puzzles that need solutions 156; report 167–168; requests from treating professionals 150–151; response to referrals 151–153; role of psychologists 154–156; summary 168–174; test batteries 158–167
conduct problems 123
conflict-sharing 143–145
consciousness 34–35
court system 150–151
creative pursuits in psychotherapy 38–41
cultural continuity/identity (in genograms) 97–98
current mood 5–6, 106, 108–109

D-A-P *see* Draw-A-Person technique
D-A-P-R *see* Draw-A-Person-In-The-Rain
DAS *see* Draw-a-Story procedures
depression 90–91, 134–135
developmental sequences 27, 30–32
Diagnostic Drawing Series (DDS) 47, 48–49
DiLeo, J. H. 30, 59–60
doors (of houses) 60
Draw-A-Family 81–83
Draw-A-Person (D-A-P) technique 47; *see also* human figures
Draw-A-Person-In-The-Rain (D-A-P-R) 7–8, 40, 41, 75, 77–81, 169–170
Draw-a-Story (DAS) procedures 47

Draw Your Current Mood 5–6, 106, 108–109
Draw Your Ideal Self 105–107, 173–174
Draw Yourself (with friends) 103
Draw Your World 101–102
DSM-5 49, 131–132

Emotional and Cognitive Art Therapy Assessment (LECATA) 47
emotional disturbance (D-A-P technique) 71
emotional indicators 34–36
Etude medico-legale sur la folie 37
everyday objects 56–57
everyday practice 1–24
eyes 69–70

Family-Centered-Circle-Drawing (F-C-C-D) 86–88
family drama 58–62
family drawing procedures 81–91
family evaluations 142–143
family shields 99–100
F-C-C-D *see* Family-Centered-Circle-Drawing
FEATS *see* Formal Elements Art Therapy Scale
feet (D-A-P) 72
fences around houses 60
figure slanting (D-A-P) 72
fingers (D-A-P) 72
Fitness for Duty Evaluations 150–151
Formal Elements Art Therapy Scale (FEATS) 49
foundations of clinical drawings 25–55; art therapy 41–50; cognitive maturation 32–34; creative pursuits in psychotherapy 38–41; developmental sequences 27, 30–32; emotional indicators 34–36; history 25–26; physiological maturation 26–29; psychology 37–50; symbols of mental illness 37
free drawings 163
Freud, S. 37–38, 47

Gantt, L. 42, 47
Garcia-Preto, N. 97–98
Gardner, H. 26–27, 34
Generalized Anxiety Disorder 129
genograms 97–99
Gerson, R. 97
Gil, E. ix–xv, 42, 97
Gillespie, J. 89
Giordano, J. 97–98
glaring eyes (D-A-P) 69–70
goals and motivation 14
Golomb, C. 34

Goodenough, F. 42, 43, 47, 66, 68
gutters (of houses) 60

hair pulling 129
Halstead–Reitan Neuropsychological Battery 160
Hammer, E. F. 34–35, 43, 47
hands (D-A-P) 72
Hanvik, L. J. 42
Harris, D. 31, 47, 66, 68
heads (D-A-P) 72
HIV/AIDS 18
hospitalization 117–118
hostility 69–70, 165–166
house drawings 58–62
House–Tree–Person (H-T-P) 47, 56–93
human figures 56–57, 66, 68–73
Hyperactivity Disorder *see* Attention Deficit Hyperactivity Disorder

ideal self 105–107, 173–174
identification of presenting problems 153–154
identity (genograms) 97–98
Individual Educational Plan (IEP) 68–69
information gathering for interviews 115–118
insight 10
inspiration 17–20
intake interviews 124–127
intellectual quotient (IQ) scores 43, 68, 159
interpersonal approaches: broadening of 94–95; engagement 16–17
interviews 115–147; benefits and limitations 139–140; crux of 123–124; enhancement to practitioners 145–146; initial 119–121; types 124–129
IQ *see* intellectual quotient scores

Jung, C. 37–38

Kellogg, R. 32
Kinetic-Family-Drawing (K-F-D) 83–86
Kinetic–House–Tree–Person (K-H-T-P) 74–76
kinetic school drawings 103–105
Klopfer, W. G. 46–47
Knoff, H. M. 104
Koppitz, E. 30, 32–33, 46
Kris, E. 34
Kwiatkowska, H. 41

large sized human figures (D-A-P) 72
lawyers 150–151
legs (D-A-P) 72
Levick Emotional and Cognitive Art Therapy Assessment (LECATA) 47

Levy, B. 42
line quality (D-A-P) 72
lips (D-A-P) 69–70
Luquet, G.H. 27
Luria–Nebraska Neuropsychological Battery 160

McGoldrick, M. 97–98
Machover, K. 69
McNeish, T. J. 71
Malchiodi, C. A. 27, 30, 34, 41–42
maturation: cognitive 32–34; physiological 26–29
memory: Draw Your World 101–102; timelines 95–96; trauma interviews 130
mental illness 37
mental status exams (MSE) 126, 128–129
Miami-Dade County School system, Florida 47
Minnesota Multiphasic Personality Inventory (MMPI) 161
mood 106, 108–109, 128
Morgan, C. D. 162
Mother-and-Child (drawings) 89–91
mouth (D-A-P) 72
Multiple Personality Disorder 43, 101–102, 129
Murray, H. A. 162

Naglieri, J. A. 71
National Institute of Mental Health (NIMH) 41
neurodevelopmental art therapy (NDAT) 42
neuropsychological testing 160

Obsessive Compulsive Disorder (OCD) 90–91
orientation (mental status exams) 128

Peabody Individual Achievement Test 160
personality inventories 160–161
Person-in-the-Rain 7–8, 40, 41, 169–170
Person Picking an Apple from a Tree (PPAT) 47, 49–50
Phillips, P. D. 103
Piaget, J. 27, 47
picture interpretation technique *see* Thematic Apperception Test
Pietrowski, Z. 34–35
poor integration of body parts (D-A-P) 71
Posttraumatic Stress Disorder (PTSD) 42, 130–134, 136, 161
PPAT *see* Person Picking an Apple from a Tree

Prinzhorn, H. 37
problem definition/resolution 110–112
problem-solving 10
projective techniques 34–35, 37, 161–162
Prout, H. T. 103, 104
psychology 37–50; *see also* comprehensive psychological evaluations
psychosis 47
PTSD *see* Posttraumatic Stress Disorder
"public masks" 17–18
pulling out of hair 129

reassurance 7–9
recollections (timelines) 95–96
referrals 150–153, 157–158
reliability (of psychological evaluations) 157
reliving (trauma interviews) 130
Reynolds Suicide Ideation Scale 19–20
Roberts Apperception Test 162
roofs (of houses) 61
Rorschach test 43, 81, 86–87, 162
Rubin, J. 38

Sarbaugh, M. E. 103–104
Schizophrenia 43, 101–102, 129
self-loathing 15–16
sexual abuse 137–139
sexuality 70
shading (D-A-P) 71
sharing of conflicts 143–145
shoulders (D-A-P) 72
shutters (of houses) 61
Silk, A. M. J. 27, 30
Silver Drawing Test 47, 48
small sized human figures (D-A-P) 72
sneering lips (D-A-P) 69–70
Stanford–Binet Tests 68
stories: DAS procedures 47; *see also* Thematic Apperception Test
substance abuse 122
suicide 19–20, 149
symbols of mental illness 37

Tabone, C. 47
Tardieu, L. 37
TAT *see* Thematic Apperception Test
Taulbee, E. S. 46–47
teeth (D-A-P) 69–70
temperament 11–13
test batteries 158–167
The Clinical Applications of Projective Drawings 43, 47
Thematic Apperception Test (TAT) 43, 81, 162, 171, 173

They Could Not Talk and So They Drew (Levick) 47
Thomas, G. V. 27, 30
timelines 95–96
Tinnin, L. 42
Tools of the Trade 47
Tourette's Syndrome 90–91
transparencies (D-A-P) 72
trauma interviews 130–131, 133–137
Trauma Symptom Checklist for Children (TSCC) 131, 135–137
Trauma Symptom Inventory (TSI) 131, 133–135
tree drawings 63–67
Trichotillomania 129

Ulman, E. 42
unconsciousness 34–35, 38

validity (of psychological evaluations) 157

walkways (of houses) 61
walls of houses 61
Wechsler Intelligence Scale for Children (WISC-V) 68, 159, 169
Wide Range Achievement Test 160
windows of houses 61
Wolff, W. 81
Woodcock–Johnson psycho-education test batteries 160